Lecture Notes in Computer Science 6711

Commenced Publication in 1973
Founding and Former Series Editors:
Gerhard Goos, Juris Hartmanis, and Jan van Leeuwen

Jan Camenisch   Costas Lambrinoudakis (Eds.)

Public Key Infrastructures, Services and Applications

7th European Workshop, EuroPKI 2010
Athens, Greece, September 23-24, 2010
Revised Selected Papers

 Springer

Volume Editors

Jan Camenisch
IBM Research - Zurich
Saeumerstrasse 4
8803 Rueschlikon
Switzerland
E-mail: jca@zurich.ibm.com

Costas Lambrinoudakis
University of Piraeus
Department of Digital Systems
18532 Piraeus
Greece
E-mail: clam@unipi.gr

ISSN 0302-9743   e-ISSN 1611-3349
ISBN 978-3-642-22632-8   ISBN 978-3-642-22633-5 (eBook)
DOI 10.1007/978-3-642-22633-5
Springer Heidelberg Dordrecht London New York

Library of Congress Control Number: 2011934789

CR Subject Classification (1998): K.6.5, C.2, E.3, D.4.6, J.1, K.4.4

LNCS Sublibrary: SL 4 – Security and Cryptology

Typesetting: Camera-ready by author, data conversion by Scientific Publishing Services, Chennai, India

Printed on acid-free paper

Springer is part of Springer Science+Business Media (www.springer.com)

Preface

This book presents the proceedings of the 7th European Workshop on Public Key Infrastructures, Services and Applications (EuroPKI 2010) that was held in Athens, Greece during September 23–24, 2010. The European Workshop on Public Key Infrastructures, Services and Applications aims at hosting novel, significant and technical-quality advancements in research and practical aspects of PKI and at providing an international interface for researchers and practitioners to exchange information. The workshop continues from previous events held in Samos (2004), Kent (2005), Turin (2006), Mallorca (2007), Trondheim (2008) and Pisa (2009).

The advances in the information and communication technologies (ICT) have raised new opportunities for the implementation of novel applications and the provision of high-quality services over global networks. The aim is to utilize this 'information society era' to improve the quality of life for all citizens, disseminating knowledge, strengthening social cohesion, generating earnings and finally ensuring that organizations and public bodies remain competitive in the global electronic marketplace. Unfortunately, such a rapid technological evolution cannot be problem free. Concerns are raised regarding the 'lack of trust' in electronic procedures and the extent to which 'information security' and 'user privacy' can be ensured. Public key infrastructure (PKI) is probably one of the most important items in the arsenal of security measures that can be brought to bear against the aforementioned growing risks and threats. Furthermore, public key cryptography (PKC) services and applications make steady inroads into the various information security solutions needed, providing genuine benefits in selected application areas.

The conference program included one keynote speech and six technical papers sessions. The keynote speech, entitled "Data Privacy in Outsourcing Scenarios," was delivered by Pierangela Samarati from the University of Milan (Italy). In response to the EuroPKI 2010 call for papers, 41 papers were submitted. Each paper was reviewed by three members of the Program Committee, on the basis of their significance, novelty, technical quality, and PKI / PKC relevance. At the end of the reviewing process, only 14 papers were selected for presentation. Therefore, the acceptance rate of the workshop was 34%. The accepted high-quality papers covered a broad range of topics, from authentication mechanisms and privacy preserving techniques to electronic signature schemes and from privacy and identity management to public key infrastructure and public key cryptography applications.

We thank the attendees for coming to Athens to participate and debate the new emerging advances in this area. We would also like to thank all the members of the Program Committee, as well as the external reviewers, for their constructive and insightful comments during the review process. Moreover, we would like to express our gratitude to the members of the Organizing Committee for their continuous and valuable support. Finally, we would like to thank all of the authors that submitted papers for the event and contributed to an interesting set of conference proceedings.

September 2010   Jan Camenisch
                                                       Costas Lambrinoudakis

Organization

General Co-chairs

Dieter Gollmann   Hamburg University of Technology–TUHH,
                                           Germany

Stefanos Gritzalis   University of the Aegean, Greece

Program Committee Co-chairs

Jan Camenisch   IBM Research – Zurich, Switzerland

Costas Lambrinoudakis   University of Piraeus, Greece

Program Committee Members

I. Agudo	University of Malaga (Spain)
L. Batina	Katholieke Universiteit Leuven (Belgium)
D. Chadwick	Kent University (UK)
M. Cremonini	Università degli Studi di Milano (Italy)
S. De Capitani di Vimercati	Università degli Studi di Milano (Italy)
C. Diaz	Katholieke Universiteit Leuven (Belgium)
R. Di Pietro	University of Rome III (Italy)
S. Farell	Trinity College Dublin (Ireland)
S. Furnell	University of Plymouth (UK)
D. Galindo	University of Luxembourg (Luxembourg)
J. Gonzalez-Nieto	Queensland University of Technology (Australia)
J. Guajardo	Philips Research Europe (The Netherlands)
J. Hoepman	Radboud University Nijmegen (The Netherlands)
S. Katsikas	University of Piraeus (Greece)
S. Kent	BBN Technologies (USA)
D. Kesdogan	University of Siegen (Germany)
E. Konstantinou	University of the Aegean (Greece)
D. Lekkas	University of the Aegean (Greece)
A. Lioy	Politecnico di Torino (Italy)
J. Lopez	University of Malaga (Spain)
D. M'Raihi	Verisign (USA)
F. Martinelli	National Research Council (Italy)
S. Mauw	University of Luxembourg (Luxembourg)
C. Meadows	NRL (USA)

A. Meliones	University of Piraeus (Greece)
C. Mitchell	Royal Holloway, University of London (UK)
S. Mjølsnes	Norwegian University of Science & Technology (Norway)
Y. Mu	University of Wollongong (Australia)
D. Naccache	ENS (France)
S. Nikova	Katholieke Universiteit Leuven and University of Twente (Belgium, The Netherlands)
C. Ntantogian	University of Athens (Greece)
M. Pala	Dartmouth College (USA)
O. Pereira	UCL (Belgium)
G. Pernul	University of Regensburg (Germany)
D. Polemi	University of Piraeus (Greece)
B. Preneel	Katholieke University Leuven (Belgium)
S. Radomirović	University of Luxembourg (Luxembourg)
P. Rizomiliotis	University of the Aegean (Greece)
P. Samarati	Università degli Studi di Milano (Italy)
R. Scandariato	Katholieke Universiteit Leuven (Belgium)
S. Smith	Dartmouth College (USA)
Y. Stamatiou	University of Ioannina (Greece)
C. Xenakis	University of Piraeus (Greece)
J. Zhou	Institute for Infocomm Research (Singapore)

Organizing Committee

P. Najera	University of Malaga (Spain)
E. Darra	University of Piraeus (Greece)
N. Vrakas	University of Piraeus (Greece)
D. Anastassopoulou	University of Piraeus (Greece)

External Reviewers

G. Alpár	Radboud University Nijmegen (The Netherlands)
W. Alrodhan	Royal Holloway, University of London (UK)
C. Ardagna	Università degli Studi di Milano (Italy)
J. Balasch	Katholieke Universiteit Leuven (Belgium)
T. Barth	University of Siegen (Germany)
M. Bourimi	University of Siegen (Germany)
R. Brinkman	Katholieke Universiteit Leuven and University of Twente (Belgium)
C. Broser	University of Regensburg (Germany)
J. Camenisch	IBM Zurich Research Laboratory (Switzerland)

G. Costa	National Research Council (Italy)
F. Demertzis	University of Piraeus (Greece)
J. Doumen	Katholieke Universiteit Leuven (Belgium)
C. Fritsch	University of Regensburg (Germany)
O. Gmelch	University of Regensburg (Germany)
F. Guo	University of Wollongong (Australia)
H. Guo	Beihang University (China)
L. Ibraimi	Katholieke Universiteit Leuven and University of Twente (Belgium)
M. Jacobs	Radboud University Nijmegen (The Netherlands)
H. Jonker	University of Luxembourg (Luxembourg)
T. Karantjias	University of Piraeus (Greece)
M. Kohlweiss	Katholieke University Leuven (Belgium)
A. Lehmann	IBM Zurich Research Laboratory (Switzerland)
L. Marconi	University of Rome III (Italy)
A. Pashalidis	Katholieke Universiteit Leuven (Belgium)
V. Pham	University of Siegen (Germany)
S. Rea	Dartmouth College (USA)
A. Rial	Katholieke Universiteit Leuven (Belgium)
D. Sun	Queensland University of Technology (Australia)
Q. Tang	Katholieke Universiteit Leuven and University of Twente (Belgium, The Netherlands)
A. Tsochou	University of Piraeus (Greece)
N. Verde	University of Rome III (Italy)
G. Weaver	Dartmouth College (USA)
A. Yautsiukin	National Research Council (Italy)

Table of Contents

Session 5: Identity Management

Session 6: PKI and PKC Applications

PorKI: Portable PKI Credentials via Proxy Certificates*

Massimiliano Pala, Sara Sinclair, and Sean W. Smith

Computer Science Department
PKI/Trust Lab, Dartmouth College
6211 Sudikoff, Hanover, NH 03755, US
{pala,sinclair,sws}@cs.dartmouth.edu

Abstract. Authenticating human users using public key cryptography
provides a number of useful security properties, such as being able to
authenticate to remote party without giving away a secret. However,
in many scenarios, users need to authenticate from a number of client
machines, of varying degrees of trustworthiness. In previous work, we
proposed an approach to solving this problem by giving users portable
devices which wirelessly issue temporary, limited-use proxy certificates to
the clients. In this paper, we describe our complete prototype, enabling
the use of proxy credentials issued from a mobile device to securely authenticate users to remote servers via a shared (or otherwise not trusted)
device. In particular, our PorKI implementation combines out-of-band
authentication (via 2D barcode images), standard Proxy Certificates, and
platform attestation to provide usable and secure temporary credentials
for web-based applications.

Keywords: Mobile Authentication, Usable Security, Website Authentication, Proxy Certificates, PKI.

1   Introduction

Usability is critical to the success of a secure computer system [19]. In particular, the user's experience in performing common actions—such as authenticating
to the system—has a strong impact on their overall engagement with the system [15]. Authentication schemes based on public key cryptography offer more
rigorous security guarantees than passwords, but the overhead costs of obtaining
credentials and configuring them for use on commodity machines makes PKI essentially unusable in many domains. Moreover, there is no clear-cut way to use
a private key on a potentially untrustworthy workstation without exposing that
key to compromise.

---

* This work was supported in part by Intel Corporation and by the NSF, under grant
CNS-0448499. The views and conclusions contained in this document are those of
the authors and should not be interpreted as necessarily representing the official
policies, either expressed or implied, of any of the sponsors.

J. Camenisch and C. Lambrinoudakis (Eds.): EuroPKI 2010, LNCS 6711, pp. 1–16, 2011.
© Springer-Verlag Berlin Heidelberg 2011

At the same time that these challenges prevent PKI from gaining wide adoption among end users, we are becoming increasingly dependent on remote systems to store and process sensitive data (e.g., in the cloud). As this dependence grows, so too does our awareness that password-based authentication is glaringly insufficient.

This work. We therefore propose a novel approach to user authentication from a client machine. Our solution—named *PorKI* because it enables long-term PKI credentials to be portable across machines—leverages the user's smart phone as a credential repository, and generates limited-use proxy certificates for short-lived key-pairs for use on potentially untrustworthy workstations. This paper focuses on an implementation of PorKI targeted at authentication to web-based resources; we also present software for the workstation that allows the user to authenticate to websites using the proxy certificate she generates on her smart phone.

Paper Organization. In Section 2 we summarize related work and briefly survey existing mechanisms for user authentication on the web. We describe the design of the PorKI system in Section 3, and discuss details of our implementation in Section 4. How to enable PorKI authentication in Web Applications is discussed in Section 5. Finally, Section 6 provides our conclusions proposals for future work.

2 Related Work

This is a brief overview of related work; for a more complete treatment, see the earlier paper on the design of PorKI [14].

The predominant mechanism for authenticating users on the web is the classic secret password, despite its vulnerability to phishing and other attacks. RSA's SecureID [12] adds an additional factor of authentication, although deploying tokens may not be appropriate for all organizations. Smartcards and USB PKI tokens face similar cost and logistical challenges; moreover, a compromised workstation can take advantage of the access to the user's keypair, even with user- and system-level controls in place [7]. Instead of reducing the size of the Trusted Computing Base (TCB) to fit a secure co-processing unit as in the SHEMP project [6], our work uses an external device (i.e. a smart phone) as a personal TCB.

Work by Wu et al [9] leverages a cell phone and a trusted third party to protect credentials from the workstation. Different from our solution, their solution requires the user to input data to authenticate a specific session instead of automatically generate short-lived strong proxy credentials while authenticating to a remote server. Sharp et al. [13] augment the workstation interface with a trusted browser on the user's mobile device, which can then be used to securely enter passwords or other sensitive information. Garriss et al. [5] present a system with which a user can use a mobile device to verify the identity and integrity of software on the workstation; after the verification process is complete, the user may be more confident about sharing his credentials with the machine.

PorKI's system for establishing a trusted channel of communication between devices—via the mobile device's camera and a 2D barcode displayed on the workstation—is similar to that of the Grey System [8]. In their work, the authors use the discovery functionality of Bluetooth and barcode images to securely transfer ephemeral keys or self-signed certificates. In our work, we leverage their technique to allow pairing of the devices over IP network (i.e., without requiring the Bluetooth discovery properties)—but we differ by providing support for standard proxy credentials (proxy certificates) for web-based applications.

2.1 Proxy Certificates

The problem of exposing a user's credentials when accessing services on public or shared computers is well-known. As the sharing of strategic resources grows beyond a single campus or organization (e.g. in computing grids), the need grows to provide simple ways to use short-lived or ad-hoc credentials demands for usable solutions.

We think that the usage of a mobile device and the possibility to easily transfer proxy-credentials to the shared device provide a better security paradigm and a more usable solution.

To allow for simple authentication delegation, the IETF standardized Proxy Certificates allows a user to issue herself a certificate which enables only a subset of the permissions present in her long-lived identity certificate. Proxy Certificates use the X.509 standard with the prescriptions described in RFC 3820 [18]. Proxy Certificates bind a public key to a subject name, as normal identity certificates do. The use of the same format as X.509 public key certificates allows Proxy Certificates to be compatible with existing protocols and libraries which significantly eases implementation. However, unlike a public key certificate, the issuer (and signer) of a Proxy Certificate is an End Entity (EE) or another Proxy Certificate rather than a Certification Authority (CA). Therefore, Proxy Certificates can be created dynamically without requiring the normally heavy-weight vetting process associated with obtaining EE certificates from a CA. Intuitively, this approach is safe because it only permits the EE to delegate a subset of its own identity and privileges to this new, temporary keypair.

As the standard mandates, the subject name of a Proxy Certificate is scoped by the subject name of its issuer to achieve uniqueness. This is accomplished by appending a CommonName relative distinguished name component (RDN) to the issuers subject name. This means that the *subject* of the proxy certificate (or *Distinguished Name*) has to include the user's original one plus an additional *CommonName* (CN) field whose value is, usually, set to "Proxy". Moreover, the user can include only a subset of her own identity certificate permissions into her proxy credentials. That is, let ϕ be the set of original permissions in the user's certificate χ and ϕ' the set of permissions present in the proxy certificate χ'. Then the set of allowed permissions ψ is a subset of the one present in the user's certificate χ as restricted by the proxy certificate's permissions, i.e. $\psi = \phi \cap \phi'$. In particular, the user can limit the validity period, the Key/Extended Key usage, and embed a usage policy.

By using proxy certificates, temporary strong short-lived credentials can be easily issued (matching temporary, short-lived key-pairs). This approach limits the exposure of the user's credentials to a very short temporal window, thus allowing their usage also on shared computing devices as their expiration guarantees that they can no longer be used beyond the intended period. Although this approach has been deployed within some communities, such as scientific grid computing, its main drawback is that revocation of these type of certificates is very inconvenient. Therefore, such approaches(e.g., [2]) completely avoid publishing revocation information. Moreover, although requesting a new certificate is a quite frequent operation (because of the limited validity period), the process can be either quite cumbersome on the user part or rely on very lightweight authentication procedures.

Although already standardized, proxy certificates are not yet widely adopted outside specific communities of users, such as grid computing.

3   System Design

Suppose Alice wants to authenticate to a remote relying party Bob through a client workstation W that neither Alice nor Bob trust completely. Alice could use a PKI-equipped USB token—but this requires that W contain drivers for this token, and (what's worse) can expose Alice's key to malicious use by W [7].

PorKI enables Alice to do this without exposing her identity private key— but without having to do any complicated work or assuming anything special hardware properties of W. In particular, our work combines the usability and ubiquity of mobile devices, the security of out-of-band communication for secure key management, and the compatibility of legacy X.509-based authentication with proxy-credentials delegation.

In PorKI, the main idea is to generate and transfer ad-hoc proxy credentials (i.e., the proxy certificate and the corresponding private key) from a mobile device (such as a smart phone) to W (e.g., a shared lab computer or an internet-cafe terminal). These newly generated credentials can be used to securely authenticate Alice to Bob via standard protocols (e.g., SSL, TLS, or DTLS) applications already use. By using the proxy keypair, the Alice's long-term one is kept safe on the mobile device and never transferred to the shared device W.

In our work, we identified three main components, i.e. (1) the mobile device application, (2) the shared device extension that manages PorKI's operations, and (3) Proxy Certificates enabled services and applications. In this section we focus on the description of the first two components. We provide considerations on leveraging the information embedded in the user's proxy credentials in section 4.

PorKI in a Nutshell. The user activities required to issue proxy-credentials via PorKI is depicted in Fig. 1. The mobile device is paired with the shared one (e.g., Internet station) via barcode images generated on the latter that carry the channel authentication information needed to secure the communication between the devices. Once a secure communication channel has been established between

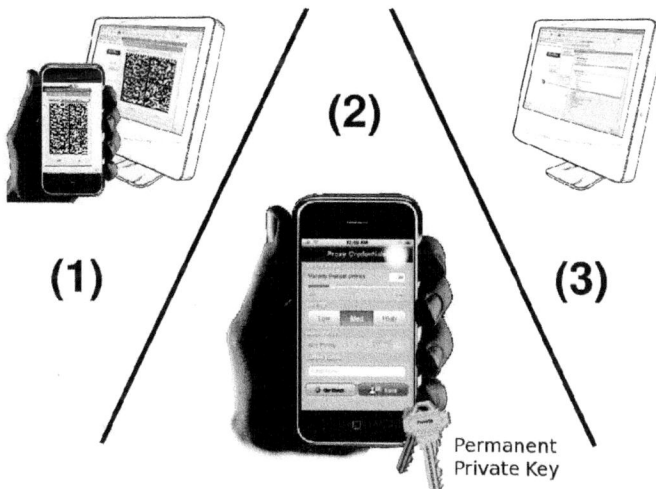

Fig. 1. User interactions with PorKI: first (1) the user pairs the mobile device and the shared workstation using the former's camera to read the barcode displayed on the latter. Next (2) she has the option to modify the parameters according to which the proxy certificate with be generated; when she taps the *send* (highlighted) button, the credentials are transferred. The user can now (3) use her short-term credentials in the browser on the shared workstation to authenticate to web resources.

the two devices (via this pairing), trust measurements about the shared one (eg., TPM attestation) are transferred to the mobile device and embedded into the proxy credentials. Then, the new certificate and keypair are transferred back to the paired device together with the full chain of certificates up to the trust root.

As described later in 3.2, we extended the Firefox browser to act as the PorKI-enabled application on the shared device. Once PorKI is activated and the proxy-credentials are transferred to the browser on the shared device, the user can authenticate herself to web applications by using her new proxy-credentials.

3.1 Smart Phone Application

PorKI leverages the possibility to securely store the user's long credentials into a mobile device that the user is acquainted with. In particular, as phones and other smart devices like iPods or PDAs are very popular, we leverage the user's familiarity with these devices in order to provide usable proxy credentials.

Assumptions. To securely pair the mobile device with the shared one (W), we assume that:

- The shared resource W has a display capable of displaying images of 400 by 400 pixels. Since we use black and white images, the display does not need color capabilities.

- The mobile device is capable of taking VGA resolution pictures. Although it is possible to use lower resolutions for detecting the barcode displayed on the shared resource, the usage of VGA resolution reduces the detection error rates and increases the usability of the mobile application. We notice that today even low-cost mobile phones carry camera with higher resolution.
- The mobile resource is capable of contacting the shared resource via IP (e.g., over wifi, 3G, or EDGE networks).

As the third assumption is quite important, it requires further discussion. To transfer the shared device's trust measurement and the proxy credentials back to the shared device, PorKI needs a secured communication channel between the two devices. In our previous work [14], we focused on the usage of bluetooth [1] as the out-of-band channel for transferring the user's proxy credentials, but this proved to be too restrictive as most of the shared resources (eg., desktop computers) do not come with bluetooth capabilities. Therefore, we divided the pairing process into two separate phases. During the first one, we transfer only the information needed to establish the secure communication channel (a symmetric 128-bit key) by using barcode images as the out-of-band channel. During the second phase, we establish the secure channel and transfer the information back and forth the two devices.

In other words, we use the out-of-band communication only for transferring the shared resource's (W) network address and the encryption/integrity key to securely pair the devices (i.e., setup the encrypted communication channel). Subsequent data transfers happen via IP communication. This assumption is reasonable as the two devices are physically in the same location and, in many cases, share the same LAN segment. Although this approach cannot be applied to every possible scenario (e.g., because of the presence of firewalls), we think it is the least restrictive assumption possible.

The User Interface. In PorKI, we designed the user interface in order to minimize the steps required by the user to issue and transfer the proxy credentials among devices. The application workflow is as follow:

1. The User starts the application and take a picture of the barcode image displayed on the shared resource display
2. The application automatically decodes the information from the image and establishes the secure communication channel (via TLS)
3. The User selects one of the stored credentials on the mobile device and sets the validity period of the proxy credentials via a simple bar selector
4. The mobile application generates the new keypair and issues the new proxy certificate.
5. The mobile device sends the proxy credentials in an encrypted PKCS#12 file to shared device over the authenticated communication channel

It is to be noted that the required level of interaction with the mobile device application is sensibly low (steps 1 and 3). In fact, compared to other solutions that require pairing the two devices via bluetooth, our approach based on barcode images proved to be quite effective.

```
id-porki          OBJECT IDENTIFIER ::= { id-pkix 50 }
     -- Object Identifier for the porkiDeviceInfo extension

porkiDeviceInfo ::= SEQUENCE {
     retrievedAt                 GeneralizedTime,
       -- time when the Info has been collected
     retrievedBy                 INTEGER,
       -- identifier for the component which gathered
       -- the device information
     data                        SEQUENCE OF OCTET STRING }
```

Fig. 2. ASN.1 notation for the `porkiDeviceInfo` extension that is used in the proxy certificate to store the shared device information

Proxy Credentials. By being able to directly issue proxy credentials (as opposed to have to request them from a third party), it is possible to embed the shared device's authentication information in the proxy certificate. For this purpose, we identified a new extension (i.e., porkiDeviceInfo) that allows for unstructured content to be embedded. In our application, we include a simple XACML assertion that carries information about the shared device that have been gathered by the shared device's PorKI application (i.e., the Firefox extension). The ASN.1 notation for the extension syntax is reported in Figure 2. This extension carries several fields. The `retrievedAt` is the time at which the measurement is performed. The value of this field can be used to evaluate the freshness of the information. In particular, it is possible to use cached values if the measurement is sufficiently recent, thus allowing for shorter communication between the paired devices if a recent pairing has recently took place. In `retrievedBy` we store the identifier of the component that performed the measurement. We identify with 0 the mobile device—the core of trust for PorKI. The browser extension is identified by 1, while any external component is identified by 2. Currently, the trust measurements are performed directly on the shared device and then transferred to the mobile device. In future versions of PorKI, we envisage gathering more reliable information about the shared device by performing a remote attestation of the platform [17]. If a remote attestation is performed by the mobile device, a higher level of trust for the performed measurements can be adopted by the web application. In this case, the presence of the `retrievedBy` field allows the relying party (e.g., the web application) to raise or lower its confidence in the porkiDeviceInfo contents. Ultimately, if the remote attestation cannot be performed (e.g., because of the lack of the TSS stack on the shared device), the current mechanism based on self-attestation on the shared device can be used as fallback option.

Location-Aware Certificates. In PorKI, we enabled the possibility to embed location information in the proxy-credentials. In fact, if the mobile device provides support for GPS or GSM positioning, the information is embedded in the proxy certificate in the form of another extension. For this, we identified

```
certIssuingLocation ::= SEQUENCE {
     latitude                  UTF8String,
         -- latitude information
     longitude                 UTF8String,
         -- longitude information
     elevation                 INTEGER,
         -- elevation (in meters) information
     levelOfAccuracy           INTEGER
         -- level of accuracy (in meters)
}
```

Fig. 3. ASN.1 notation for the `certIssuingLocation` extension. The information carried in this extension can be used for authentication, authorization and auditing purposes

the `certIssuingLocation` extension as defined in Figure 3. Because the level of accuracy of GPS/GSM positioning is usually very low inside buildings, the location information includes the `levelOfAccuracy` field which has to be taken in consideration when the location information is consumed. Also in this case, because the mobile device is the source of trust in PorKI, the location information embedded in the proxy credentials can be considered trustworthy under the assumption that the device is not subject to a GPS spoofing attack. Although we notice that this attack is easy to carry out [16] and that there is no protection against it in current GPS receivers, it is possible to detect GPS spoofing attack by combining and analyzing location information gathered through both the GSM and the GPS networks. On mobile devices that do not provide the possibility to access a second source of location information (e.g., PDAs), several proposals have been made on how to fix this problem [4, 10]. We hope that the next generation of GPS receivers will provide also authentication information to allow applications to recognize the level of trustworthiness of the signal (e.g., by using information about the time, noise level and strength's of the GPS signal, reported accelerations' sanity checks).

In PorKI, both authentication and authorization engines of web applications could use the location information to grant or restrict access to specific resources depending on the physical location of the user. The information collected by the mobile device, could be of value for several scenarios. Besides using the user's position for authorization purposes, this information could be used later on for auditing purposes.

3.2   The Browser Extension

In our work, a central component is the PorKI application that enables the shared device to transfer and install the temporary proxy credentials.

Because our implementation is aimed at providing support for web-based applications, we chose to develop the PorKI application as an extension for the Firefox browser. This choice has several side-benefits. First, the installation of extensions for the browser is quite an easy process and users are already used to

Fig. 4. Barcode image generated by the PorKI application. The image encodes the shared device IP address and the shared session key.

it. Moreover, the extension code can be digitally signed thus allowing for code verification and automatic updates.

Although our choices were driven by the specific example scenario of Alice authenticating to a Web site operated by Bob, the general design of the PorKI application can easily be applied to other contexts. For example, operating systems could provide an update/extension process for their certificates store that would allow the installation/creation of a PorKI-enabled store. It is out of the scope of this work to discuss all the possibilities offered by the different OSes or software distribution technologies.

Out-of-Band Data. The browser extension is responsible to generate the barcode image (Figure 4) that is used to setup the secure communication channel between devices. As the first step, the shared device generates a session key that is used to establish the encrypted and integrity-checked channel with the mobile device. The same key is also used to decrypt the PKCS#12 file that contains the proxy credentials. Together with the generated symmetric key (3DES), the network IP address of the shared device is embedded in the 2D barcode that is displayed to the user when she requires to transfer/generate a new proxy credential. Once the secure communication is established between the two devices, the PorKI application sends the details about the shared device to the mobile one. This data can be in any format and is meant to be consumed by the web-application. It is to be noted that, besides initiating the process, the user is not asked to interact with the PorKI application on the shared device.

4   Implementation Details

During the development of PorKI, we identified two main challenges: providing support for Proxy Certificates across operating systems and devices, and enabling the usage of Proxy Certificates for SSL/TLS authentication in Firefox.

To address the first issue, we used and enhanced LibPKI [11] to support proxy certificates. In particular, we added support for PKCS#12 tokens manipulation and proxy certificates profiles management.

The second issue proved to be difficult to solve as much legacy software does not allow easily extension of the crypto APIs in order to support proxy certificates. The main problem in adding support for proxy certificates is the path building process. In fact, according to RFC 5280 [3], an End Entity (EE) cannot sign certificates. Therefore, the path construction and validation for a proxy certificate fails in crypto libraries that do not explicitly support them. Thus, solving this problem can potentially require to directly patch large parts of the browser software. Fortunately, this was not required in our implementation. As we describe in 4.2, we leverage the properties of Firefox's certificates store to alter the normal behavior of the browser and convince it to use the imported proxy credentials as normal identity certificates.

4.1   iPhone and Proxy Certificates via LibPKI

In order to develop the PorKI mobile application, we needed a platform that was able to provide the required functionality out of the box or that would allow us to port existing software to the device in an easy fashion. Fortunately, the iPhoneOS and its development environment allow for UNIX programs to be ported by using open-source tools like GCC. In particular, to address our needs for cryptographic functionality, we were able to compile LibPKI by using the iPhone SDK (v2.0, v3.0, and v3.1.3). The possibility of using LibPKI instead of the native cryptographic functionality built into the iPhoneOS helped us in:

- reducing the size and complexity of the iPhone application
- support proxy-certificate creation easily
- building secure connection channel with the shared device via the provided URL interface

For encoding and decoding barcode images, we used libdmtx[1]. We managed to port this library to the iPhoneOS as well as MacOS X and Linux operating systems. Because all the other libraries we rely on are already available across these systems by default (e.g., libxml2, pthreads, and OpenSSL), we decided to use the same set of tools to develop both the iPhone application and the browser's extension.

[1] The DMTX library is available at http://www.libdmtx.org/

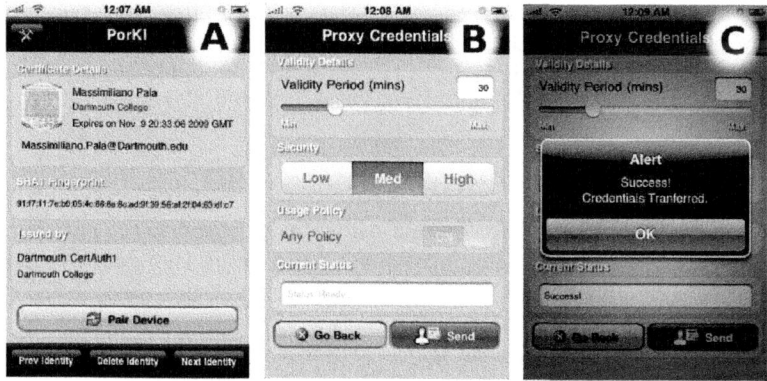

Fig. 5. PorKI's user interface on the iPhone: (a) the identity certificate display view, (b) the proxy-credential issuing view, and (c) communication box for the successful transfer of the proxy credentials

Touch User Interface. The PorKI UI on the iPhone provides a usable and clean interface that minimizes the required user interaction. Figure 5 provides some screenshots of the interface. At first, the PorKI application allows the user to select the identity to be used to generate the proxy credentials in the main screen (A). After that, the user can use the "Pair Device" button to initiate the pairing of the device. The standard iPhone picture-taking interface is then displayed and, after the picture is taken, the proxy-credential issuing interface (B) is displayed. In the current version, the user can select the validity period (in minutes) of the proxy credentials and the key length—in the form of a simple "weak", "medium", and "strong" selector—only. In future versions we will explore how to provide the user with meaningful information required to decide about which policy information to be embedded in the proxy certificate. After the validity period is chosen, a tap on the "Send" button will send the newly issued credentials to the shared device and imported into the browser automatically. A simple confirmation popup (C) is displayed to the user upon successful transfer. In case of an error, an appropriate message is displayed instead.

The PKCS#12 ***Contents.*** Because the PKCS#12 format is meant to provide a container for identity certificates, it does not explicitly support proxy-certificates. This means that there is no specific "bag" where the proxy-certificate should be stored in. We decided to put the proxy-certificate in the identity-certificate bag and push the identity-certificate in the CA's one. As specified in more details in 4.2, this allowed us to identify the proxy-certificate as a CERT_TYPE_PROXY_USER while the user's identity one as a CERT_TYPE_PROXY_CA.

The current version of the iPhone application does not allow a user to import her own credentials from an external source. In the prototype we simply embedded several identity certificates in the form of encrypted PKCS#12 files. In our future work, we plan to leverage the URI interface in LibPKI to transfer the user's long term credentials from an external repository to the mobile device via different transport protocols (e.g., ldap, https, mysql, postgresq, ssh). By using this approach, a simple URI can be used to configure the application. Both the Firefox Extension and the iPhone source code are available from the project's repository[2].

4.2   The PorKI Firefox Extension

The PorKI extension for Firefox is responsible (a) to generate the pairing images, (b) to import the proxy-credentials, and (c) to enable the usage of the newly issued proxy credentials and setting the appropriate trust configuration in the application store.

Our Firefox extension has two main parts. First, there's the lower-level functionality developed in C++. These functionality are then wrapped by using the XPCOMM interface and exposed to the top layer via JavaScript calls. The usage of LibPKI as our cryptographic provider sensibly contributed to reduce the size of the C++ code. In particular, the compiled part of the Firefox extension is only 1160 lines of code (the JavaScript part is 500 lines of code).

Lower Level Functions. The PorKI lower level API exposes a very restricted number of functions to the upper level. In particular, we expose the following:

- `GetLocalAddr()` provides the IP address of the shared device
- `GenHexKey()` generates the shared key
- `GenBarCode()` generates the barcode image and stores it in a local directory on shared device
- `GetUserProxy()` opens the communication channel with the mobile device and stores the retrieved PKCS#12 file
- `ImportProxyCertDB()` — imports the proxy-credentials into Firefox's certificate store and sets the appropriate trust configuration

among these, the most interesting function is the latter. In fact, during the design of PorKI we planned to extend Firefox in order to:

- correctly import a proxy certificate
- enable the proxy-certificate to be used as a normal user certificate

Because Firefox provides the possibility to interact with its certificate store and, most importantly, to extend the SSL/TLS callbacks, in our original design we planned to use both of these features to enable the usage of proxy-credentials for normal browsing operations.

Because of the lack of documentation on the internals of Firefox, the best implementation strategy was not clear. After studying the NSS library (the security library that provides the cryptographic functionality to Firefox) internals, we realized that Firefox heavily relies on the library to store, retrieve, and verify certificates. The proxy-credentials import process has been divided into two functions: `ImportNSSKeypair()`, and `ImportNSSCertificate()`. The first function

---

[2] http://mm.cs.dartmouth.edu/porki/

Table 1. Trust Settings for PorKI's Imported Certificates in Firefox Trust Store

Certificate Type	Trust Flags
CERT_TYPE_CA	CERTDB_TRUSTED_CA, CERTDB_VALID_CA, CERTDB_TRUSTED
CERT_TYPE_EMAIL	CERTDB_VALID_PEER
CERT_TYPE_SERVER	CERTDB_VALID_PEER
CERT_TYPE_PROXY_CA	CERTDB_TRUSTED_CA, CERTDB_TRUSTED_CLIENT_CA CERTDB_VALID_CA, CERTDB_SEND_WARN, CERTDB_TRUSTED
CERT_TYPE_PROXY_USER	CERTDB_VALID_PEER, CERTDB_SEND_WARN CERTDB_TRUSTED, CERTDB_USER

takes care of importing the private key and set the usage flags in the store. The second one, takes care of importing a certificate in the appropriate store. In PorKI we use the following types of certificates during our import process:

- CERT_TYPE_PROXY_USER, which identifies the proxy-certificate issued by the mobile device
- CERT_TYPE_PROXY_CA, which identifies the user's identity certificate (the certificate used to sign the proxy credentials)
- CERT_TYPE_CA, which identifies any other CA certificate in the chain of certificates up to the user's root CA

When parsing the contents of the PKCS#12 file, the certificates are imported into the Firefox store according to their type. In particular, after retrieving a reference to the default certificate store, our ImportNSSCertificate() function sets the trust flags in the NSS object. Table 1 provides a list of all the trust settings for the different type of certificates and their trust settings. Because of the lack of documentation about the meaning and the effects of each trust setting, we performed some tests to discover the right set of trust settings. Specifically, after importing the certificate with the CERT_ImportCerts() function, by setting the appropriate trust settings via the CERT_ChangeCertTrust() NSS function, PorKI is able to correctly import the proxy credentials and have Firefox to correctly verify the full chain of certificates. Surprisingly, this automatically enables the usage of the proxy credentials in Firefox also for browsing activities. We note that enabling proxy-certificates usage in the NSS library was easier than expected.

Higher Level Functionality. The high-level functionality are provided via the JavaScript portion of the Firefox extension. In particular, we use an Icon on the status bar that the user can interact with. By left-clicking on the Icon, the user activates the generation of the barcode image (openBarCode()), while a right-click on the PorKI icon simply opens up the Certificate Dialog where the user can verify her own certificates and identity settings. Figure 6 shows the default Certificate Dialog correctly showing the details of a proxy certificate generated with PorKI.

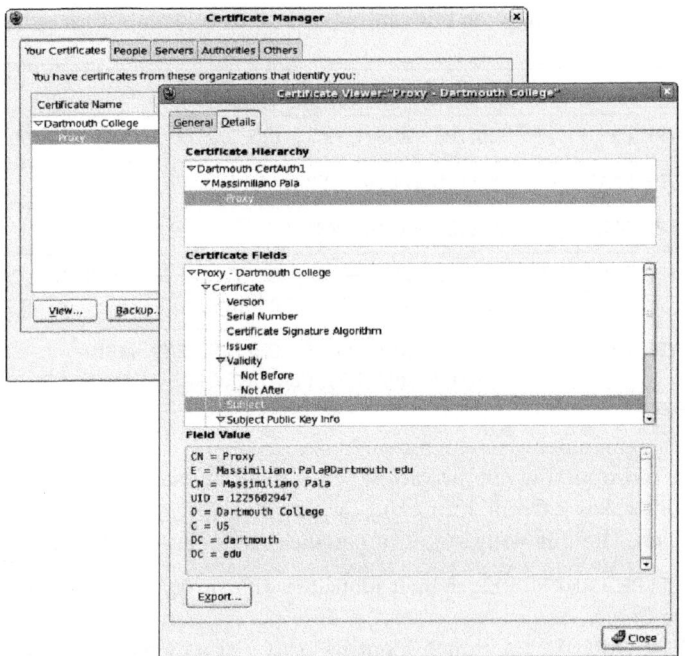

Fig. 6. The Proxy Certificate installed on Firefox as displayed by the standard certificate selector

5   Enabling PorKI Authentication in Web Applications

In order to evaluate the usability of the PorKI system, we evaluated the impact on configuring some PKI-enabled web applications to accept our proxy-credentials instead of the user's identity certificate. In particular, we evaluated a widely adopted systems: GridWiki.

This software is used by many communities of users or researchers to exchange information about their interests or work. We choose this specific software because it supports user authentication via X.509 certificate out of the box.

Our purpose was to determine how difficult would it be to enable the usage of PorKI's proxy credentials (standard X.509 proxy certificates) in GridWiki, and how usable would the user's experience be. Specifically, we installed GridWiki on a Linux machine running Apache v2.2.6.

Because Apache uses the OpenSSL library as its cryptographic provider, in order to enable the support for proxy-certificates for SSL/TLS, we just needed to set the OPENSSL_ALLOW_PROXY_CERTS environment variable in the server's startup script. This simple change allowed existing users (users that already registered themselves on the wiki page) to login into the Wiki by using their proxy credentials instead of their regular certificates. Also, no problems were reported when new users registered on the wiki by using their proxy credentials directly.

As reported earlier in this paper, it is interesting to notice how simple the whole setup process was, both from the sysadmin and the user perspectives.

6   Conclusions and Future Work

This work represents a new approach to end-user key management. The PorKI system allows average users to authenticate to remote web resources with their PKI credentials; moreover, it allows those users to authenticate from workstations of varying trustworthiness without exposing their long-term keypair to attack. The tool is flexible, usable, and based on widely-accepted PKI standards; because it also leverages a popular mobile platform and a lightweight browser extension, it can be easily deployed in a variety of settings.

As described in Section 3, we envision using the mobile device to perform remote attestation of the workstation (similar to work by Garriss et al. [5]) during the negotiation of the short-term credentials. Having more trustworthy information about the workstation would allow the remote party stronger confidence in providing the user with access to the sensitive data. As in the SHEMP project [6], we can also envision crafting custom policies to govern the types of access that may be performed using a given set of short-term credentials; we anticipate that corporate organizations who allow their employees to access company systems from personal workstations would have a particular interest in this sort of fine-grained access management.

References

1. Bluetooth SIG: Specification of the Bluetooth System, Core Version 1.2 (2003), http://www.bluetooth.org/
2. Cholia, S., Genovese, T., Skow, D.: Profile for SLCS X.509 Public Key Certification Authorities with Secured Infrastructure (2009), http://www.tagpma.org/files/SLCS-2.1b.pdf
3. Cooper, D., Santesson, S., Farrell, S., Boeyen, S., Housley, R., Polk, W.: Internet X.509 Public Key Infrastructure Certificate and Certificate Revocation List (CRL) Profile. RFC 5280 (May 2008), http://www.ietf.org/rfc/rfc5280.txt
4. El-Bakry, H.M., Mastorakis, N.: Design of Anti-GPS for Reasons of Security. In: CIS 2009: Proceedings of the International Conference on Computational and Information Science 2009, pp. 480–500. World Scientific and Engineering Academy and Society (WSEAS), Stevens Point (2009)
5. Garriss, S., Cáceres, R., Berger, S., Sailer, R., van Doorn, L., Zhang, X.: Trustworthy and Personalized Computing on Public Kiosks. In: MobiSys 2008: Proceeding of the 6th International Conference on Mobile Systems, Applications, and Services, pp. 199–210. ACM, New York (2008)
6. Marchesini, J.: Shemp: Secure Hardware Enhanced MyProxy. Ph.D. thesis, Dartmouth College, Hanover, NH, USA (2005)
7. Marchesini, J., Smith, S.W., Zhao, M.: Keyjacking: The Surprising Insecurity of Client-Side SSL. Computers & Security 24(2), 109–123 (2005)

8. McCune, J.M., Perrig, A., Reiter, M.K.: Seeing-Is-Believing: Using Camera Phones for Human-Verifiable Authentication. In: SP 2005: Proceedings of the 2005 IEEE Symposium on Security and Privacy, pp. 110–124. IEEE Computer Society, Washington, DC, USA (2005)
9. Wu, M., Garfinkel, S., Miller, R.: Secure Web Authentication with Mobile Phones. In: MIT Project Oxygen: Student Oxygen Workshop (2003)
10. Mundt, T.: Two Methods of Authenticated Positioning. In: Q2SWinet 2006: Proceedings of the 2nd ACM International Workshop on Quality of service & Security for Wireless and Mobile Networks, pp. 25–32. ACM, New York (2006)
11. Pala, M.: The LibPKI project. Project Homepage, https://www.openca.org/projects/libpki/
12. RSA: RSA SecurID Two-Factor Authentication. RSA Solution Brief (2010)
13. Sharp, R., Madhavapeddy, A., Want, R., Pering, T.: Enhancing Web Browsing Security on Public Terminals using Mobile Composition. In: MobiSys 2008: Proceeding of the 6th International Conference on Mobile Systems, Applications, and Services, pp. 94–105. ACM, New York (2008)
14. Sinclair, S., Smith, S.W.: PorKI: Making User PKI Safe on Machines of Heterogeneous Trustworthiness. In: Annual Conference on Computer Security Applications, vol. 0, pp. 419–430 (2005)
15. Singh, S., Cabraal, A., Demosthenous, C., Astbrink, G., Furlong, M.: Password Sharing: Implications for Security Design Based on Social Practice. In: CHI 2007: Proceedings of the SIGCHI Conference on Human Factors in Computing Systems, pp. 895–904. ACM, New York (2007)
16. Tippenhauer, N.O., Rasmussen, K.B., Pöpper, C., Čapkun, S.: Attacks on Public WLAN-based Positioning Systems. In: MobiSys 2009: Proceedings of the 7th International Conference on Mobile Systems, Applications, and Services, pp. 29–40. ACM, New York (2009)
17. Trusted Computing Group: TCG Specification Architecture Overview. Specification, Revision 1.4 (August 2007), http://www.trustedcomputinggroup.org/files/resource_files/ AC652DE1-1D09-3519-ADA026A0C05CFAC2/TCG_1_4_Architecture_Overview.pdf
18. Tuecke, S., Welch, V., Engert, D., Pearlman, L., Thompson, M.: Internet X.509 Public Key Infrastructure (PKI) Proxy Certificate Profile. RFC 3820 (Proposed Standard) (June 2004), http://www.ietf.org/rfc/rfc3820.txt
19. Whitten, A., Tygar, J.D.: Why Johnny Can't Encrypt: a Usability Evaluation of PGP 5.0. In: Proceedings of the 8th USENIX Security Symposium, p. 14. USENIX Association, Berkeley (1999)

A New Revocable Secret Handshake Scheme with Backward Unlinkability*

Yamin Wen[1,2] and Fangguo Zhang[1,**]

[1] School of Information Science and Technology
Sun Yat-sen University, Guangzhou 510275, P.R. China
isszhfg@mail.sysu.edu.cn
[2] School of Mathematics and Computational Science
Guangdong University of Business Studies, Guangzhou 510320, P.R. China
yamin.wen@gmail.com

Abstract. Secret handshake schemes allow the members of a certain organization can anonymously authenticate each other. In this paper, a new revocable secret handshake scheme with backward unlinkability is presented. Our new scheme achieves the impersonator resistance against Group Authority (GA), such that group members are protected from being impersonated and framed by a malicious GA. Also the revocation is obtained in the new scheme, as well as the unlinkability and the traceability. Moreover, the anonymity of revoked members is improved so that the past transcripts of revoked members remain private, i.e., *backward unlinkability*. Our new scheme is provably secure in the random oracle model by assuming the intractability of $q+1$ Square Roots Problem and Decisional Bilinear Diffie-Hellman Problem. We stress that the improved anonymity of revoked members answers the open problem of the backward unlinkability on secret handshakes, which is left by Jarecki and Liu at CRYPTO 2009.

Keywords: Mutual authentication, Secret handshakes, Unlinkability, Revocation.

1 Introduction

With a rapid development of online applications via public networks, privacy is more and more noticed by people. Privacy-preserving authentication plays a pivotal role among the whole privacy concerns. In an anonymous authentication system, a user can prove himself (prover) to others (verifier) that he obtains a valid credential from a trusted Certification Authority (CA) without leaking any private information. A well-known method for realizing the uni-directionally privacy-preserving authentication is anonymous credentials [6]. Unfortunately,

---

* This work is supported by the the National Natural Science Foundation of China (No. 60773202, 61070168).
** The corresponding author.

J. Camenisch and C. Lambrinoudakis (Eds.): EuroPKI 2010, LNCS 6711, pp. 17–30, 2011.

uni-directionally anonymous authentications still have to exchange the information about the trusted CA (affiliation). In some sensitive applications, the leakage of affiliation is not acceptable for privacy concerns. A typical example is that members of FBI want to secretly authenticate each other. The prover will reveal his affiliation if and only if the verifier holds the same one, and vice versa. Therefore, it is necessary to seek a mutually anonymous authentication solution, which can not only protect the identity information of participants, but also provide a privacy-preserving property on their affiliations. *Secret Handshake*, which has been introduced by Balfanz *et al.* [2], is exactly designed for realizing mutually anonymous authentication on public networks.

Derived from the pioneering publication of Balfanz *et al.* [2], many two-party secret handshake schemes have been proposed from different cryptographic primitives. For instances, CA-oblivious encryption [7], ElGamal signature [17] and RSA [13]. All those works use one-time pseudonyms to ensure the unlinkability of secret handshakes which are executed by the same members. In addition, it is straightforward for Group Authority (GA) to trace and revoke its members because GA knows all one-time pseudonyms of members. However, one-time pseudonyms based schemes require more storage and computation costs in practice. Moreover, since it knows all secret information of group members, GA is able to impersonate and frame its members for malicious behaviors. Thus the anonymity against GA can be hardly achieved by using one-time pseudonyms.

Based on reusable credentials, Xu and Yung [15] first offered a secret handshake scheme which has a "weaker" unlinkability than the schemes from one-time pseudonyms. By using identity-based encryption [14], Ateniese *et al.* [1] presented the first efficient unlinkable secret handshake scheme with reusable credentials. Afterwards, Jarecki and Liu [8] proposed a revocable secret handshake scheme with unlinkability via broadcast encryption. Yet Jarecki and Liu's scheme [8] is impractical for the following reasons. Firstly, the scheme [8] requires that all groups have the same numbers of revoked members synchronously. Secondly, the number of group public keys are increased linearly with the number of group members. Moreover, by using reusable credentials, GA cannot completely trace members' behaviors anymore because of the randomness of transcripts from executed handshakes. Hence all above works based on reusable credentials will have advantage of the unlinkability, which implies that even GA cannot link and trace group members' behaviors. On the other hand, it also becomes difficult to add the revocation of malicious members to the untraceable schemes from reusable credentials.

Nevertheless, a practical secret handshake scheme should realize similar security properties as a group signature scheme. Namely, secret handshakes with reusable credentials are required to be traceable, revocable and unlinkable. Recently, Kawai *et al.* [10] proposed the definition of strong anonymity for secret handshakes at ISPEC 2009, which takes malicious GA into consideration. They constructed an unlinkable secret handshake scheme with reusable credentials, which supports strong detector resistance and co-traceability by using group signature with message recovery. However, the revocation mechanism is not explicitly considered in their scheme. In CRYPTO 2009, Jarecki and Liu [9] proposed a practical unlinkable secret handshake scheme, which supports both revocation and traceability with reusable credentials. But Jarecki and Liu's scheme [9] still exists two limitations. Firstly, GA still generates all secret information for every group member by using of verifier-local revocation group signature [5]. Hence, it is easy for a malicious GA to impersonate and frame a member in its group. For strong security, it is necessary to eliminate the possibility of GA's malicious behaviors. Secondly, the anonymity of revoked members cannot be guaranteed in Jarecki and Liu's scheme [9]. Namely, once a member is revoked, all past transcripts of the member can be recognized and traced by adversary after running revocation checking. As shown in [11], the property is also considered as *backward unlinkability*. It has been left by Jarecki and Liu [9] as an open question if there exists a secret handshake scheme with backward unlinkability.

Our Contributions. Inspired by Kawai *et al.*'s scheme [10] and Jarecki and Liu's scheme [9], a new construction of revocable secret handshake scheme, which is named by RSH, is presented. Compared to the related schemes [9,10], the contributions of our new scheme are two-fold. Firstly, the security of RSH is improved by consideration of a malicious behavior of GA. Namely, RSH can protect group members from being impersonated and framed by malicious GA, which is not considered by Jarecki and Liu's scheme [9]. Our new method is to apply a two-party secure computation protocol between GA and user when GA issues group credential to each user. Secondly, revocation mechanism is appended to the secret handshake scheme, which is not achieved by Kawai *et al.*'s scheme [10]. In addition, the anonymity of RSH is enhanced in view of revoked members, which allows the past transcripts of revoked members still keeping anonymous, i.e., *backward unlinkability*. Therefore, the new scheme is a practical revocable secret handshake scheme, which answers the open problem left by Jarecki and Liu at CRYPTO 2009 [9].

Organization. The remainder of this paper is organized as follows. In Section 2, we recall some preliminaries related to our work. In Section 3, the definition and security properties of secret handshakes are reviewed. In Section 4, RSH is presented together with its security analysis, and then the performance of the related schemes is compared. Section 5 concludes the paper.

2   Preliminaries

2.1   Bilinear Pairing

Let $\mathbb{G}$ be a (multiplicative) cyclic group of prime order p and g is a generator of $\mathbb{G}$. A one-way map $e : \mathbb{G} \times \mathbb{G} \to \mathbb{G}_T$ is a bilinear pairing if the following conditions hold. *Bilinear:* For all $g \in \mathbb{G}$, s.t., g is a generator of $\mathbb{G}$, and $a, b \in \mathbb{Z}_p$, $e(g^a, g^b) = e(g, g)^{ab}$. *Non-degeneracy:* $e(g, g) \neq 1$. In other words, if g generates $\mathbb{G}$, then $e(g, g)$ generates $\mathbb{G}_T$. *Computability:* There exists an efficient algorithm for computing $e(u, v)$ for all $u, v \in \mathbb{G}$.

2.2   Complexity Assumptions

Definition 1 (Decisional Bilinear Diffie-Hellman (DBDH) Problem [11]). *Let* $\mathbb{G}, \mathbb{G}_T$ *be cyclic groups of prime order p along with a bilinear map* $e : \mathbb{G} \times \mathbb{G} \to \mathbb{G}_T$, *and let* $g \in \mathbb{G}$ *be generator of* $\mathbb{G}$. *The DBDH problem is* (t, ϵ)-*hard if all t-time adversaries* $\mathcal{A}$ *can solve the DBDH problem with the following advantage:*

$$\mathtt{Adv}_{\mathcal{A}}^{DBDH} = |\Pr[\mathcal{A}(g, g^a, g^b, g^c, e(g,g)^{abc} = 1)] \\ - \Pr[\mathcal{A}(g, g^a, g^b, g^c, e(g,g)^d) = 1]| < \epsilon$$

where $a, b, c, d \leftarrow_R \mathbb{Z}_p^*$.

DBDH Assumption: We say that the DBDH assumption holds if there exists no algorithm can solve the DBDH problem with a non-negligible advantage in a polynomial time bound. In other words, for $g \in \mathbb{G}$ and $a, b, c, d \leftarrow_R \mathbb{Z}_p^*$, distinguish between tuples of the form $(g, g^a, g^b, g^c, e(g,g)^{abc})$ and $(g, g^a, g^b, g^c, e(g,g)^d)$ is infeasible.

Definition 2 ($q+1$ Square Roots Problem ($q+1$-SRP) [16]). *Let* $(\mathbb{G}, \mathbb{G}_T)$ *be two cyclic groups of prime order p. For an integer q, and* $x \in_R \mathbb{Z}_p, g \in \mathbb{G}$, *given*

$$\{g, \alpha = g^x, h_1, \cdots, h_q \in \mathbb{Z}_p, g^{(x+h_1)^{\frac{1}{2}}}, \cdots, g^{(x+h_q)^{\frac{1}{2}}}\},$$

compute $g^{(x+h)^{\frac{1}{2}}}$ *for some* $h \notin \{h_1, \cdots, h_q\}$.

$q + 1$-**SR Assumption:** We say that the $q + 1$-SR assumption holds if there exists no algorithm can solve the $q + 1$-SRP with a non-negligible advantage in a polynomial time bound.

3   Definition and Security Properties

Secret handshake scheme (denoted by SHS) operates in an environment which consists of a set of groups managed by a set of group authorities, and a set of users $U_1, \cdots, U_n$ registered into some groups. Based on the definitions in [2,9], our scheme consists of the following probabilistic polynomial-time algorithms:

- SHS.Setup: The Setup algorithm selects a security parameter κ to generate the public parameters **params** common to all subsequently generated groups.
- SHS.CreateGroup: CreateGroup is a key generation algorithm executed by GA to establish a group G. It takes **params** as input, and outputs group public key and private key (gpk_G, gsk_G).
- SHS.AddMember: AddMember is a two-party protocol run by user and GA. GA plays a role of the CA for the group, which issues credential for a legitimate member of the group. Assuming that GA can add n users to the group, each user generates his own private/public keys and revocation tokens $(usk[i], upk[i], urt[i])$ for each $i \in [1, n]$. After verifying the users' real

identities, GA interacts with users and corporately computes signatures on users' secret keys as their credentials. Consequently, each user can get credential $cred_i$ for $i \in [1, n]$ from GA and become a member of the group after the protocol.

- SHS.Handshake: Handshake is a two-party authenticate protocol executed by a pair of anonymous members (A, B), where (A, B) are possible members who may belong to different groups. The protocol inputs the anonymous member's secrets $(usk[i], cred_i, gpk_i)$ and other public information. The output of the protocol for each member is either "1" or "0". If A and B belong to the same group (i.e., $gpk_A = gpk_B$), the output is "1" and a session key K will be produced which can be used for subsequent secure communication between the two members.

- SHS.TraceMember: TraceMember is a polynomial time algorithm which is executed by the trace authority of GA. The protocol outputs the identity of member U, whilst a transcript of secret handshake involved with member U is submitted.

- SHS.RemoveMember: RemoveMember is a polynomial time algorithm which is authorized by the trace authority of GA. It takes its current Revocation List (RL) and U's revocation tokens as the inputs, whilst outputs an up-to-date RL that includes new revocation records.

Security properties. A secret handshake scheme should obey the basic security properties: *Completeness, Impersonator Resistance, Detector Resistance* and *Unlinkability*. Borrowed from [10,9], the formal definitions of these properties in our scheme are presented as follows.

Completeness. It requires that the SH protocol always outputs "1" when any interactive participants U_i and U_j honestly execute the Handshake protocol and satisfy the authentication policy of the counter-party, respectively.

Impersonator Resistance (IR). Intuitively, any adversary who attempts to impersonate a member of one group cannot succeed with non-negligible probability. As described in [9], this property implies the traceability. If a participant executes a successful secret handshake, the participant's identity can be derived from the corresponding transcript. Formally, the property is defined in the following game Game^{IR} between an adversary $\mathcal{A}$ and a challenger $\mathcal{B}$:

- **Init:** The adversary $\mathcal{A}$ first sets Chosen = $\{G^*, i^*\}$. Then $\mathcal{B}$ simulates Setup, CreateGroup and AddMember, and sends group public keys and up-to-date RL to $\mathcal{A}$.
- **Queries:** $\mathcal{A}$ can make the following queries, such that the responses will be simulated by $\mathcal{B}$.
  - **Corruption Queries:** The corruption list Cor is initialized as $\emptyset$. The adversary $\mathcal{A}$ can query CreateGroup and AddMember for the secret information of some groups and members, except for Chosen. $\mathcal{B}$ will response the simulated information and update the corruption list Cor.

- **Handshake Queries:** The adversary $\mathcal{A}$ can make queries on the Handshake protocol with the group members. The transcripts of the queried members can be generated by $\mathcal{B}$. During a handshake, $\mathcal{A}$ can query the hash functions used in the Handshake protocol. In particular, $\mathcal{A}$ can request non-interactive proof of knowledge on a random message for any member at the current interval.
- **Challenge:** The challenger $\mathcal{B}$ acts as the group member i^* of G^* and executes handshake protocol with the adversary $\mathcal{A}$. $\mathcal{A}$ attempts to convince $\mathcal{B}$ that $\mathcal{A}$ is a legitimated member of the group G^*.
- **Output:** If the adversary $\mathcal{A}$ on half of a member i in the group G^* succeeds in executing Handshake with $\mathcal{B}$, the output of the game is "1". Otherwise, the output is "0". Note that it is required that $\mathcal{A}$ never queried any secret information with respect to the member i of the group G^*, i.e., $i \cap \mathsf{Cor} = \emptyset$.

Let $\mathtt{Adv}_{\mathcal{A}}^{IR} = \Pr[\mathsf{Game}^{IR} = 1]$, we say that SHS satisfies the impersonator resistance if the function $\mathtt{Adv}_{\mathcal{A}}^{IR}$ is negligible for any polynomially-bounded adversary.

Remark on Impersonator Resistance against GA. Since the GA issues group credentials for members and holds all secret information of every member in most of previous schemes [2,7,9], GA can impersonate one of its group members and execute a successful handshake with other members. Considering the malicious behavior of GA, GA can frame its group member while the group member never did that behavior. Therefore, it is necessary to strengthen the impersonator resistance, i.e., impersonator resistance against GA, which is not explicitly discussed in the schemes [9,10]. It means that even though GA can generate dummy members and succeed in handshaking, GA is still not able to frame that the handshakes run by the dummy members are generated by other genuine members. In the following section, we will present a new secret handshake scheme to achieve the improved property.

Detector Resistance (DR). Any adversary cannot succeed with a non-negligible probability to detect the affiliation information when he activates a Handshake with a legitimate member. Formally, the property is defined in the following game Game^{DR} between an adversary $\mathcal{A}$ and a challenger $\mathcal{B}$:

- **Init:** The adversary $\mathcal{A}$ first sets Chosen $= \{i_0, G_0, i_1, G_1\}$. Then $\mathcal{B}$ simulates Setup, CreateGroup and AddMember, and sends group public keys together with revocation lists of all groups to $\mathcal{A}$.
- **Queries:** $\mathcal{A}$ can make the following queries, such that the responses will be simulated by $\mathcal{B}$.
  - **Corruption Queries:** The corruption list Cor is initialized as $\emptyset$. The adversary $\mathcal{A}$ can query CreateGroup and AddMember for the secret information of some groups and members, except for Chosen. Thus, $\mathcal{B}$ will response the simulated information and update the corruption list Cor.
  - **Handshake Queries:** The adversary $\mathcal{A}$ can make queries on the Handshake protocol with the group members. The transcripts of the queried members can be generated by $\mathcal{B}$. During a handshake, $\mathcal{A}$ can query the

hash functions used in the Handshake protocol. In particular, $\mathcal{A}$ can request non-interactive proof of knowledge on a random message for any member at the current interval.

- **Challenge:** The challenger $\mathcal{B}$ selects a random bit $\phi \leftarrow \{0,1\}$. And then $\mathcal{B}$ acts as the member i_ϕ in the group G_ϕ and executes handshake protocol with the adversary $\mathcal{A}$. $\mathcal{A}$ attempts to distinguish which group $\mathcal{B}$ belongs to.
- **Output:** The adversary $\mathcal{A}$ outputs ϕ' as its guess of ϕ.

Let $\mathrm{Adv}_{\mathcal{A}}^{DR} = |\Pr[\mathrm{Game}^{DR}(0) = 1] - \Pr[\mathrm{Game}^{DR}(1) = 1]|$, we say that SHS satisfies the detector resistance if the function $\mathrm{Adv}_{\mathcal{A}}^{DR}$ is negligible for any polynomially-bounded adversary.

Unlinkability. Anyone except GA could not distinguish whether two instances of SH protocol are executed by the same honest member. In addition, GA will never link two executions run by the same member, unless it carries out the TraceMember algorithm. Thus, the TraceMember algorithm can be authorized by a separate trace authority of GA in order to improve the unlinkability. In the security definition of SHS [9], the privacy property explicitly implies both the unlinkability and the detector resistance. The formal definition of unlinkability is easily derived from Game^{DR} of detector resistance when the "Challenge" phase is executed twice. Let ϕ_0 and ϕ_1 be the random bits of the two challenges, respectively. If $\phi_0 = \phi_1$, let $\phi = 1$, else let $\phi = 0$. Therefore, the adversary outputs ϕ' as its guess of ϕ to distinguish the two different challenges. We say that SHS satisfies the unlinkability if the probability of outputting the correct ϕ' is negligible for any polynomially-bounded adversary.

Remark on Backward Unlinkability. If a group member is removed from his group, i.e., his revocation token is added to the RL, the anonymity of the revoked member before the revocation is desirable to be sustaining (i.e., *backward unlinkability*). It means that even after a member is revoked, all past handshake behaviors produced from the revoked member remain private and unlinkable. The formal definition of the property is easily obtained by revising the Chosen and "Challenge" phases of Game^{DR}, which is similar to *backward unlinkability* in [11]. However, Jarecki and Liu's scheme [9] is executed by adopting the group signature with verifier-local revocation introduced by Boneh and Shacham [5], which cannot achieve backward unlinkability of revoked members. Therefore, backward unlinkability of revoked members will be achieved in the following scheme.

4   A New Revocable Secret Handshake Scheme with Backward Unlinkability

In this section, a new revocable secret handshake scheme with backward unlinkability (which is denoted by RSH) will be described. First we will present the construction of the RSH scheme. Second, the security and performance analysis are discussed in the following subsections, respectively.

4.1   The RSH Scheme

In the construction of our scheme, we borrow the ideas from Nakanishi and Funabiki's group signature scheme in ASIACRYPT 2005 [11] and two-party secure computation protocol [3]. Since secret handshakes are private mutual authentications, the group signature with public verification can not be directly used to construct secret handshake scheme. Therefore, we have to modify the group signature to a non-interactive proof of knowledge with message recovery adapted to our secret handshake scheme, denoted by PROOF. The key idea of PROOF is to abandon public verifications of messages, whilst messages can only be recoverable but not verifiable right after receiving the proofs. Moreover, the verification of a recovered message is delayed to execute in the second round of interactive handshake phase. Consequently, a message can be recovered and verified correctly if and only if the receiver and signer are in the same group. The RSH scheme is designed as follows.

- Setup: Given a security parameter κ, the algorithm runs

$$Setup(1^{\kappa}) \rightarrow \texttt{params} = (\mathbb{G}, \mathbb{G}_T, g, p, e, H_1, H_2, F, F^{-1}, T, \tau_1, \cdots, \tau_T),$$

  which are shared by all participants in the whole secret handshake system. Here g is a generator of a subgroup $\mathbb{G}$ of prime order $p \equiv 3(mod\ 4)$. In addition, $H_1 : \{0,1\}^* \rightarrow \mathbb{G}$ and $H_2 : \{0,1\}^* \rightarrow \mathbb{Z}_p^*$ are two cryptographic hash functions. $F : \mathbb{G} \rightarrow \mathbb{Z}_p$ is an injective mapping from $\mathbb{G}$ to $\mathbb{Z}_p$, and $F^{-1} : \mathbb{Z}_p \rightarrow \mathbb{G}$ is its inverse. T is the number of time intervals in the secret handshake system, and $\tau_j \leftarrow_R \{0,1\}^*$ represents the j-th time interval for each $j \in [1, T]$.
- CreateGroup: GA chooses group secret key $gsk = s \leftarrow_R \mathbb{Z}_p^*$, and generates group public key $gpk = g^s$.
- AddMember(n, T): Assuming that GA can add n members to the group in T time intervals, GA issues credentials for each member by executing two-party interactive protocol as follows.

  1. If a user U_i wants to join the group, first he generates his own private/public key pair $(usk[i] = x_i \in_R \mathbb{Z}_p^*, upk[i] = g^{x_i} \in \mathbb{G})$. And then he calculates his revocation tokens $urt[i][j] = B_{ij} = h_j^{x_i}$, where $h_j = H_1(\tau_j)$ for each time interval τ_j such that $j \in [1, T]$. Hence, he sends B_{ij} and $upk[i]$ together with other necessary information(e.g., the user's public key certificate) to GA for identity verification, where the user's public key $upk[i]$ can be verified by the certificate signed by a trusted authority (e.g., CA in PKI).
  2. GA authenticates the user's identity information and verifies $e(B_{ij}, g) \overset{?}{=} e(h_j, upk[i])$ for each $j \in [1, T]$. If the verification succeeds, GA will store B_{ij} as the user's revocation tokens and updates the member list. Note that member and revocation lists can be maintained by a separate trace authority of GA. Afterwards, GA and the user U_i execute the following protocol to issue a group credential, which is similar to

the two-party protocol in [3]. Let Keygen, HEn, HDe be an additively homomorphic semantically secure encryption scheme, "$\bigoplus$" denotes the homomorphic operation on ciphertexts. For a ciphertext $e1$ and an integer r, $e1 \bigotimes r$ denotes "adding" $e1$ to itself r times.

- GA generates $\mathsf{Keygen}(1^\kappa) \rightarrow (sk_{hom}, pk_{hom})$. He computes $e_1 = \mathsf{HEn}(pk_{hom}, gsk)$ which can be regarded as a commitment on gsk, and then sends e_1 and pk_{hom} to the user U_i, together with a zero knowledge proof that e_1 and gpk are committed to the same secret value.

- The user U_i selects $\gamma \leftarrow_R \mathbb{Z}_p^*$ and computes $r_1 = \gamma^2$. U_i chooses $r_2 \leftarrow_R \{0, ..., 2^\kappa p\}$ and sends $e_2 = ((e_1 \bigoplus \mathsf{HEn}(pk_{hom}, x_i)) \bigotimes r_1) \bigoplus \mathsf{HEn}(pk_{hom}, r_2 p)$ to GA. Furthermore, U_i should provide a proof of knowledge (PK) on x_i, so that GA can be convinced that the commitment e_2 and his public key $upk[i]$ are committed to the same x_i as well as committed correctly, denoted by $\pi^U = PK\{x_i : upk[i] = g^{x_i} \land e_2 = \mathsf{HEn}(pk_{hom}, r_1(x_i + gsk) + r_2 p)\}$.

- If GA checks the proof π^U successfully, its private output will be $z = r_1(x_i + s) = \mathsf{HDe}(sk_{hom}, e_2)$. Otherwise, the output will be $z = \bot$. If $z \neq \bot$ and $z \in QR_p$, then GA calculates and sends $cred_i' = g^{z^{\frac{1}{2}}}$ (if $z \notin QR_p$, $cred_i' = g^{(-z)^{\frac{1}{2}}}$) to U_i.

- U_i computes $cred_i = cred_i'^{\gamma^{-1}} = g^{(x_i + s)^{\frac{1}{2}}}$ or $cred_i = g^{(-x_i - s)^{\frac{1}{2}}}$, and then verifies that the credential is valid by testing $e(cred_i, cred_i) \stackrel{?}{=} e(gpk \cdot upk[i], g)$ or $e(cred_i, cred_i) \stackrel{?}{=} e(gpk \cdot upk[i], g)^{-1}$. Note that the credential $cred_i = g^{(x_i + s)^{\frac{1}{2}}}$ can be regarded as Zhang et al.'s short signature [16] from GA.

Consequently, the user U_i obtains a valid group credential from GA, while GA would not know the member's private key and authentic credential. Compared to the Jarecki and Liu's scheme [9], RSH lifts the trust level of GA so that GA does not need to hold all secret information of its members. Namely, GA would not be able to impersonate and frame any other valid members, which is similar to the exculpability or non-frameability in group signatures [4]. The direct reason is that the members' secret keys are hidden from GA and hence, GA cannot forge any proof of knowledge on those secret keys. Furthermore, even if GA generates a dummy member $\mathcal{U}$ and claims that a malicious handshake produced by $\mathcal{U}$ is executed by an innocent member U_i, the member U_i can deny the malicious accusation as follows. Since GA uses the existing revocation tokens to trace a member's identity at the j-th time interval, a malicious GA provides the $\mathcal{U}$'s revocation token at the j-th time interval as the proof of U_i's malicious behavior. However, U_i can provide a public verifiable proof that the discrete logarithm of his public key g^{x_i} on g (i.e., private key) is not equal to the corresponding discrete logarithm of $\mathcal{U}$'s revocation token on h_j. Since U_i's public key has been authorized by a trusted authority, the malicious claims from GA are publicly distinguishable because of U_i's denial proof. Hence the strong impersonator resistance against a malicious GA is obtained in RSH.

- Handshake: Supposing A and B are two members who want to execute a secret handshake protocol to authenticate each other without leaking their privacy at time interval τ_j. Member A runs the protocol with $usk[A] = x_A$, $cred_A$ and gpk_A which are created by group G_A, and member B runs it with $usk[B] = x_B$, $cred_B$ and gpk_B which are created by group G_B. For simplicity, we only consider the credential as the form of $cred_i = g^{(x_i+s)^{\frac{1}{2}}}$. The protocol proceeds as follows:

1. $A \rightarrow B : \{\texttt{PROOF}(x_A, cred_A)[k_A]\}$

   (a) A chooses $r_A \leftarrow \mathbb{Z}_p^*$, $k_A = g^{r_A}$.

   (b) A selects $\ell, t \leftarrow_R \mathbb{Z}_p^*$, and computes $T_1 = cred_A^\ell, T_2 = g^{\ell^2}, T_3 = e(g^{x_A}, h_j)^t, T_4 = g^t$.

   (c) A selects $r_\ell, r_t, r_{x_A}, r_\alpha, r_\beta \leftarrow_R \mathbb{Z}_p^*$, and computes $R_1 = g^{r_\ell}$, $R_2 = T_2^{r_{x_A}} \cdot g^{-r_\alpha}$, $R_3 = e(g, gpk_A)^{r_\ell} \cdot e(g, g)^{r_\alpha}$, $R_4 = e(g, h_j)^{r_\beta}$, $R_5 = g^{r_t}, R_6 = T_4^{r_{x_A}} \cdot g^{-r_\beta}$, where $\alpha = x_A \cdot \ell^2, \beta = x_A \cdot t$.

   (d) A computes $c' = H_2(\texttt{params}, gpk_A, \tau_j, R_1, R_2, R_3, R_4, R_5, R_6)$ and $c = c' \oplus F(k_A)$.

   (e) A computes $s_\ell = r_\ell + c \cdot \ell^2, s_{x_A} = r_{x_A} + c \cdot x_A, s_t = r_t + c \cdot t$, $s_\alpha = r_\alpha + c \cdot \alpha, s_\beta = r_\beta + c \cdot \beta$.
   Finally, A sends $\texttt{PROOF}(x_A, cred_A)[k_A] = (T_1, T_2, T_3, T_4, s_\ell, s_{x_A}, s_t, s_\alpha, s_\beta, c)$ to B. Note that $\texttt{PROOF}(x_A, cred_A)[k_A]$ is the partial zero-knowledge proof of $(x_A, cred_A)$, which can be regarded as a message recoverable variant of group signature on k_A without public verification. The message can be recovered by using the correct group public key. Since the soundness of the recovered message cannot be verified in the step, B cannot distinguish which group A belongs to. Therefore, B has to provide his proof of group credential to A for implementing secret handshakes.

2. $B \rightarrow A : \{\texttt{PROOF}(x_B, cred_B)[k_B], V_B\}$

   (a) B acquires the revocation list RL_j of his group and checks if A is not revoked at the time interval τ_j. The revocation check is achieved by verifying $T_3 \neq e(T_4, B_{ij})$ for all $B_{ij} \in RL_j$ after getting (T_3, T_4) from A.

   (b) B chooses $r_B \leftarrow \mathbb{Z}_p^*$ and computes $k_B = g^{r_B}$.

   (c) Similarly, B also generates a proof knowledge on k_B : $\texttt{PROOF}(x_B, cred_B)[k_B]$, which is also the partial zero-knowledge proof of $(x_B, cred_B)$.

   (d) If A does not pass the revocation check, B will generate a random value $V_B \leftarrow_R \mathbb{Z}_p^*$ as verification response. Otherwise, B will recover k_A' from $\texttt{PROOF}(x_A, cred_A)[k_A]$ by using his group public key gpk_B and computes a verification value V_B as follows.

- B retrieves $\tilde{R}_1 = g^{s_\ell} \cdot (T_2)^{-c}$, $\tilde{R}_2 = T_2^{s_{x_A}} \cdot g^{-s_\alpha}$, $\tilde{R}_3 = e(g, gpk_B)^{s_\ell} \cdot$
  $e(g,g)^{s_\alpha} \cdot (\frac{1}{e(T_1, T_1)})^c$, $\tilde{R}_4 = e(g, h_j)^{s_\beta} \cdot T_3^{-c}$, $\tilde{R}_5 = g^{s_t} \cdot T_4^{-c}$, $\tilde{R}_6 =$
  $T_4^{s_{x_A}} \cdot g^{-s_\beta}$.
- B computes the challenge
  $\tilde{c}' = H_2(\mathtt{params}, gpk_B, \tau_j, \tilde{R}_1, \tilde{R}_2, \tilde{R}_3, \tilde{R}_4, \tilde{R}_5, \tilde{R}_6)$.
- B recovers the key $k'_A = F^{-1}(c \oplus \tilde{c}')$. As described in the above step, B does not know whether the recovered message is correct.
- B will verify the value V_B if $V_B = H_2((k'_A)^{r_B} || k_B || 0)$.

Finally, B sends both $\mathtt{PROOF}(x_B, cred_B)[k_B]$ and V_B to A.

3. $A \rightarrow B : V_A$

   (a) A acquires the revocation list RL_j of his group and checks if B is not revoked at the time interval τ_j. The revocation check is also achieved by verifying $T_3 \neq e(T_4, B_{ij})$ for all $B_{ij} \in RL_j$ after getting (T_3, T_4) from B.

   (b) If B is revoked at time interval τ_j, A responds a random value $V_A \leftarrow_R \mathbb{Z}_p^*$ as well. Otherwise, A retrieves k'_B from
   $\mathtt{PROOF}(x_B, cred_B)[k_B]$ by using his own group public key gpk_A.

   (c) A verifies V_B with the equation $V_B \stackrel{?}{=} H_2((k'_B)^{r_A} || k'_B || 0)$. At this phase, A can verify the soundness of the recovered message from B. But the verification depends on B also correctly recovered the message from A. Therefore, the equation holds if and only if A and B belong to the same group, i.e., $gpk_A = gpk_B$. Thus, A will output "1" and send $V_A = H_2((k'_B)^{r_A} || k_A || 1)$ to B. Else A outputs "0" and responds a random value $V_A \leftarrow_R \mathbb{Z}_p^*$ to B.

   (d) B verifies V_A with the following equation $V_A \stackrel{?}{=} H_2((k'_A)^{r_B} || k'_A || 1)$. B outputs "1" only if the above equation holds, else B outputs "0".

- TraceMember: When dispute happens, the trace authority of GA first retrieves the proof information T_3 and T_4 from a transcript of a secret handshake instance at time interval τ_j. And then it checks $T_3 \stackrel{?}{=} e(T_4, B_{ij})$ for all B_{ij} in the member lists to identify who has executed the malicious secret handshakes, where R_{ij} for each $j \in [1, T]$ is corresponding to the member U_i and his public key $upk[i]$.

- RemoveMember: The procedure is responsible for the update of the revocation list for each time interval after tracing some malicious group members or receiving some members' revocation requests. In order to remove a member U_i at time interval $\tau_{j'}$, the trace authority of GA firstly looks up the member U_i's information from its member list. And then it removes the member's revocation tokens $urt[i][j] = B_{ij}$ for all $j \geq j'$ to the RL of its group. Consequently, other unrevoked group members can execute revocation check under the updated RL to identify whether the counter-party is revoked. Particularly, the revocation tokens before the time interval $\tau_{j'}$ are not added in the updated RL and will not satisfy the revocation check equation. Moreover, it is infeasible to deduce the previous revocation tokens B_{ij} for all $j < j'$

from the revocation tokens B_{ij} for all $j \geq j'$ that have been added in the updated RL at the time interval $\tau_{j'}$. Therefore, the past transcripts of revoked members still remain unrecognized and private, which solves the open problem proposed by Jarecki and Liu's scheme [9] in CRYPTO 2009 to a certain extent.

Completeness. If A and B belong to the same group (i.e., $gpk_A = gpk_B$), both A and B will recover the original message $k'_A = k_A$ and $k'_B = k_B$ as described in the above scheme. Thus, the corresponding verification values from both members can be verified successfully. Hence, A and B complete a successful secret handshake protocol. A session key $K = H_2(g^{r_A \cdot r_B} || k_A || k_B)$ is also agreed for the following two-party communications. Note that any adversary cannot distinguish the session key. Furthermore, our scheme is easily extended to achieve dynamic matching such that the authentication policy of each member is not limited to the same group. As long as their authentication policies are matching, both members can recover the correct messages by applying their target group public keys according to authentication policies.

4.2   Security

Now we provide the security results on the new construction RSH with respect to the Impersonator Resistance, Detector Resistance and Unlinkability described in Section 3. Due to the length restriction, the proofs of the theorems are omitted.

Theorem 1. *If there exists an adaptive adversary $\mathcal{A}$ can (t, ϵ)-breaks the Impersonator Resistance of RSH, then there exists an algorithm $\mathcal{B}$ can solve the $(q + 1)$-SRP in polynomial time t' with a non-negligible probability ϵ', such that*

$$t = t', \epsilon' \geq \frac{n - q_A}{n^2} \cdot \frac{\epsilon^2}{q_H},$$

where n denotes the maximal number of group members in one group, q_A denotes the number of queries for AddMember, and q_H is the number of queries for hash function H_2.

Theorem 2. *If there exists an adaptive adversary $\mathcal{A}$ can $(t, \frac{1}{2} + \epsilon)$-breaks the Detector Resistance and Unlinkability of RSH, then there exists an algorithm $\mathcal{B}$ can solve the DBDH in polynomial time t' with a non-negligible advantage $\epsilon' \geq (\frac{1}{nT} - \frac{q_P q_H}{p}) \cdot \epsilon$, where n denotes the maximal number of group members in one group, T denotes the maximal number of time intervals in the whole secret handshake system, q_P denotes the number of queries for PROOF, q_H is the number of queries for hash function, p is the prime order of $\mathbb{G}$.*

4.3   Performance

Here we analyze the performance of RSH by considering of its communication and computation costs. We note that the Jarecki and Liu's scheme [9] only gives a generic construction, which is not easy to be implemented because the representations of the commitments and the conditional oblivious transfer for every elements in one representative vector. Hence, we just describe the performance comparison between our scheme and Kawai *et al.*'s scheme [10]. Without losing the generality, we choose the order p to be 170-bit prime, and the representations of $\mathbb{G}$ and $\mathbb{G}_T$ are 171 and 1020 bits, respectively [5].

- **Communication Costs.** In RSH, each member needs transmit 3 elements from $\mathbb{G}$, 1 element from $\mathbb{G}_T$ and 7 elements from $\mathbb{Z}_p^*$ that includes one response verification information V. It is about $1020 + 171*3 + 170*7 = 2893$ bits. In Kawai *et al.*'s scheme [10], without considering revocation check, it is about $171*5 + 170*12 = 2795$ bits. We note that 1020 bits from $\mathbb{G}_T$ in our scheme are used for achieving revocation with backward unlinkability, which is necessary for practical application. Therefore, although RSH spends slightly more bits in communications, it is valuable for realizing the revocation mechanism.

- **Computation Costs.** In the three-rounds handshake protocol of RSH, each member requires 19 multi-exponentiations and 4 bilinear pairing computations, where 3 bilinear pairing computations can be pre-computed. Moreover, for the sake of revocation check, each member needs $|RL_j|$ bilinear pairing computations. In comparison, the Kawai *et al.*'s scheme [10] requires 27 multi-exponentiations, 7 bilinear pairing computations for each member. Similarly, if we do not consider revocation checking problem, our scheme can take better efficiency. However, it is necessary to authenticate the revocation status of counter-party in practical secret handshakes. Hence, the trade-off is reasonable in order to adapting our secret handshake scheme to more practical applications.

5 Conclusion

In this paper, we have proposed a new revocable secret handshake scheme, which supports revocation with backward unlinkability and impersonation against malicious GA. The revocation with backward unlinkability solves the open question left by Jarecki and Liu to a certain extension. In future work, a practical approach is to design an unlinkable secret handshake scheme which satisfies the verification costs of revocation are sub-linear to the number of revoked members. It is also a challenge work to design a practical secret handshake scheme without using the random oracle in the security proof.

References

1. Ateniese, G., Blanton, M., Kirsch, J.: Secret handshakes with dynamic and fuzzy matching. In: Network and Distributed System Security Symposium, NDSS, pp. 159–177 (2007)
2. Balfanz, D., Durfee, G., Shankar, N., Smetters, D., Staddon, J., Wong, H.: Secret handshakes from pairing-based key agreements. In: IEEE Symposium on Security and Privacy, pp. 180–196 (2003)

3. Belenkiy, M., Camenisch, J., Chase, M., Kohlweiss, M., Lysyanskaya, A., Shacham, H.: Randomizable proofs and delegatable anonymous credentials. In: Halevi, S. (ed.) CRYPTO 2009. LNCS, vol. 5677, pp. 108–125. Springer, Heidelberg (2009)
4. Boneh, D., Boyen, X., Shacham, H.: Short group signatures. In: Franklin, M. (ed.) CRYPTO 2004. LNCS, vol. 3152, pp. 41–55. Springer, Heidelberg (2004)
5. Boneh, D., Shacham, H.: Group signatures with verifier-local revocation. In: ACM CCS, pp. 168–177 (2004)
6. Camenisch, J., Lysyanskaya, A.: An efficient system for non-transferable anonymous credentials with optional anonymity revocation. In: Pfitzmann, B. (ed.) EUROCRYPT 2001. LNCS, vol. 2045, pp. 93–118. Springer, Heidelberg (2001)
7. Castelluccia, C., Jarecki, S., Tsudik, G.: Secret handshakes from CA-oblivious encryption. In: Lee, P.J. (ed.) ASIACRYPT 2004. LNCS, vol. 3329, pp. 293–307. Springer, Heidelberg (2004)
8. Jarecki, S., Liu, X.: Unlinkable secret handshakes and key-private group key management schemes. In: Katz, J., Yung, M. (eds.) ACNS 2007. LNCS, vol. 4521, pp. 270–287. Springer, Heidelberg (2007)
9. Jarecki, S., Liu, X.: Private mutual authentication and conditional oblivious transfer. In: Halevi, S. (ed.) CRYPTO 2009. LNCS, vol. 5677, pp. 90–107. Springer, Heidelberg (2009)
10. Kawai, Y., Yoneyama, K., Ohta, K.: Secret handshake: Strong anonymity definition and construction. In: Bao, F., Li, H., Wang, G. (eds.) ISPEC 2009. LNCS, vol. 5451, pp. 219–229. Springer, Heidelberg (2009)
11. Nakanishi, T., Funabiki, N.: Verifier-local revocation group signature schemes with backward unlinkability from bilinear maps. In: Roy, B. (ed.) ASIACRYPT 2005. LNCS, vol. 3788, pp. 533–548. Springer, Heidelberg (2005)
12. Pointcheval, D., Stern, J.: Security proofs for signature schemes. In: Maurer, U.M. (ed.) EUROCRYPT 1996. LNCS, vol. 1070, pp. 387–398. Springer, Heidelberg (1996)
13. Vergnaud, D.: RSA-based secret handshakes. In: Ytrehus, Ø. (ed.) WCC 2005. LNCS, vol. 3969, pp. 252–274. Springer, Heidelberg (2006)
14. Waters, B.: Efficient identity-based encryption without random oracles. In: Cramer, R. (ed.) EUROCRYPT 2005. LNCS, vol. 3494, pp. 114–127. Springer, Heidelberg (2005)
15. Xu, S., Yung, M.: K-anonymous secret handshakes with reusable credentials. In: ACM CCS, pp. 158–167. ACM, New York (2004)
16. Zhang, F., Chen, X., Susilo, W., Mu, Y.: A new signature scheme without random oracles from bilinear pairings. In: Nguyên, P.Q. (ed.) VIETCRYPT 2006. LNCS, vol. 4341, pp. 67–80. Springer, Heidelberg (2006)
17. Zhou, L., Susilo, W., Mu, Y.: Three-round secret handshakes based on ElGamal and DSA. In: Chen, K., Deng, R., Lai, X., Zhou, J. (eds.) ISPEC 2006. LNCS, vol. 3903, pp. 332–342. Springer, Heidelberg (2006)

SOMA: Self-Organised Mesh Authentication

Foivos F. Demertzis, Christos Xenakis

University of Piraeus, Department of Digital Systems,
80 Karaoli Dimitriou Street, PC 18534, Piraeus, Greece
{fdemertz,xenakis}@unipi.gr
http://www.ds.unipi.gr

Abstract. Community mesh networks have emerged rapidly in every metropolis around the world, however many of the security methods applied are counter-intuitive and usually disrupt the autonomous characteristics of the mesh nodes. In SOMA we present a structured Peer-to-Peer solution providing authentication service based on a scalable, self-organized and fully distributed Web-of-Trust. Our proposal is a hybrid Public Key Infrastructure build on top of Chord, allowing each agent to place its own trust policy while keeping the autonomous characteristics the nodes intact. Our goal is to create a large-scale authentication system for mesh networks without the need of a Trusted Third Party. We leave the decision of whom to trust in each agent independently taking advantage of the overlay to alleviate the shortcomings of traditional Web-of-Trust models. This is achieved by using the overlay as a meta-structure to infer trust relationships. The possible attacks and limitations of our proposal are also investigated and discussed.

Keywords: Mesh Networks, Public Key Infrastructure, Web-of-Trust, Peer-to-Peer.

1 Introduction

Community mesh networks have emerged in every metropolis around the world, where the comprising nodes share resources and services while working in an autonomous fashion. These mesh networks are based on independent, computational powerful, wireless ad-hoc, multi-hop nodes. Identity management is the cornerstone for the establishment of trust in any network, and as such mesh networks are of no exception. In such networks, authentication credentials are usually exchanged in a bi-directional and symmetric fashion between two or more parties. Nodes that wish to communicate securely, first need to establish some form of trust, which is based on the fact that initially the two parties are distrusted. Therefore, to establish a secure channel of communication and authenticate the exchanged data, a node first and foremost should be able to prove the authenticity of the identification credentials of the party in question.

These community mesh networks comprise of a decentralised infrastructure that can scale to many thousands. In this work, we focus on fully or semi-planned, long-term wireless ad-hoc networks similar to the many community

J. Camenisch and C. Lambrinoudakis (Eds.): EuroPKI 2010, LNCS 6711, pp. 31–44, 2011.

Wireless Metropolitan Networks (WMNs). The nodes use wireless multi-hop transmissions to communicate, based on IEEE 802.11 and are computationally strong enough, such as the ones found at the edges of community WMNs (e.g., Athens WMN [1], MIT's Roofnet [2]).

1.1   Motivation

Currently, many security models have been proposed for mesh networks, but most of these are counter-intuitive and usually disrupt the autonomous characteristics of the mesh nodes. The use of a centralised Public Key Infrastructure (PKI) approach is fundamentally incompatible with the decentralised open nature of the mesh network's topology. Many traditional PKI solutions delegate trust to a Trusted Third Party (TTP). Single Certification Authority (CA) and replicated CAs are not viable for community mesh networks. The former is not a scalable architecture and neither is fault tolerant. The latter, introduces increased security risk, by providing additional attack vectors. This is due to the fact that an adversary can gain access to the CA's private key by compromising even a single of the replicated CAs.

A plethora of the proposals use empowered nodes either involving the organisational aspects of the network or its trust management. Implementing such a solution for mesh networks that scale to many thousands would inevitably lead us to inefficiency, bottlenecks and points of failure. By delegating trust decisions to an external third party, distributed or otherwise, we would inevitably lose the individuality and autonomy of the mesh nodes. Hence, we propose SOMA a system that has self-organization, autonomy and scalability as its principal design co-ordinates.

1.2   Our Contribution

SOMA is a certificate-based authentication infrastructure that aims to create a large-scale secure authentication system for mesh networks without the need of a TTP. We aim at creating a self-organised, efficient and scalable authentication infrastructure, without sacrificing the autonomous characteristics of the nodes. Hence, our work focuses on building on top of a self-organised, structured Peer-to-Peer, Web-of-Trust [3] infrastructure. The proposed system leaves the decision of whom to interact with and why to place trust on each of the agents, independently. It provides a policy-based system, which can also be the basis for a more complex reputation based model. Such a model can include a variety of relationships and metrics, which is out of the scope of this paper.

In SOMA, we make use of structured Peer-to-Peer in contrast to unstructured flooding based protocols, e.g., Gnutella [4], due to the fact that the nodes are mostly static. Therefore, using a structured Peer-to-Peer approach, such as Chord [5], a node is given access to a scalable holistic view of the mesh. In addition, building an efficient Web-of-Trust infrastructure, which exploits collective knowledge in a self-organised way, fits better to the studied autonomous network architecture. Using Chord, we gain mathematically provable scalability and great thoroughly investigated static resilience [5], which is a mandatory requirement for an identity management system. SOMA is based on a PGP-like [3] architecture, where the nodes create the public and private keys themselves. Issuing and managing of the key material is done locally and digital certificates are issued using only the collective information of the overlay routing architecture. Through certificate exchanges each node builds its keyring, storing it locally, in accordance to PGP Web-of-Trust. In contrast to hierarchical PGP, we do not use neither a central nor a distributed CA, and we avoid completely delegation of trust to a TTP. Hence, each of the agents uses its keyring independently, placing their trust depending on the identification credentials gathered. A node, after assessing the certificates on its keyring and evaluating the identity of the communicating parties, will use these credentials to establish a secure communication channel.

The basic operations and goals of our solution stem from the fact that we wish to have no empowered nodes. From a security design point of view, our goals are similar to the ones found in most public-key based schemes, authentication, data integrity, confidentiality and non-repudiation. Most community WMNs are open and each peer individually decides what services to offer in the mesh. Therefore, our authentication mechanism has to impose no barriers to entry and, in addition, keep the autonomy of the nodes intact. We take advantage of the consistent hashing, employed by many structured Peer-to-Peer overlays and we use the overlay look-up protocol to infer the trust relationships between the autonomous peers.

In the next chapter we will examine some of the related work and background that has been put into distributing PKIs. Section 3 presents our authentication system called SOMA. Section 4 presents an evaluation including discussion of the security issues and closely examines possible attack scenarios. Finally, section 5 summarizes important points and outlines the conclusions drawn.

2   Related Work

The notion of a distributed Public Key Infrastructure (PKI) to provide authentication service for ad-hoc networks has been coined around for many years. A lot of interest and research has been put into creating efficient scalable infrastructures, that do not sacrifice the autonomous characteristics of the comprising nodes. Research has mainly been put into mobile ad-hoc networks (MANETs) where mobility is a limiting factor, and in wired systems the central PKI is distributed using threshold cryptographic schemes [6]. In this section, we summarize the most important literature that has been proposed for tackling public key management in ad-hoc networks. We also do a critical appraisal on issues that we will be investigating through SOMA.

In 1999 L. Zhou and Z. Haas [7] proposed the first Distributed Certification Authority (DCA) for ad-hoc networks, based on threshold cryptography. We refer to this work because it was the foundation for many DCA implementations that followed and hence, have similar limitations abated to an extent depending on the specifics of each approach. The architecture proposed by Zhou and Haas has an arbitrary number of server-nodes and combiner nodes that constitute the DCA. Without delving into the technical details, these server-nodes would divide between them the private key of the CA. The server-nodes would follow a (n, t+1) scheme, needing t+1 out of n shares to recover the secret parts of the divided private key, as per Shamir's secret sharing scheme [6]. All the nodes in the system would also have a public key/secret key pair that the DCA would be responsible to certify. Subsequently, the server-nodes involved would sign with their share of the private key a partial signature and submit these pieces to a combiner node that produces the final signature.

There are several limitations with this approach, most importantly, it does not scale since it is semi-distributed. Furthermore, it uses empowered nodes, which are not self-organized, but rather depend on an off-line authority to empower them. The nodes require an off-line assignment of Unique Universal Identifiers (UUIDs). The proposed system does not provide a solution in case of connectivity problems between the nodes since it was out of its scope. Large-scale changes in topology have a detrimental effect both on the system security and its performance. This is due to the fact that security comes with a trade-off to availability and hence, a method needs to be devised to re-organise the number of shares, required to construct the secret key.

Similar in concept to Zhou and Z. Haas is by Kong et al. [8], which alleviates the availability issues, by not using combiner nodes, but exposes the system to Sibyl attacks [9]. More work in similar grounds has been done in [10] an extension proposed by Zhou et al. for use on the Internet. Furthermore, Yi and Kravets [11][12][13] propose a DCA based on threshold cryptography. The main points of their proposal being that the nodes requiring certification contact t+1 nodes instead and make use an efficient β-unicast method for dissemination instead of flooding.

All the aforementioned proposals do not scale well and are not fully self-organized, hindering the autonomous characteristics of a mesh network. One different approach that uses certificate chaining similarly to the PGP Web-of-Trust was proposed by Hubaux et al. [14][15][16] for MANETs. They developed a self-organised solution for key management in ad-hoc networks, where each user has authority and issues public-key certificates to other users. Key authentication is done via the exchange of certificate graphs. Each user stores all the certificates from other users and evaluation of valid certificate chains is done through merging their individual certificate repositories. The certificate dissemination that takes place is done in ad-hoc flooding basis, taking into account the mobility of the users, which is integral for the convergence of the certificate graph. This introduces a delay in the initial stages of network and can cause problems when there are insufficient trust relationships. More work on certificate chaining schemes similar to Hubaux et al. was done in [17] were the authors propose a hierarchical Binary Tree based solution with certificate chaining for MANETs.

Other related work that focuses on different requirements can be found in identity based encryption schemes in [18], [19]. In addition, overlay DCAs have been proposed that use DHT (Distributed Hash Table) to provide the primitives needed to create a distributed storage of the key material and the underlying management infrastructure. In SOMA, on the other hand, we do not use storage of a DHT as a core component. A DHT solution can be found on [20], in which the authors propose a statistical quorum based mechanism to probabilistically get certificates of the overlay and decide on their authenticity. Moreover, on [21] they propose the use of threshold cryptography to distribute the CA functionality. They derive and delegate trust by distributing the certificate directory and the private key of the CA in many nodes, divided into segments of trust. In both these structured Peer-to-Peer solutions DHT provides a distributed storage for the key material and the underlying management infrastructure, distributing the directory and the private key of the CA. We, on the other hand, focus on the autonomy of the nodes, each acting independently using a Web-of-Trust.

3   SOMA

In this section we present our proposal and the rationale behind our design choices. Furthermore, we proceed in analysing the steps taken for the formation of a mesh network and the authentication protocol specifics that will be followed by the nodes.

3.1   Overview

We wish to build an authentication infrastructure in the presence of active adversaries, so that the nodes can verify the public keys and their authenticity via chains of trust. Our system is build on top of Stoica's Chord [5]. Chord is a structured overlay protocol, that provides a look up interface based on consistent hashing over a circular (modulo) identifier space. Using a key, Chord maps that key onto a node. Chord is normally used as the basis for providing some DHT functionality. On a DHT that is based on Chord, we can normally store (key,value) pairs as we would in every other locally stored hash table and retrieve the data back, based on our key. Consistent hashing uses a one-way function (e.g., SHA1, SHA2) to map both the keys and the node IDs (e.g., IP-addresses) uniformly distributed in the same identifier space. A key look-up in Chord returns the IP address for that key. It is scalable, taking O(log N) communication hops and keeps O(log N) state per node, where N is the total number of nodes in the system.

The benefits inherited from Chord can be summarised:

– A simple scalable lookup algorithm based on consistent hashing.
– A robust overlay that is robust on node joins and failures.
– A stabilisation protocol.

Our proposal is targeted on multi-hop, ad-hoc networks that display transitive trust relationships between the comprising nodes. This can be extrapolated further saying that as a community WMN, the nodes will build a PGP Web-of-Trust and exhibit characteristics similar to Small-World graphs [22]. Moreover, even-though the nodes themselves will not often be neighbours of one another, most nodes will be reachable from every other by a significantly smaller number of hops, compared to the network size. This is usually achieved by short-cuts between the nodes.

We use the overlay network as a meta-structure that efficiently creates the transitive relationships, so that the nodes can deduce the chains of trust between them in a self-organised and scalable manner. Hence, when the Chord protocol is used as the basis of a Web-of-Trust model and certificates are stored in local keyrings, we can safely reach the conjecture that a node would be able to find a chain of certificates in $O(\log N)$ time and in $O(\log N)$ number of certificates for any trust path given. Ideally, a peer requiring a secure authenticated service to another peer would be able to deduce a valid chain of trust, with the same complexity as would a simple look-up do in Chord. Therefore, SOMA builds a self-organised distributed authentication service, based on the aforementioned idea and tailors it to the needs of the mesh networks.

The SOMA architecture comprises the mesh nodes, forming a virtual ring overlay. Each node has a unique ID that encompasses its physical and logical address. A node wishing to join SOMA requires to know one node that is already in the ring (e.g., its bootstrapping node to the mesh network). Subsequently, each node is able to exchange certificates and establish trust relationships with the rest of the nodes in SOMA. The overlay structure forms the framework for the transitive trust relationships and each node exchanges certificates with the nodes that is directly responsible for routing. When a node requests a PGP chain of certificates to another node, following the overlay routing, will result to an efficient trust path discovery.

The nodes in the mesh form logical ring. The main components of a node in SOMA are listed below:

- A logical ID that is directly correlated to its physical ID.
- A PGP keyring.
- A finger table providing efficient lookups and captures the inter-node certificate relationships.
- A list of successors and a cache of IP addresses that provide resilience against attacks and failures.

In SOMA, we assume that the nodes will use TCP and are assigned static IP addresses. The network is assumed vulnerable by adversaries at all times. The TCP communication messages are reinforced with authenticated DiffieHellman session keys. The certificate exchange between two parties is done using 2-pass strong authentication. The PGP messages and certificate format details follow the OpenPGP Message Format [23] or any compliant format.

3.2   Initialization and Bootstrapping

When a new node n wishes to join the mesh network and use the authentication service, it must first create a public/secret key pair Pk_n/Sk_n . Furthermore, n will produce a self-signed certificate $Cert_n$, which is done locally and without any CA involvement. Then it bootstraps to the network, by contacting one of its direct one hop links in the mesh n'. These one hop links serve as trust-anchors and short-cuts in the overlay ring. They are considered initially trusted since usually in community WMNs for a node to join the network it has to contact another peer directly for bootstrapping, address resolution, antenna alignment etc. Therefore, we can safely assume that the node n can verify the identity of n', its introducer, as authentic at least to the extent of connecting the peer n to the mesh.

To extrapolate further on the above, the side channel (e.g., physical contact or other direct channels) between two peers, performs the role of an off-line CA. n' being the bootstrapping node of n will sign the authenticity of the key Pk_n and n will sign the authenticity of $Pk_{n'}$. The certificate will follow the PGP format details and n' will then put in its keyring the certificate $Cert_{n\Rightarrow n'}$. Additionally, n will hold in its keyring $Cert_{n'\Rightarrow n}$ as in the PGP Web-of-Trust. Hence, at the start we have direct one-hop relationships which are bi-directionally verified by n and its introducing nodes.

To join a SOMA ring a node needs to generate a new unique ID. The unique ID of node n is ID_n and will be derived by hashing the concatenation of node's n public key and its network address $ID_n = h(Pk_n||IP_{address\ of n})$. This identifier ID_n will be the key that uniquely identifies node n in SOMA's circular identifier space. Node n will then use the produced ID_n to connect to the overlay. The authenticated introducer in SOMA is in fact what the initial contact link is to the Chord ring. n' will learn node's n successor by looking up ID_n and n will proceed with building its finger table, as described in the following section.

3.3   Node Join and Stabilisation

For n to join SOMA it will need to setup its finger table. A finger table is a list of pointers to IDs in the overlay. Instead of holding a single pointer to the next node, $n.finger = ID_{next\_node}$, a list of m nodes is maintained, $n.finger(m)$, with their logical inter-node distance increasing exponentially. This provides the efficient look up mechanism. Typically, on each of the entries, associations and additional information will be stored. For instance, each ID in the finger table will be associated with a corresponding certificate from the local keyring and a physical address. Moreover, the nodes will need to take past transactions into account, therefore, for each of the fingers n will record a trustworthiness metric and a cache of IP addresses encountered thus far. The finger table of a node can be viewed as a map holding the IDs that a node can use as certificate paths in SOMA. Therefore, the finger table will comprise the nodes that it has exchanged certificates with and that is responsible for their correct routing. In more details, the $n.finger(i)$ is the ith entry of the finger table for the node n and will hold the $n + 2^{i-1}$ ID and physical address that succeeds n on the circular identifier space, where $1 \leqslant i \leqslant 160$ (for SHA1 with arithmetic modulo 2^{160}).

Hence, when n joins the ring and since each node holds O(log N) state in each finger table, to holistically capture the new entry more nodes in SOMA need to propagate the change. Similarly to the original Chord look up, for a certificate path discovery to be successful, only the successor pointers of the finger table need to be correct. The finger table mechanism serves only in lookup efficiency, not its correctness. The finger table needs to be kept up to date with new entries so that certificate look ups scale logarithmically. When node n joins, the steps taken are:

1. Initialization of the predecessor and the finger table entries of n by establishing authenticated relations through a chain of trust.
2. Update the fingers and predecessors of the existing nodes to reflect the addition of n.

The first step for the joining node n will be to initialize its finger table and find its virtual position in the ring. Node n calls $n.join(ID_{n'})$, where node n' is its introducer. This will make n' to do a Chord look-up of ID_n in the ring and return back to n the key/address of its successor s. The successor s is the first finger in the finger-table of n, $n.finger[1] = s$. In addition n' will provide n with a PGP certificate $Cert_{n' \Rightarrow n}$ so that it can associate its credentials with s. Finally, node n will set $n.successor \rightarrow s$.

The join mechanism of SOMA changes the periodic stabilisation protocol in Chord. The procedures $stabilize()$, $notify()$ and $fix\_fingers()$ run periodically to notify the overlay nodes for the new entry, accomplishing the steps 1 and 2. After finding its successor, n will proceed with $n.stabilize()$ so that it can exchange its credentials with its successor and propagate the information on the new join. We can think of $stabilize()$ as a protocol working on linked list, that uses certificates for authentication and updates the linked list when there is a new entry.

The stabilization runs periodically in the background by all nodes. The first step for $n.stabilize()$ is for n to notify node s that $n.successor \rightarrow s$ using the certificate provided by n'. Node s will proceed with checking the validity of the supplied credentials and call $s.findCertChain(n')$ (more details in section 3.4). The validation mechanism includes checking the public key, the address, the signatures, the timestamps and if any of the certificates in the chain is revoked. If s finds that all are correct, it sets $s.predecessor \rightarrow n$ else will request for another valid PGP certificate. Moreover, when the original predecessor of node s, node y runs $stabilize()$, it will ask for $s.predecessor$, s will then return to y that n is its new successor. Node y in turn will $notify()$ n. Node n will reply back providing the certificate chain by n'. Node y will similarly check the supplied chain leading to n. After the above stabilizations finish, n will set $n.predecessor \rightarrow y$ and y will have $y.successor \rightarrow n$.

After, the establishment of correct associations with the successor and predecessor, $fixFingers()$ which also runs periodically by the nodes, refreshes the finger table entries. The procedure is repeated for each of the non-trivial ring intervals in the finger table. Which are the ones containing non-virtual distinct nodes. The procedure of $n.fixFingers()$ is as follows: *For each $i \in m$: $finger[i] = findCertChain(finger[i])$*, where m=number of bits used as index (e.g. SHA1 m=160 bits). The procedure to find a certificate chain to another node is done through the $findCertChain(target\_node)$ and follows original Chord $find\_successor()$ algorithm, as described in the following section.

3.4   Certification

When n wishes to authenticate with a peer, it will require a valid chain of trust. In an established SOMA with N number of peers, n will hold all the routing information that is needed on its finger table, similarly to Chord. In addition, n will hold a keyring with all the public keys and information that will allow it to make decisions, based on a trust metric. When two nodes need to mutually authenticate, they construct a certification request and exchange their credentials using the following:

1. $A \longmapsto B : Cert_A, n_1, t_1, ID_B, data_1, (n_1, t_1, ID_B, data_1)Sk_A$
2. $B \longmapsto A : Cert_B, n_2, t_2, ID_A, data_2, (n_2, t_2, ID_A, data_2)Sk_B$

$Cert_{A,B}$ are the respective node certificates. $n_{1,2}$ are nonces and $t_{1,2}$ are expiration timestamps used to ensure freshness and that they were received in a valid time-frame. The $data_{1,2}$ can include a session key encrypted with the receiver's public key and also other information related with the origin of data and implementation specifics.

When n wishes to verify the credentials of a node p, it will have to get a trust chain leading to p. Therefore n will first check if p is already in its finger table or if p is an introducer for n. If any of the two hold true, then n will have a chain of certificates from the stabilisation protocol leading to p that can be directly verified for its validity. If ID_p is not included in its finger table, then node n will make a certificate chain lookup to find the PGP chain to p.

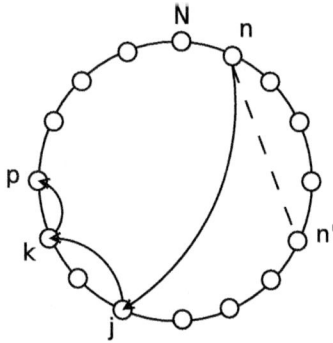

Fig. 1. An example of the logical representation of SOMA ring with N nodes

Following the above, n with ID_n has introducer ID_n' and wants to authenticate the certificate of p (Fig. 1). Node n finds a certificate chain to ID_p, by sending a *findCertChain()* request to an intermediate node j, *j.findCertChain(p)*. Node j is chosen because ID_j is the closest finger that precedes ID_p in n's finger table and hence in the circular identifier space. Node n has already exchanged credentials with node j at join/stabilisation. Upon receiving the request by n, j will look in its finger table finding that the closest preceding finger is k and will reply with this information back to n providing also the certificate containing $Cert_{j \Rightarrow k}$. Finally, node n will ask $k.findCertChain(ID_p)$ similarly returning to n the final link $Cert_{k \Rightarrow p}$. As a result, n receives on each query a certificate that will allow it to build a chain of trust up until ID_p, with each time reducing the distance half-way through. Node n logarithmically gets closer to the target ID_p, building the needed trust path.

3.5   Revocation

In every PKI, dealing with the revocation of certificates can be a technical challenge. In SOMA a node can implicitly or explicitly revoke its published certificate. An implicit revocation by a node takes place when a certificate is allowed to naturally expire. Each issued certificate has a predetermined lifetime. When its expiration time passes it will no longer pass any validation tests taken by the nodes and hence, the certificate will be considered implicitly revoked. If a node is aware that its private key has been compromised, it can explicitly revoke the certificate for the public key in question. This is done by using a revocation certificate and without introducing a complex reputation scheme. Each node, creates and stores safely (e.g. in external media) a revocation certificate that will be used as insurance in case of a key compromise. The revocation certificate will be used to effectively separate the ID/node relationship for that node in the ring.

The node that revoked its certificate does not need to send the revocation request certificate to all the nodes in SOMA. The only interested parties in the revocation scheme are the ones that point in their finger table to the revoked key. Therefore, the node only needs to provide the revocation certificate to its predecessor and exchange it through the stabilisation protocol with all the nodes that update their finger table to the node itself. In this way, the Certificate Revocation List (CLR) is build conjointly with the keyring for each node and will propagate to all the nodes that require it. Furthermore, when a node requires to check if a certificate is currently revoked, then it only needs to proceed with the normal lookup operation. The nodes along the SOMA ring will provide the revocation certificate if has been published.

4   Evaluation

4.1   Security Analysis

The design characteristics of SOMA focus on decentralisation through self-organisation, scalability and robustness against malicious behaviour. In this section we analyse the shortcomings and possible attack scenarios regarding the certificate mechanism, the control and use of key material and, finally, the overlay routing itself.

Node Join. When a node joins the ring, a malicious bootstrapping node could attempt to provide false credentials to the rest of the SOMA nodes. This attack would be negated in our case, since the node's public key and physical IP address is connected with its logical ID on the ring. Any false credentials provided by the bootstrapping node would require a valid certification chain, which it can not forge due to the certificate digital signatures.

Certificate Chain. A node wanting to find a certificate chain to another node, needs to authenticate first, a chain of intermediate nodes. These intermediate nodes have valid IDs and the digital certificates provide authentication and non-repudiation for the each node in the certificate path. The consistent hashing mechanism between the physical and the logical address provides a simple defence against impersonation and Sibyl attacks. If one of the nodes, misbehaves or simply creates multiple identities, it will be detected, since the certificates are bound to their address. Therefore, this node can simply be ignored and move on the previous node preceding the target node in the finger table. As long as a single node in the finger table follows the protocol the authentication can proceed. Moreover, an integrated reputation model would help in dealing with misbehaving nodes accordingly to the predefined rules.

Denial of Service. If a node joins a SOMA ring, where the majority of the nodes are malicious, then its identity even though could not be forged, the authentication service for that node could be potentially disrupted through denial of service (DoS). Against DoS attacks, SOMA is resilient due to the fact it uses consistent hashing to distribute the logical identities of the nodes. Therefore, malicious nodes would require a large majority to be able to control the full certificate log n path. This is due to the fact that the IDs are mapped using consistent hashing where the standard hardness assumptions for the chosen hash function apply.

Credential Exchange. An attack directly on the certificate exchange is thwarted by the use of nonces and timestamps, which ensure freshness, and prevent man in the middle attacks (MITM). Additionally, the inclusion of origin and target data safeguards against certificate hijacking and all forms of impersonation.

Overlay attack. Attacks on the routing protocol, itself, can be hard to avoid if the majority of nodes are malicious. Even though impersonation is averted through the logical-physical address relationship of the public key certificates, a DoS attack could potentially disrupt the overlay as a whole. In such a case, a reputation model would provide the necessary insight to marginalise or expel malicious nodes. Attacks on the network infrastructure itself could include churn attacks and potential network failures from the malicious nodes. Against such attacks, SOMA is resilient by requiring at least one correct node in the finger table for correct routing. In addition, instead of using a single successor, employing successor lists will provide additional routes and mitigate the effects of overlay attacks.

4.2   Critical Appraisal

SOMA provides authentication service, data integrity, confidentiality and non-repudiation for the nodes. But to have, a fully self-organised network, a policy model such as the one proposed is not enough to guarantee sound decision making. A reputation system would need to be integrated in the model as a monitoring mechanism. This integration can be easily achieved in the form of a trustworthiness metric in the finger table of the nodes. The reputation model would provide additional insight and better informed reasoning that would be based on predefined rules for trust establishment. Our system is designed so that it can incorporate a reputation model for the nodes to decide whether or not to place their trust. Such an extension can be through observations or recommendations by the peers themselves. The integration of such a model on top of SOMA will be investigated in future work.

SOMA is a hybrid solution based on structured Peer-to-Peer to tackle the limitations that arise in threshold cryptography, random walks and pure Web-of-Trust solutions. It utilises the collective knowledge gained by structured peer-to-peer overlays and combines it with a certificate chaining solution to create an autonomous self-organised authentication system suitable for our goals. By taking advantage of the mathematical guaranties of the Chord infrastructure, path discovery for the chain of trust building becomes scalable to many thousands of nodes and with bounded path traversal latency. Chord is application agnostic and utilises consistent hashing in the same way we apply it in SOMA, therefore SOMA can guarantee $O(\log N)$ authenticated certificate chain depth, routing efficiency for certificate discovery of $O(\log N)$ communication hops and $O(\log N)$ state per node as it was seen in the certification example in (Fig. 1).

In SOMA, there are no centralised authorities and no empowered nodes because it would limit the autonomy of the nodes and disrupt the nature of a mesh network. We do not adopt any form of threshold cryptography, since it would introduce an unnecessary trade-off between security and scalability. To extrapolate further on the $(n, t+1)$ schemes, an open mesh network has many thousands of nodes and hence, we can not assume that an adversary would not compromise $t+1$ nodes in any given time frame. Moreover, we would need appropriate adaptive control mechanisms to calculate the thresholds, depending on the dynamics of the network topology, churn and number of nodes in the system. Therefore, we avoid the risk that complex voting or threshold based schemes introduce.

5   Conclusions

This paper has proposed a large-scale authentication system for mesh networks without the need of a TTP. SOMA builds on top of Chord to provide us with performance guaranties. Our proposal, allows each node to decide its own trust policy while keeping its autonomy intact. We have shown how the overlay can be used as a meta-structure to infer trust relationships and not as the means to provide distributed directory storage. Wireless ad-hoc networks have inherent vulnerabilities, the nodes can always be considered susceptible to security attacks and to physical capture. Thus, in creating SOMA we took into account the security of the network as a whole and provided the building blocks for establishing trust without relying on centralised authorities. Finally, the possible attacks and limitations of our proposal were discussed, providing the grounds for future work.

References

1. AWMN: Athens Wireless Metropolitan Network, www.awmn.gr
2. Bicket, J., Aguayo, D., Biswas, S., Morris, R.: Architecture and Evaluation of an Unplanned 802.11b Mesh Network. In: 11th Annual International Conference on Mobile Computing and Networking (2005)
3. Zimmermann, P.: The Official PGP Users Guide. The MIT Press, Cambridge (1995)
4. Gnutella RFC v0.4, http://rfc-gnutella.sourceforge.net/index.html
5. Stoica, I., Morris, R., Karger, D., Kaashoek, M. F., Balakrishnan, H.: Chord: A Scalable Peer-to-Peer Lookup Service for Internet Applications. In: ACM SIGCOMM Technical Conference (2001)
6. Shamir, A.: How to Share a Secret, vol. 22(11), pp. 612–613. ACM, New York (1979)
7. Zhou, L., Haas, Z.: Securing Ad-hoc Networks. IEEE Network 13(6), 24–30 (1999)
8. Kong, J., Zerfos, P., Luo, H., Lu, S., Zhang, L.: Providing Robust and Ubiquitous Security Support for Mobile Ad-hoc Networks. In: 9th International Conference on Network Protocols (ICNP) (November 2001)
9. Douceur, J.R.: The Sybil Attack. Springer, Microsoft Research, One Microsoft Way (2002)
10. Zhou, L., Schneider, F., Renesse, R.: COCA: A Secure Distributed Online Certification Aauthority. ACM Transactions on Computer Systems (TOCS) 20(4), 329–368 (2002)
11. Yi, S., Kravets, R.: Practical PKI for Ad-hoc Wireless Networks. Department of Computer Science. University of Illinois, USA (2001)
12. Yi, S., Kravets, R.: Key Management for Heterogeneous Ad-hoc Wireless Networks. In: 10th IEEE International Conference on Network Protocols (ICNP) (2002)
13. Yi, S., Kravets, R.: MOCA: Mobile Certificate Authority for Wireless Ad-hoc Networks. In: 2nd Annual PKI Research Workshop (2003)
14. Capkun, S., Hubaux, J., Buttyn, L.: Mobility Helps Security in Ad-hoc Networks. In: Mobile Ad Hoc Networking and Computing (MobiHoc) (2003)
15. Capkun, S., Buttyn, L., Hubaux, J.: Self-organized Public-key Management for Mobile Ad-hoc Networks. IEEE Transactions on Mobile Computing 2(1), 52–64 (2003)
16. Capkun, S., Hubaux, J., Buttyn, L.: Mobility Helps Peer-to-Peer Security. IEEE Transactions on Mobile Computing 5(1), 43–51 (2006)

17. Kambourakis, G., Konstantinou, E., Gritzalis, S.: Binary Tree Based Public-Key Management for Mobile Ad Hoc Networks. In: Proceedings of the ISWCS 2008 5th IEEE International Symposium on Wireless Communications Systems, Reykjavik, Iceland, pp. 687–692. IEEE, Los Alamitos (October 2008)
18. Boneh, D., Franklin, M.: Identity-based Encryption from the Weil Pairing. In: Kilian, J. (ed.) CRYPTO 2001. LNCS, vol. 2139, p. 213. Springer, Heidelberg (2001)
19. Bobba, R.B., Eschenauer, L., Gligor, V., Arbaugh, W.: Global Telecommunications Conference, GLOBECOM 2003, December 1-5. IEEE, Los Alamitos (2003)
20. Aberer, K., Datta, A., Hauswirth, M.: A Decentralised Public Key Infrastructure for Customer-to-Customer E-commerce. International Journal of Business Process Integration and Management 1(1), 26–33 (2005)
21. Avramidis, A., Kotzanikolaou, P., Douligeris, C.: Embedding a Public Key Infrastructure into the Chord Overlay Network. In: López, J., Samarati, P., Ferrer, J.L. (eds.) EuroPKI 2007. LNCS, vol. 4582, pp. 354–361. Springer, Heidelberg (2007)
22. Watts, D.J., Strogatz, S.H.: Collective Dynamics of 'small-world' Networks. Nature 393, 440–442 (1998) doi: 10.1038/30918
23. Open PGP November 2007/RFC 4880, http://tools.ietf.org/html/rfc4880

A Privacy-Preserving Secure Service Discovery Protocol for Ubiquitous Computing Environments*

Jangseong Kim[1], Joonsang Baek[2], Kwangjo Kim[1], and Jianying Zhou[2]

[1] Department of Information and Communications Engineering,
KAIST, Daejeon 305-714, Korea
{jskim.withkals,kkj}@kaist.ac.kr
[2] Institute for Infocomm Research, Singapore 138632, Singapore
{jsbaek,jyzhou}@i2r.a-star.edu.sg

Abstract. Recently, numerous service discovery protocols have been introduced in the open literature. Unfortunately, many of them did not consider security issues, and for those that did, many security and privacy problems still remain. One important issue is to protect the privacy of a service provider while enabling an end-user to search an alternative service using multiple keywords. To deal with this issue, the existing protocols assumed that a directory server should be trusted or owned by each service provider. However, an adversary may compromise the directory server due to its openness property.

In this paper, we suggest an efficient method of membership verification to resolve this issue and analyze its performance. Using this method, we propose a privacy-preserving secure service discovery protocol protecting the privacy of a service provider while providing multiple keywords search to an end-user. Also, we provide performance and security analysis of our protocol.

1 Introduction

Since hundreds of devices and services may surround end-users in ubiquitous computing environment, any prior knowledge about nearby environment (*i.e.*, a list of wireless access points and accessible services) could be useful to satisfy the service requirements of an end-user and choose proper services [1]. Using this knowledge, an end-user can find an alternative service and replace the current service with new one if the current service is no longer available. However, this knowledge cannot be provided to end-users due to their mobility, which may violate their desire for service continuity. This is one of important requirements why we should consider a service discovery protocol for ubiquitous computing environment.

Most existing service discovery protocols [2–6] consist of three major components: end-user, service provider, and directory server. To obtain the access

---

* This work was done while the first author was visiting I²R, supported by I²R's Postgraduate Attachment Program.

J. Camenisch and C. Lambrinoudakis (Eds.): EuroPKI 2010, LNCS 6711, pp. 45–60, 2011.

information of a service, an end-user sends a query message to a directory server. A service provider periodically stores the access information of its own service in the directory server. After obtaining the access information of the target service, the end-user accesses the service. The directory server stores or provides proper service access information for simplified trust management and scalability: each end-user and service provider should identify and trust the directory server only rather than many services and end-users.

As the directory server should be accessible by anyone and placed in public place, the adversary can compromise the directory server to obtain private information of an end-user or service provider. However, the service provider can check whether the directory server gives wrong searching result, which causes the compromised directory server to operate properly against all requests. From this, we consider the directory server to be a semi-honest entity. In short, the directory server may seek to gather any sensitive information of an end-user or service provider, identify which entity submits the given keywords, and impersonate the target entity while giving correct searching result of the given keywords.

Any end-user could be one of the service providers in photo-image sharing or personal music broadcasting applications, and thus the privacy of a service provider should also be protected. To preserve the privacy of an end-user and service provider together, an authentication server, believed to be trusted third party, is required to take a role of signer and verifier in blind signature scheme.

Based on these observations, the system for ubiquitous computing environment should satisfy the following security requirements.

Mutual authentication. Mutual authentication between an end-user and service provider is required to identify whether the communicating party is a legitimate entity or not.

Anonymity and accountability. An end-user wants to preserve the private information (*i.e.*, identity, service usage, and *etc*) during service discovery while presenting their legitimacy and access permission. Similarly, the service provider wants to protect the private information (*i.e.*, identity, service access information, service presence information, and *etc*) from non-subscribers of the service. Although anonymous authentication can protect the privacy of an end-user and service provider, it also can help a malicious user access several services without permission.

Differentiated access control. Although a service provider wants to provide differentiated services based on access privilege of his/her subscribers, anonymous communication through an authentication server allows the server to access the subscription information of the service provider which should be protected.

Efficient keyword search on encrypted data. As many services may exist in ubiquitous computing environments, keyword search is required to allow an end-user to specify a target service satisfying the service requirements of the end-user. However, it can violate the privacy of a service provider. Anyone can access the stored service information if proper access control is not enforced. Simple solution is to store the service information and its corresponding keywords in directory server after encrypting them. Still, this approach has three limitations: complexity of key distribution, heavy computational overhead of a directory server, and information leakage by the semi-honest directory server.

Lightweightness. As one of the main characteristics in ubiquitous computing environment is heterogeneity, cryptographic protocols should be lightweight from the view of communication and computation cost.

Let us consider the following example illustrating the convenience of service discovery protocol and its disadvantages: A famous researcher is visiting a university to give a special talk. If the researcher needs to find a place where she will give a talk and to print out some lecture notes, she should access the Internet and find out what type of printers are available. While a service discovery protocol can automatically detect and configure these service, which spares the researcher any manual setup operations, the researcher may have to reveal her sensitive information (*e.g.*, purpose, identity, and access permission) to the service provider and directory server. This disadvantage can happen when the service discovery protocol does not satisfy security requirements (*i.e.*, confidentiality, integrity, and access control). Also, the protocol supporting the security requirements still causes this disadvantage if the compromised directory server (or authentication server) disclose the received information to the adversary. However, as the previous work [5, 6] does not address this problem, we require a privacy-preserving secure service discovery protocol.

In this paper, we propose an efficient approach of membership verification which evaluates an encrypted polynomial representation of a given set. When the set is a keywords list to specify a service, our approach can support multiple keywords search without leaking sensitive information of the service provider. Also, our approach can remove the privacy concern regarding the abuse of subscription information by the administrator in the authentication server when the set is a subscriber list to ensure access control. Based on these results, we propose a privacy-preserving secure service discovery for ubiquitous computing environment. Moreover, our protocol provides various security-related features and is suitable for establishing a security framework for ubiquitous computing environment.

The root of this paper is organized as follows: In Section 2, we discuss the related work. After explaining our assumption and notation used in this paper, we present our membership verification with its performance and security analysis in Section 3. Then, we explain our privacy-preserving service discovery protocol in Section 4. Also, we provide performance and security analysis of our protocol in Section 5. Finally, we conclude this paper in Section 6.

2 Related Work

2.1 Secure Service Discovery

To address these privacy and security issues, Czerwinski *et al.* [5] proposed a scheme which was called "Secure Service Discovery Service". The scheme consisted of end-user, discovery server, and service provider. Through directory server, regarded as trusted entities, an end-user and service provider authenticated each other. However, they should expose their own identities and service access information during service lookup and service announcement.

In 2006, Zhu *et al.* [6] proposed the PrudentExposure model for a secure service discovery protocol. This approach can preserve the privacy of end-users and service providers based on a Bloom filter. Also, end-users should bind themselves to a nearby agent and transfer all their identities to the agent via a secure channel. However, this approach has several limitations. **First**, additional communication cost is incurred to bind and transfer end-users' identities to an agent. **Second**, privacy leakage occurs among insiders even though the model is designed to preserve sensitive information for an end-user and service provider. **Third**, the end-user should perform two public key encryptions (or decryptions) and one signing operation *whenever* he/she sends a lookup message. Although the agent near the end-user should perform this computation, we need to take into account the cost of removing privacy concern that the nearby agent can identify the user's service selection and obtain all messages between the end-user and service provider as a computational cost of the end-user. **Finally**, each service provider should have his/her own directory server.

2.2 Multiple Keywords Search on Encrypted Data

A keyword search on encrypted data is introduced to share audit log and email on a public server while minimizing information leakage. Previous protocols [7–9] have three common entities in their system models: a data provider, public server, and data retriever. The data provider generates shared information and stores it on a public server in an encrypted form. Only an entity having a proper trapdoor (*i.e.*, access permission) can retrieve the stored information. This approach can remove a strong security assumption that a directory server should be trusted. However, no access control is provided [10] and the server can link two different sessions to the same group using the relationship between the stored data and the submitted trapdoor.

To provide access control only, Yau *et al.* [10] proposed an idea to convert the searching of the sets to an evaluation of polynomial representations of a given set [11, 12] using BGN encryption [13]. Interestingly, this approach can address the second problem due to non-deterministic property of BGN encryption. However, the proposed approach is not efficient in view of computational overhead. Denote S_1 and S_2 by a set of access keys and a set of keywords, respectively. Then, the data retriever should compute $(\mid S_1 \mid + \mid S_2 \mid +1)$ exponent multiplications and BGN encryptions [13] per each query.

2.3 BGN Encryption [13]

In 2005, Boneh *et al.* proposed a new homomorphic encryption scheme supporting unlimited additive operations and one multiplicative operation on encrypted data. The proposed encryption scheme enables one entity to evaluate the encrypted data without revealing the content of encrypted data. We review the BGN encryption scheme in brief.

In BGN encryption, all operations are done on two cyclic groups G and G_1 with the same order $n = q_1 q_2$, where q_1 and q_2 are two large prime numbers. The public key PK_{BGN} is g and $h = g^{\mu q_2}$ under the group G, where μ is a random integer. The encryption of m_i, $m_i + m_j$, and $m_i m_j$ can be computed as $g^{m_i} h^{r_i}$, $g^{m_i} h^{r_i} g^{m_j} h^{r_j}$, and $e(g^{m_i} h^{r_i}, g^{m_j} h^{r_j})$ where T is a non-zero random number less than q_2, $m_i \in \mathbb{Z}_T$ be i^{th} message, r_i is i^{th} random number, and e is a bilinear mapping from $G \times G$ to G_1, respectively. The expected decryption time using Pollard's lambda method is $\tilde{O}(\sqrt{|T|})$ although the authentication server has the private key, $SK_{BGN} = q_1$.

3   Membership Verification

We convert membership verification to set search by evaluating of a polynomial representing a given set [11, 12], where the set contains the service subscriber list.

Compared to membership verification cost of the previous work [10], which relies on the number of access keys and subscribers, our membership verification cost is reduced to the number of subscribers. In this point, we argue that our membership verification is an efficient approach. Note that access keys in our scheme are used to derive K_{rk} which is used to encrypt the access information of the target service and can be derived from the list of hidden encryption keys $g^{r-ak_1}, \cdots, g^{r-ak_p}$ using each subscriber's access key ak_i where i is an index of each end-user.

3.1   Assumption and Notation

We assume that an end-user can control the source addresses of the outgoing Medium Access Control (MAC) frames since this assumption is a prerequisite for anonymous communications. A detailed method for this modification is covered by Gruteser et al. [14]. Table 1 illustrates the notations used throughout this paper.

The AS (or SP) issues SID, a polynomial $f(x)$ with degree t, access key ak_i, $E[i + r, PK_{BGN}, G_1]$, and ID_t to service provider (or end-user). Using the received information, the end-user or SP can generate their MT.

The SP stores SID list and polynomials for membership verification to the AS in an encrypted form. If there is any change in the stored information, the SP updates the stored information.

Finally, PK_{AS}, ID_{AS} and PK_{BGN} are assumed to be known to all entities.

3.2   Polynomial Generation

For a set $S_1 = w_1, w_2, \cdots, w_p$, a polynomial with degree t, $f(x)$ for S_1 is defined as the following:

$$f(x) = \begin{cases} -r & x = w_i \in S_1 \\ -r' & x = w_i \notin S_1, \end{cases}$$

where r and $r'(r' \neq r)$ are random integers. Here, $w_i \in \mathbb{Z}_T$ is a user account of ith subscriber (or keywords) if $f(x)$ is used for membership test in AS (or DS). Figure 1 presents an example of generating a polynomial. A public SP means that the service is well-known to all or some of all entities in a single administration domain and presence information of the service is not important. However, a private SP indicates that the service is known to some selected entities and

Table 1. Notations

AS / DS / SP	Authentication Server / Directory Server / Service Provider
$Credential$ / ID_A	A ticket for entity authentication / An identifier of entity A
n / U	A user's access frequency / End-user
PK_A / SK_A	A public key of entity A / A private key of entity A
PK_{BGN}	A public key under BGN encryption scheme [13] owned by AS
MT	A ticket for indicating subscribers of the target SP
DMV	A ticket for Discovery Membership Verification
S	A set of selected numbers the length where $\mid S \mid \geq 2n$
SID	A service type identifier describes a selected subset of the available service pool and includes an polynomial identifier for membership test
SK_{BGN}	A private key under BGN encryption scheme [13], which is owned by AS and distributed to DS for membership test
C^i or C_A^i, $i = 0, 1, \cdots$	A series of authorized credentials generated by entity A
$CertA$	A certificate that binds entity A with A's public key
j^i or j_A^i, $i = 1, 2, \cdots$	A series of a user's number selections generated by entity A
$K_{A,B}$	Shared secret key between entities A and B
$E\{m, K_A\}$	A message m is encrypted by a symmetric key K_A
$E[m, PK_A]$	A message m is encrypted by an entity A's public key
$D[m, SK_A]$	A message m is signed by an entity A's private key
$E[m, PK_{BGN}, \mathbb{G} \text{ or } \mathbb{G}_1]$	A message m is encrypted by the public key PK_{BGN} on cyclic group $\mathbb{G}$ or $\mathbb{G}_1$ and the ciphertext is $g^m h^r$ or $g_1^m h_1^r$ where $g_1 = e(g, g)$ and $h_1 = e(e, h)$
$H(m)$	A hash value of message m using SHA-1
R^i or R_A^i, $i = 1, 2, \cdots$	A series of nonces generated by entity A where $\mid R^i \mid \geq 64$-bit.

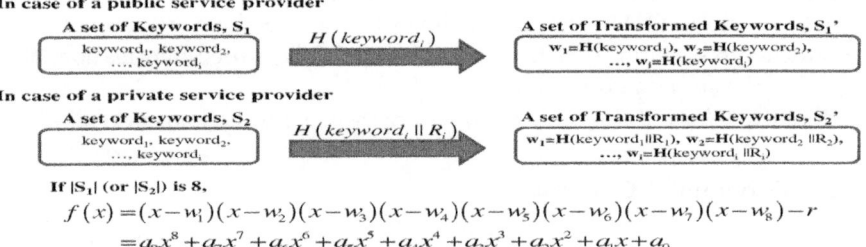

Fig. 1. An example of polynomial generation

presence information is important. By concatenating a nonce with the given keywords and distributing the nonce to each subscriber, the private SP can hide a relationship between own service and the given keywords as shown in Figure 1.

3.3 Polynomial Evaluation

For membership verification, an end-user submits w_i and $i+r$ to the membership verifier. Then, the membership verifier can check whether the user belongs to one of the service subscribers by computing $i+r+f(w_i)$. Only if $1 \leq i+r+f(w_i) \leq p$, the user is one of the service subscriber where p is the number of subscribers of target service.

However, we want to hide the detailed information of membership function from the AS, DS, and non-subscribers of the service. That's why the SP encrypts the polynomial $f(x)$' coefficients with public key PK_{BGN} on cyclic group $\mathbb{G}$ and $i+r$ with public key PK_{BGN} on cyclic group $\mathbb{G}_1$. Also, the user encrypts $1, w_i^1, w_i^2, \cdots, w_i^t$ with public key PK_{BGN} since BGN encryption supports only one multiplicative operation on encrypted data. Then, the membership verifier performs the following steps:

1. Set $z = 1$.
2. Compute $C = \prod_{v=1}^{t-1} e(E[a_v, PK_{BGN}, \mathbb{G}], E[(w_j)^v, PK_{BGN}, \mathbb{G}])$.
3. Compute $C' = C \cdot E[a_0, PK_{BGN}, \mathbb{G}_1] \cdot E[(w_j)^t, PK_{BGN}, \mathbb{G}_1] \cdot E[i+r, PK_{BGN}, \mathbb{G}_1]$
4. Repeat the following steps until $z \leq p$.
   (a) If $C'^{(SK_{BGN})} = e(g, g)^{(z \cdot SK_{BGN})}$, return z.
   (b) $z = z + 1$
5. Return 0.

Using $f(x) = a_t \cdot x^t + a_{t-1} \cdot x^{t-1} + \cdots + a_1 \cdot x + a_0$ and the homomorphic properties of the BGN encryption scheme, we can change $\prod_{v=1}^{t-1} e(E[a_v, PK_{BGN}, \mathbb{G}], E[(w_j)^v, PK_{BGN}, \mathbb{G}])$ to C in the above procedure. By assuming that a_t and a_0 are both 1, C' in the above step (3) is the same as $E[i+r, PK_{BGN}, \mathbb{G}_1] \cdot E[f(w_j), PK_{BGN}, \mathbb{G}_1] = E[(i+r) + f(w_j), PK_{BGN}, \mathbb{G}_1]$.

3.4 Performance Analysis

To obtain the processing time of membership verification, we generate a polynomial $f(x)$ with different degree i and implement our polynomial evaluation method

Table 2. Processing time of membership verification when $|PK_{BGN}| = 512$ bits and $p = 20$

Degree of a polynomial $f(x)$		i=2	i=3	i=4	i=5	i=6	i=7	i=8
Processing time (ms)	1st user	48.5	85.9	121.8	159.4	195.3	232.8	270.3
	11th user	112.5	148.5	184.3	220.3	257.8	296.8	332.8

using pairing based cryptography library [15] under Intel®Core ^{TM}2 2.13GHz CPU, 1GB RAM and Microsoft Windows XP Professional Service Pack 3.

Table 2 shows the processing time of membership verification procedure. Rather than showing membership verification request of all subscribers of the target service, we present the request of $1st$ (or $11th$) end-user. As increasing the degree of a given polynomial $f(x)$, the number of pairings in step (2) and exponent multiplications in step (4) will be increased. That's why the processing time of membership verification is increased linearly. In addition, the communication cost increases linearly with the degree of a given polynomial $f(x)$. Therefore, we suggest that each SP should divide his own subscribers to several subsets based on access privilege and desired performance of our membership verification.

Let assume that Alice provides a printing service based on two different privileges such as heavy and light user. In each privilege, 30 legitimate users are subscribing the printing service. If 3 degree of polynomial $f(x)$ is sufficient to satisfy Alice's desired performance, for each privilege Alice generates 10 polynomials where the degree of polynomial $f(x)$ is 3 and each polynomial has 10 different subscribers. For membership verification, each end-user should submit $E[(i + r), PK_{BGN}, \mathbb{G}_1]||E[(w_1), PK_{BGN}, \mathbb{G}] ||E[(w_1)^2, PK_{BGN}, \mathbb{G}_1]$ where i is the index value of an end-user among the target service subscribers and r is a random number. Then, the message size of submitted membership information is $3 \times |PK_{BGN}|$. However, we can reduce the message size by sending the x-coordinate of membership information to $1.5 \times |PK_{BGN}|$. Since PK_{BGN} is a point on cyclic group G, the encrypted result is also one of points on cyclic group $\mathbb{G}$ or $\mathbb{G}_1$ where a point consists of x-coordinate and y-coordinate. Therefore, we can reduce the communication cost and processing delay to the desired performance of the service provider. Moreover, this approach will help us to support differentiated access control.

4   Our Protocol

Before describing our protocol in detail, we illustrates our system architecture and activities of each entity in Figure 2. Our protocol consists of four phases: entity registration, service registration, discovery, and service access. Through

Fig. 2. System architecture for ubiquitous computing environment

entity registration phase, an entity (*e.g.*, end-user or SP) obtains his/her authorized credential preserving the privacy of the entity. The AS verifies the legitimacy of the entity using the received MT. In service registration phase, a service provider stores his/her service and proper information, which are required to verify the legitimacy of the end-user, to the DS. Using his/her credential and DMV, the end-user can find the registered service and obtain proper information to access the service in discovery phase.

Note that the DS can authenticate itself and shares a fresh session key with the AS though entity registration phase and entity authentication phase. Using the shared session key, the DS can make the communication with the AS to be secure. From now, we assume that the communication between the DS and AS is secure.

4.1 Entity Registration Phase

Only if the entity is a legal entity having proper permission to access a service or provide his/her service, the AS authorizes the received credential. To hide the relationship between the authorized credential and the entity's real identity we apply blind signature technique. Figure 3 depicts entity registration phase.

To verify whether the entity is a legitimate one and has proper permission to access or provide a service, the AS verifies the received certificate with PK_{AS} and performs our membership verification (i.e., polynomial evaluation discussed in Section 3). If the result of the entity's membership verification is non-zero integer less than p, the AS sends proper information to the entity. Otherwise, the AS discards the received message. Note that $DirectoryList$ indicates a list of the accessible and legitimate DS.

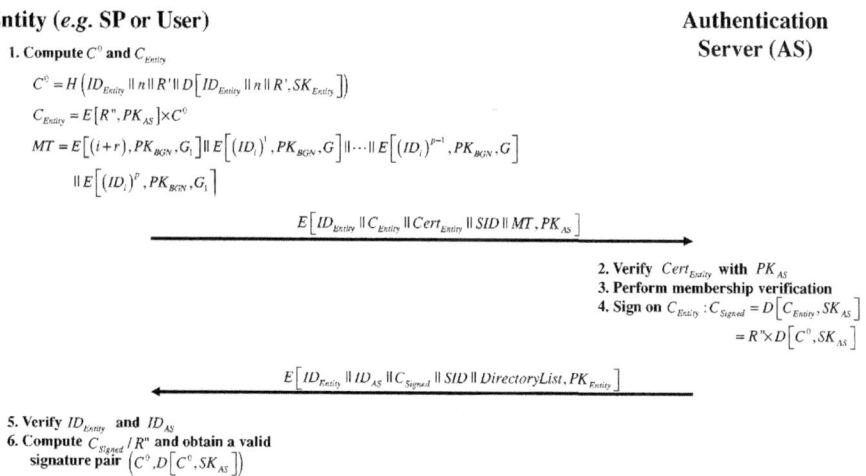

Fig. 3. Entity registration

4.2 Authentication Phase

In the entity authentication phase, each entity establishes $K_{Entity,AS}$ and $K_{Entity,DS} = H(K_{Entity,AS}||C^i||R_{DS})$.

$$K_{Entity,AS} = \begin{cases} H(C^0||PK_{AS}||R^1||j^1||SID) & \text{if } i = 1 \\ H(C^0||C^{i-1}||SID) & \text{otherwise} \end{cases}$$

To provide accountability of the authorized credential, we adopt a set of selected numbers S, which is l-bit array. In the first access request, each entity generates the set randomly. Whenever sending an ith authentication request, each entity generates a fresh nonce R^i_{Entity} and selects one random number j between 0 to $l-1$ until $j-th$ value of S is 0. Since the set is only known to the entity and AS, the adversary without knowing S cannot generate the authentication request. Therefore, we believe that our protocol can enhance security level. Note that $C^i = H(C^0||j^i||R^i)$. For entity authentication, the AS performs the following verification procedure:

1. 1st request: After decrypting the request message, the AS computes $H(D[C^0,SK_{AS}])$ and compares the result with the received $H(D[C^0, SK_{AS}])$. Only if the result is same, the AS believes that the entity has an authorized credential and computes $C1 = H(C^0||j^1||R^1)$ and stores SID, S^1, C^0, and C^1 in the database. Otherwise, the AS discards the request.
2. i^{th} request: The AS finds C^0, $S^{(i-1)}$ and SID in the database using the received $C^{(i-1)}$ and decrypts the received message with $K_{Entity,AS}$. Next, the AS verifies that the entity has the same set of selected numbers and j^i

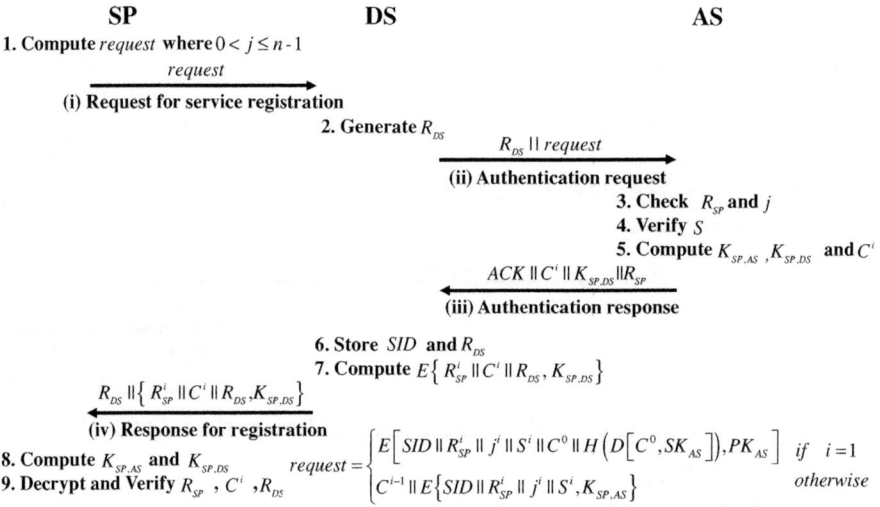

Fig. 4. Entity authentication in service registration

is not in the set. Only if the result is correct, the AS stores the received C^i and S^i. Otherwise, the AS discards it. If the entity is a legal one with proper access permission, C^i and S^i are stored in the database. As a result, the AS can verify whether the entity has an authorized credential using the received $C^{(i-1)}$.

After this verification, the AS sends a response message to the DS. Then, the DS stores proper information (*i.e.*, SID and R_{DS}) and gives a response for entity authentication request to the entity. After verifying the response message, the entity computes $K_{Entity,AS}$ and $K_{Entity,DS}$. Figure 4 illustrates this phase when the entity is a SP.

4.3   Service Registration Phase

The service registration phase consists of entity authentication and registration. Through the entity authentication phase, an SP can anonymously authenticate himself/herself to a DS and establish the shared keys, $K_{SP,AS}$ and $K_{SP,DS}$. Using $K_{SP,DS}$, the SP registers an encrypted service access information (*e.g.*, service type, service name, service description, SID list, and network address) by $K_{rk} = H(g^r)$, encrypted coefficients of $f(x)$ with PK_{BGN}, and a list of hidden encryption keys $\{g^{r_m/ak_1}, \cdots, g^{r_m/ak_p}\}$ with the directory, where r, g, and p are a random number, a generator of cyclic group G with order $n = q_1q_2$, and the number of access keys, respectively.

Also, the SP may expose polynomial identifiers, SID list, and service type to the DS when the SP wants to serve all or partial end-users enrolled in the AS. Because the exposed access information allows an end-user without any prior knowledge about nearby environment to obtain an accessible service list, this approach can support an end-user's mobility.

4.4   Discovery Phase

The discovery phase consists of three sub-steps, entity authentication, service lookup, and service selection. As the entity authentication phase has already been explained, we will skip the explanation.

Service lookup Although our keyword search is an efficient method compared to the previous approach [10], we should reduce a searching space to address scalability issue by reducing the processing time of an end-user's service lookup request in a DS or entity authentication request in the AS. Also, the end-user without having any prior knowledge may know that the same or similar type of the alternative services. That's why we use the service type as searching condition in service lookup request.

When the lookup is used to find alternative services, query is type indicating a type of the alternative services. If lookup is used to obtain service access information, query is DMV. Then, the DS finds the shared key using R_{DS}, decrypts the lookup message, and checks whether the stored SID is the same

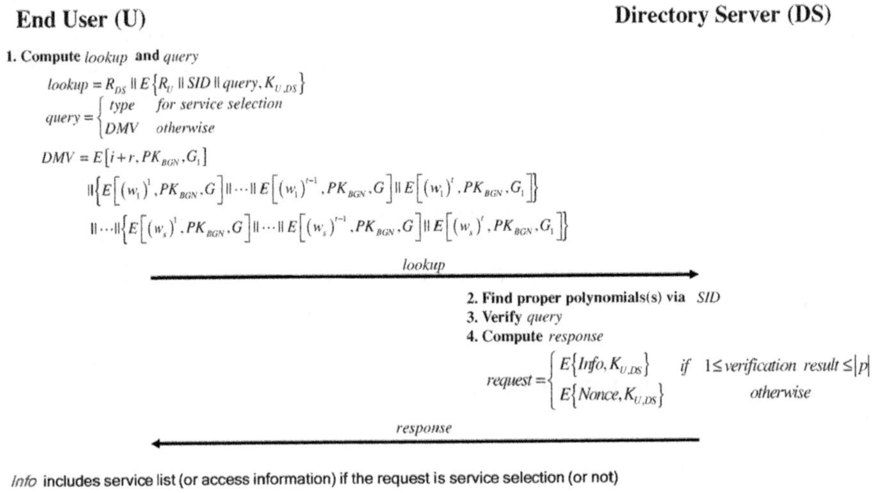

End User (U)   **Directory Server (DS)**

1. Compute *lookup* **and** *query*

$$lookup = R_{DS} \parallel E\{R_U \parallel SID \parallel query, K_{U,DS}\}$$

$$query = \begin{cases} type & \text{for service selection} \\ DMV & \text{otherwise} \end{cases}$$

$$DMV = E[i+r, PK_{BGN}, G_1]$$

$$\parallel\{E[(w_1)^i, PK_{BGN}, G] \parallel \cdots \parallel E[(w_1)^{i-1}, PK_{BGN}, G] \parallel E[(w_1)^i, PK_{BGN}, G_1]\}$$

$$\parallel \cdots \parallel \{E[(w_s)^i, PK_{BGN}, G] \parallel \cdots \parallel E[(w_s)^{i-1}, PK_{BGN}, G] \parallel E[(w_s)^i, PK_{BGN}, G_1]\}$$

lookup ————————————————————————————————→

2. Find proper polynomials(s) via *SID*
3. Verify *query*
4. Compute *response*

$$request = \begin{cases} E\{Info, K_{U,DS}\} & \text{if } 1 \leq \text{verification result} \leq |p| \\ E\{Nonce, K_{U,DS}\} & \text{otherwise} \end{cases}$$

←———————————————————————————————— *response*

Info includes service list (or access information) if the request is service selection (or not)

Fig. 5. Service lookup and its response in discovery phase

as the received SID. If the comparison is correct, the directory server performs the following steps:

1. To find alternative services: Using the type, the DS can search alternative services as some service providers expose partial access information of their services in the service registration. If any matched services exist, the DS encrypts the stored service list using $K_{U,DS}$ and sends the resulting ciphertext to the user.
2. To obtain the service access information: The DS performs membership verification procedure by evaluating the given DMV. When the verification result is not zero, the DS sends the stored access information, Em, K_{rk}, and the matched hidden key g^{r-ak_i}.

Figure 5 depicts this phase in detail.

Service selection. After the service lookup phase, the end-user may obtain a service list having the submitted service type. Then, the end-user selects one service from the list and notifies the selection to the DS. If a proper access control is enforced against the selected service, he/she should submit the proper DMV to the DS. As the detailed procedure is the same as the service lookup phase for obtaining service access information, we do not explain the procedure.

4.5 Service Access Phase

To preserve an end-user's privacy during the service access phase, an anonymous authentication protocol is required. Our protocol can support this without additional computational cost since the end-user already has the authorized credentials after the entity registration phase. The detailed procedure is similar to the entity authentication phase. The difference is that the entities participating in the authentication process are the end-user, SP, and AS.

5 Analysis of Our Protocol

In this section we analyze the performance and security-related features of our protocol.

5.1 Performance Analysis

Storage overhead. Each end-user should store $E[(i + r), PK_{BGN}, \mathbb{G}_1]$, access key, PK_{BGN}, and one 5-tuples (C^0, R^i, j^i, N, S) for service discovery and service access request. The service provider needs to save a set of polynomials $f_1(x), f_2(x), \cdots, f_k(x)$ presenting a subset of own subscriber and one 5-tuple (C^0, R^i, j^i, N, S) for service registration.

Computational overhead. Table 3(a) shows the computational overhead of our protocol. Note that p is the number of access keys in S_1, t is the number of keywords in S_2, s is the number of keywords specifying the target service and $1/N$

Table 3. Performance and security analysis

(a) Computational overhead in each phase

	Entity registration		Service registration			Discovery		
	U or SP	AS	SP	DS	AS	U	DS	AS
Public key Oper.	$(1)^\dagger + 1$	1	$(1/N)^\dagger$	0	$1/N$	$(1/N)^\dagger$	0	$1/N$
Signature Oper.	1	1	0	0	$1/N$	0	0	$1/N$
Hash Oper.	1	0	4	0	4	4	0	4
Secret Key Oper.	0	0	$(1)^\dagger + 2$	1	1	$(1)^\dagger + 3$	1	1
BGN Enc. [13]	$(p+1)^\dagger$	0	$(t+1)^\dagger$	0	0	$(s \cdot (t+1))^\dagger$	0	0
Pairing Oper.	0	$p+1$	0	0	0	0	$s{\cdot}(t+1)$	0
Exponent Oper.	0	$p+2$	$(t+1)^\dagger$	0	0	$s{\cdot}(t+1)$	$s{\cdot}(t+1)+1$	0

$\dagger$: Precomputation   Oper. : Operation   Enc. : Encryption

(b) Security-related features comparison

	Our scheme	Zhu et al. [6]	Czerwinski et al. [5]
Mutual authentication	Yes	Yes	Yes
Confidentiality & Integrity	Yes	Yes	Yes
Anonymity & non-linkability	Yes	Yes to outsiders	No
Accountability	Yes	No	No
Directory server	Not trusted	Trusted	Trusted
Access control	Yes	Easy to obtain	Yes
Scalability	Good	Not too bad	Good
Enhanced security of level	Yes	No	No
The abuse of subscription information	None	Yes	Yes

indicates that one operation is needed during N sessions. During discovery phase, the user should compute (one secret key encryption, two secret key decryptions, and four hash operations) per each discovery request while computing ($1/N$ public key encryption, one secret key encryption, $s \times (t + 1)$ BGN encryptions, and $s \times (t + 1)$ exponent multiplications) before the session. Compared with the previous protocol in [6], where the end-user should compute two public key encryptions and one signature generation, our protocol needs less computational cost.

Communication overhead. Our protocol needs four rounds during service discovery. Previous protocol in [6] also requires four rounds. To discuss with the size of communication message, let assume that SHA-1, AES-128, and ECC-160 are used as hash function, symmetric encryption scheme, and asymmetric encryption scheme, respectively. Also, service identifier is 8 bit, N is 80, the given polynomial identifier is 24 bit, and degree of polynomial is 4. Although the previous protocol [6] requires 1104 bits, which is less than our protocol (*i.e.*, 1920 bits in i^{th} request or 2016 bits in 1st request), the previous protocol does not consider that communication cost of agree on the hash functions to be used service match in advance. Also, certificate exchange between an end-user and directory server is not considered. To this point, our protocol is reasonable in communication overhead.

5.2   Security Analysis

Our protocol provides the following security-related features. In Table 3(b), we compare the security-related features of our protocol with previous work.

Mutual authentication. The end-user authenticates the AS through a public key of the AS and knowledge of the corresponding private key. Also, the AS authenticates the end-user using an authorized credential of the end-user.

Anonymity. Our protocol protects privacy of an end-user against insiders and outsiders. As the each user authenticates herself to insiders (*i.e.*, SP and DS) using authorized credentials, the insiders cannot predict who sends the service access request or lookup request. Here, insiders other than the user cannot find any relationship among the authorized credentials, in that the credentials are derived from initial credential C^0 using one-way hash function. Outsiders also cannot identify who sends the messages since all communication messages are encrypted using a shared session key.

Non-linkability. Non-linkability means that, for insiders (*i.e.*, SP and DS) and outsiders, 1) neither of them can ascribe any session to a particular end-user, and 2) neither of them can link two different sessions to the same user [16]. More precisely, non-linkability needs to prevent insiders and outsiders from obtaining an end-user's private information. Our protocol can achieve non-linkability with respect to both insiders and outsiders. First, the information to distinguish each user is never transmitted in a plaintext form. As a result, outsiders cannot associate a session with a particular user and ascribe two sessions to the same user. Second, outsiders and insiders cannot find any relationship between the exposed credentials due to the one-way hash function. Third, as the given DMV is non-deterministic, the DS cannot link two different sessions to the same user. Finally, all communications are protected by a fresh session key.

Accountability. The credentials are authorized only when the end-user is explicitly authenticated and has proper access permission on the service. By adopting a set of selected numbers, our protocol can provide a one-time usage of the authorized credentials to prevent an attacker from reusing the authorized credentials. Also, our protocol can provide good accounting capability by incorporating an accounting function.

Data confidentiality and integrity. All communications are protected by a shared session key or the receiver's public key. In this point, our protocol supports data confidentiality. Although we do not explain explicitly how to generate a key for integrity check, end-user, SP, DS, and AS can derive the key using the shared information such as a fresh session key (or the receiver's public key) and exchanged nonce. By applying HMAC with the derived key, our protocol can support data integrity.

Enhanced level of security. Every access request message contains S, randomly generated by the end-user and delivered only to the AS, to prove the actual holder of the message. Thus, an adversary is required to present S even if the adversary knows the target user's initial credential. In this point, the proposed scheme enhances the level of security.

Less the abuse of subscription information. In our protocol, the administrator can only identify the subscribers of the target service provider when he/she monitors all registration requests. However, a proper operation policy for AS can prevent illegal tracking of all registration requests. In this way, our approach reduces the privacy concern of each service provider regarding the abuse of subscription information.

6 Conclusion

In this paper, we proposed a privacy-preserving secure service discovery protocol for ubiquitous computing environment. Our main contribution is to provide an efficient membership verification procedure while preventing information leakage regarding privacy from a semi-honest directory server. Through actual performance on our membership verification procedure, we show that our protocol is practical. However, the communication cost for membership verification increases linearly as the degree of polynomial $f(x)$. To relieve this limitation we suggest that each service provider should divide all the subscribers to several subsets, which is also useful to reduce processing delay of service discovery and support differentiated access control by assigning a different privilege to each subset.

In addition, our protocol requires fewer computations compared with the previous approach in [6], while providing more useful features. Finally, our protocol is effective in establishing a security framework since the protocol can support anonymous authentication in a service access phase without additional computation cost.

References

1. Satyanarayanan, M.: Pervasive computing: Vision and Challenges. IEEE Personal Communications 8(4), 10–17 (2001)
2. Ellison, C.: Home Network Security. Intel Technology J. 6, 37–48 (2002)
3. Sun Microsystems, Jini Technology Core Platform Specification Version 2.0 (2003), http://www.sun.com/software/jini/specs/
4. Lee, C., Helal, S.: Protocols for Service Discovery in Dynamic and Mobile Networks. International Journal of Computer Research 11(1), 1–12 (2002)
5. Czerwinski, S., Zhao, B.Y., Hodes, T., Joseph, A., Katz, R.: An Architecture for a Secure Service Discovery Service. In: Proc. of Fifth Annual International Conf. on Mobile Computing and Networks (MobiCom 1999), pp. 24–35 (August 1999)
6. Zhu, F., Mutka, M., Ni, L.: A Private, Secure, and User-Centric Information Exposure Model for Service Discovery Protocols. IEEE Transactions on Mobile Computing 5(4), 418–429 (2006)
7. Boneh, D., Crescenzo, G.D., Ostrovsky, R., Persiano, G.: Public Key Encryption with Keyword Search. In: Cachin, C., Camenisch, J.L. (eds.) EUROCRYPT 2004. LNCS, vol. 3027, pp. 506–522. Springer, Heidelberg (2004)
8. Golle, P., Staddon, J., Waters, B.: Secure Conjunctive Search over Encrypted Data. In: Jakobsson, M., Yung, M., Zhou, J. (eds.) ACNS 2004. LNCS, vol. 3089, pp. 31–45. Springer, Heidelberg (2004)
9. Baek, J., Safavi-Naini, R., Susilo, W.: Public Key Encryption with Keyword Search Revisited, Cryptology ePrint Archive, Report 2005/191
10. Yau, S.S., Yin, Y.: Controlled Privacy Preserving Keyword Search. In: Proc. of ACM Symposium on Information, Computer & Communication Security (ASIACCS 2008), pp. 321–324 (March 2008)
11. Freedman, M.J., Nissim, K., Pinkas, B.: Efficient Private Matching and Set Intersection. In: Cachin, C., Camenisch, J.L. (eds.) EUROCRYPT 2004. LNCS, vol. 3027, pp. 1–19. Springer, Heidelberg (2004)
12. Kissner, L., Song, D.X.: Privacy-preserving set operations. In: Shoup, V. (ed.) CRYPTO 2005. LNCS, vol. 3621, pp. 241–257. Springer, Heidelberg (2005)
13. Boneh, D., Goh, E.-J., Nissim, K.: Evaluating 2-DNF formulas on ciphertexts. In: Kilian, J. (ed.) TCC 2005. LNCS, vol. 3378, pp. 325–341. Springer, Heidelberg (2005)
14. Gruteser, M., Grunwald, D.: Enhancing Location Privacy in Wireless LAN through Disposable Interface Identifiers: A Quantitative Analysis. Mobile Networks and Applications 10(3), 315–325 (2003)
15. Lynn, B.: Pairing Based Cryptography, http://crypto.stanford.edu/pbc/
16. Xu, S., Yung, M.: K-anonymous Secret Handshakes with Reusable Credentials. In: Proc. of the 11th ACM Conf. on Computer and Communications Security (CCS 2008), pp. 158–167 (October 2004)

Searchable Encryption for Outsourced Data Analytics

Florian Kerschbaum[1] and Alessandro Sorniotti[2]

[1] SAP Research, Karlsruhe, Germany
florian.kerschbaum@sap.com
[2] SAP Research and Institut Eurécom, Sophia Antipolis, France
alessandro.sorniotti@sap.com

Abstract. Two sets of privacy requirements need to be fulfilled when a company's accounting data is audited by an external party: the company needs to safeguard its data, while the auditors do not want to reveal their investigation methods. This problem is usually addressed by physically isolating data and auditors during the course of an audit. This approach however no longer works when auditing is performed remotely.

In this paper we present an efficient construction for a searchable encryption scheme for outsourcing data analytics. In this scheme the data owner needs to encrypt his data only once and ship it in encrypted form to the data analyst. The data analyst can then perform a series of queries for which he must ask the data owner for help in translating the constants in the queries.

Our searchable encryption scheme extends previous work by the ability to re-use query results as search tokens (query-result reusability) and the ability to perform range queries. It is efficient with $O(\log^2 n)$ work for a range query and is semantically secure relying only on Diffie-Hellman assumptions (in the random oracle model).

1 Introduction

We introduce the problem addressed in this paper by first presenting how financial auditing is traditionally performed, then exploring the privacy issues raised by the provision of auditing services remotely. We then outline the proposed solution, which makes remote auditing possible without sacrificing privacy.

From an abstract point of view, the auditor queries the accounting data and analyses the results. Even though a large amount of queries may be generated in the course of an audit, the final outcome of the audit can be as small as a few paragraphs in the company's annual report stating that everything was in order. The final report therefore details *what* was found and not *how* it was found.

Each of the two parties, the auditor and the audited company, have privacy requirements towards the other party. The company wants to preserve the privacy of data whose access is granted to the auditor for the purpose of the audit. On the other hand, what makes the auditor effective and efficient in his work are the queries he runs, which are his know-how and intellectual property. The

J. Camenisch and C. Lambrinoudakis (Eds.): EuroPKI 2010, LNCS 6711, pp. 61–76, 2011.
© Springer-Verlag Berlin Heidelberg 2011

challenge is therefore to ensure both the privacy of the data and the privacy of the queries.

The problem addressed in this paper is therefore that of performing remote auditing, a specialized case of data analytics, without sacrificing the privacy of either the data or the queries.

We describe an encryption scheme that can be used to encrypt the data, so that nothing but the result from the queries will be revealed. In our scheme, the data owner needs to encrypt his data only once and ship it in encrypted form to the data analyst. The analyst can then perform a series of queries for which he must ask the data owner for help in translating the constants in the queries.

2   Query Language and Setup

2.1   Query Language

The auditors would be able to use the following language for querying the data:

Let $t = \langle d^1, d^2, \ldots, d^n \rangle$ be a n-tuple (row) in the ledger data. Denote $t.d^i$ the i-th data item of row t. For simplicity we consider a flattened, non-normalized form of the data, where all data tables have been condensed into one flat table. Let c^i be any constant query string for $t.d^i$. The grammar for a query expression e is as follows:

```
e := e ∧ e | e ∨ e | s
s := t.dⁱ op cⁱ | t.dⁱ ops t'.dⁱ
op := ops | < | >
ops := ==
```

This grammar implies range queries $(c^i < t.d^i \land t.d^i < c'^i (c^i < c'^i))$ and keyword searches $(c^i == t.d^i)$. We write $e \models t$, if e matches the tuple t. The footprint $(\mathbb{C}_{range}, \mathbb{C}_{id}, \mathbb{F})$ of an expression e is its set $\mathbb{C}_{range}$ of used constants in range queries, its set $\mathbb{C}_{id}$ of used constants in equality queries and its set $\mathbb{F}$ of used foreign fields or keys. E.g. the query expression $t.d^1 > 2 \land t.d^1 < 6 \land t.d^2 == 4 \land t.d^3 == t'.d^3$ has the footprint $(\{2, 6\}, \{4\}, \{t'.d^3\})$. Note that the query language only represents the queries possible by the data analyst, not the security guarantee enforced by the system which we detail in Section 3.2 using a game-based definition.

2.2   Query Result Reusability

Our query language includes equality comparison of data items of two tuples; given any two encrypted tuples, one can always check whether the two are equal or not, without the need of decrypting them. This clearly implies that if a query has returned a set of tuples, each tuple in the result set can be used in turn as an equality query token: this allows subsequent keyword searches. We call this feature query result reusability.

We could go one step further and require that query results be not only reusable in equality queries but also in range queries. However we refrain from it as this would conflict with the requirements for ciphertext indistinguishability. Indeed, if this were possible, then one could always sort two resulting ciphertexts for tuples t, t' by using a returned query token $t'.d^i$ on the other ciphertext for the query $t.d^i < t'.d^i$, consequently breaking any IND-CPA-like game.

A crucial feature of the encryption system is that queries are not revealed to the encrypting party. Nevertheless the querying party can search for any range it chooses. In a completely non-interactive system these are conflicting goals. If the querier can (non-interactively) search for any range he intends to, he can binary search for the encrypted value and thereby break any encryption secure against a polynomially-bound adversary.

We therefore chose to make the translation of constants into query tokens an interactive protocol, but one that does not reveal its inputs. The query token protocol for the querier is a privacy-preserving protocol that protects the constant from the encrypting party (and the secret key from the querier). The encryption scheme preserves the privacy of the query.

2.3   Improvements over Previous Work

Our security requirements are identical to public key encryption with oblivious keyword search introduced by [8]. There is Alice who does not want to reveal its query and Bob who does not want to reveal its database. We stress that we considered this setup and developed our solution independently concurrently to [8]. Our work differs in that it is use-case driven from outsourced auditing. Consequently we introduce new functionality, namely the following two features: query result reusability and range queries.

While query result reusability is a novel concept, range queries on encrypted data have been considered in [18] and [6]. We borrow some techniques for range queries from [18], but their scheme does not lend itself to efficiently implementing blind IBE, since it reveals the plaintext in a matching query (match-revealing). Hiding the query from both, the trusted key authority and the database, is a prerequisite for our application. Their ciphertext size is logarithmic in the size of the domain $\mathbb{D}$ of the plaintext. The Boneh-Waters [6] encryption scheme supports queries for arbitrary subsets and opposed to Shi et al. hides the resulting data item in a matching query (match-concealing). It is therefore better suited for query privacy, but still a query token may reveal the data item queried for. Their ciphertext size is the full size of the range: $O(\mathbb{D})$.

Another competing approach is to use private information retrieval (PIR) [7,10,17] over single-key encrypted data. We improve over those techniques by reducing the computation complexity to polylogarithmic for range queries and the communication complexity by a factor linear in the number of queries. We know from [19] that the limiting factor in PIR is computational complexity and in the PIR approach the data owner needs to carry the computational load while in our approach the data analyst carries the higher (but less than in PIR) computational load. Boneh et al. [5] extend PIR to search on public-key encrypted data, but at a further performance expense and without the possibility for range queries.

Other secure computation protocols, such as private set intersection or Yao's millionaire's protocols are not suitable. While they perform the same functions as our searchable encryption scheme enables, the fundamental problem is that in (almost) any secure computation protocol the function is public, i.e. known to both parties. The entire point of our construction is to have one party chose the function and hide it from the other party.

Let l be the number of tuples in the database. Our encryption scheme has key size $O(|t|)$ (where $|t|$ is the number of fields in a tuple), ciphertext size $O(\log(\mathbb{D})|t|l)$, range query token size $O(\log(\mathbb{D}))$, equality query token size $O(1)$, encryption complexity $O(\log(\mathbb{D})|t|l)$, range query complexity $O(\log^2(\mathbb{D})l)$ and keyword search complexity $O(l)$.

3   Definitions

This section introduces the definitions used later in the description of our encryption scheme and also gives an explicit definition of the security of our solution.

3.1   Encryption Scheme

Definition 1. *A Searchable Encryption scheme for Outsourcing Data Analytics (SEODA) consists of the following polynomial-time algorithms or protocols:*

1. **Setup(k, Γ):** *Takes a security parameter k and tuple definition Γ and outputs a secret key K_{DO} at the data owner and a public security parameter P.*
2. **Encrypt(K_{DO}, t):** *Takes a secret key K_{DO} and a tuple t (adhering to Γ) and outputs a ciphertext C.*
3. **PrepareRangeQuery$[(c^i_{range}, c'^i_{range}), (K_{DO})]$:** *Is a protocol between the data analyst DA and the data owner DO. The analyst inputs a range from c^i_{range} to c'^i_{range} and the owner inputs a secret key K_{DO}. The output at the analyst is a range query token Q_{range} and the data owner receives no output. The protocol hides the inputs, such that the analyst will learn nothing about K_{DO} and the data owner nothing about c^i_{range}, and c'^i_{range}.*
4. **PrepareIdentityQuery$[(c^i_{id}), (K_{DO})]$:** *Is a protocol between the data analyst DA and the data owner DO. The analyst inputs a constant c^i_{id} and the owner inputs a secret key K_{DO}. The output at the analyst is an equality query token Q_{id} and the data owner receives no output. The protocol hides the inputs, such that the analyst will learn nothing about K_{DO} and the data owner nothing about c^i_{id}.*
5. **Analyze(C, $\mathbb{Q}_{range}$, $\mathbb{Q}_{id}$, e):** *Takes a ciphertext C, a set of range query tokens $\mathbb{Q}_{range}$, a set of equality query tokens $\mathbb{Q}_{id}$ and a query expression e and outputs a set $\mathbb{Q}'_{id}$ of equality query tokens.*

$$\text{Analyze}(C, \mathbb{Q}_{range}, \mathbb{Q}_{id}, e) = \begin{cases} \{\text{PrepareIdentityQuery}[(c), (K_{DO})] | \forall c \in \{c^1, c^2, \dots, c^n\}\} \\ \qquad\qquad\qquad\qquad\qquad\qquad\qquad\qquad \text{if } e \models t \\ \bot \qquad\qquad\qquad\qquad\qquad\qquad \text{w.h.p., otherwise} \end{cases}$$

where

$$P, K_{DO} = \text{Setup}(k, \Gamma)$$

$$C = \text{Encrypt}(K_{DO}, t)$$

$$\mathbb{Q}_{range} \supset \{\text{PrepareRangeQuery}[(c, c'), (K_{DO})] | c, c' \in \mathbb{C}_{range}\}$$

$$\mathbb{Q}_{id} \supset \{\text{PrepareIdentityQuery}[(c), (K_{DO})] | c \in \mathbb{C}_{id} \cup \mathbb{F}\}$$

Fig. 1. Consistency Constraint

For the encryption scheme to be searchable we impose the following consistency constraint. For each tuple $t = \langle c^1, c^2, \dots, c^n \rangle$ (defined by Γ) and each query expression e with footprint $(\mathbb{C}_{range}, \mathbb{C}_{id}, \mathbb{F})$, the above scheme must satisfy the consistency constraint from Figure 1. It basically states that the output of the Analyze algorithm is a set of equality query tokens for each value of the tuples matching the query, or the empty set if none does.

3.2   Security

Definition 2. *We say that a SEODA scheme $\mathcal{E}$ is secure if all polynomial-time adversaries $\mathcal{A}$ have at most a negligible advantage in the security game $Game_{DA}$ defined below.*

- **Setup:** The data owner runs $\text{Setup}(k, \Gamma)$ and passes the public parameter P to the data analyst (presumed adversary).
- **Query Phase 1:** The data analyst adaptively outputs a (mixed) sequence of either
  - a plain text tuple $t_1, t_2, \dots t_{q_1}$,
  - a (non-composite) range query constant $(c_1^i, c_1'^i), (c_2^i, c_2'^i), \dots, (c_{q_2}^i, c_{q_2}'^i)$, or
  - an equality query constant $c_1^i, c_2^i, \dots, c_{q_3}^i$.

  where q_1, q_2 and q_3 represent an upper bound on the number of encryption, equality and range queries that the data analyst makes. The data owner responds corresponding to the type of the query with either

  - the ciphertext $C = \text{Encrypt}(K_{DO}, t)$.
  - the range query token $Q_{range} = \text{PrepareRangeQuery}[(c^i, c'^i), (K_{DO})]$.
  - the equality query token $Q_{id} = \text{PrepareIdentityQuery}[(c^i), (K_{DO})]$.

- **Challenge:** The data analyst outputs two different plain-text tuples t_0^* and t_1^* subject to the following restrictions

- either no equality query constant c^i matches the challenge plain texts $t^*_{\{0,1\}}$ or it matches both challenge plain texts in the same dimension, i.e.

$$\forall j \in [1, q_3] \ s.t.$$
$$(c^i_j \neq t^*_0.c_i \wedge c^i_j \neq t^*_1.c_i) \vee (c^i_j = t^*_0.c_i \wedge c^i_j = t^*_1.c_i)$$

- no range query (c^i_j, c'^i_j) can distinguish the challenge plain texts $t^*_{\{0,1\}}$, i.e.

$$\forall j \in [1, q_2] \ s.t.$$
$$((c^i_j > t^*_0.c^i \wedge c^i_j > t^*_1.c^i) \vee (c^i_j < t^*_0.c^i \wedge c^i_j < t^*_1.c^i)) \wedge$$
$$((c'^i_j > t^*_0.c^i \wedge c'^i_j > t^*_1.c^i) \vee (c'^i_j < t^*_0.c^i \wedge c'^i_j < t^*_1.c^i))$$

- none of t_j's constants $t_j.c^i$ matches any constant of the challenge plain texts $t^*_{\{0,1\}}$, i.e.

$$\forall j \in [1, q_1], \forall i \ s.t. \ t.c^i \neq t^*_0.c^i \wedge t.c^i \neq t^*_1.c^i$$

The data owner flips a coin $b \in \{0, 1\}$ and encrypts t^*_b under K_{DO}. The ciphertext $C^* = \text{Encrypt}(K_{DO}, t^*_b)$ is passed to the data analyst.

- **Query Phase 2:** The data analyst continues to adaptively output plaintexts, range query and equality query constants subject to the restrictions above. The data owner responds with the corresponding ciphertexts, range and equality query tokens.
- **Guess:** The data analyst outputs a guess b' of b.

A data analyst $\mathcal{A}$'s advantage in the above game is defined as

$$Adv_{\mathcal{A}} = |Pr[b = b'] - \frac{1}{2}|$$

We need to exclude equality constant queries that match only one challenge plaintext, because they could be used in a query to distinguish the ciphertext. For the same reason we need to exclude range queries that can distinguish ciphertexts. We need to exclude encryptions of any challenge ciphertext in any scheme, since they could be decrypted to equality query tokens by matching range queries which could then distinguish the challenges.

4   Building Blocks

Let us first introduce terminology that will be used in the rest of this paper. In what follows, we denote $\mathbb{Z}^*_p = \{1, \dots, p-1\}$.

Given a security parameter k, let $\mathbb{G}_1$, $\mathbb{G}_2$ and $\mathbb{G}_T$ be groups of order p for some large prime p, where the bit-size of p is determined by the security parameter k. Our scheme uses a computable, non-degenerate bilinear map $\hat{e} : \mathbb{G}_1 \times \mathbb{G}_2 \rightarrow \mathbb{G}_T$ for which the *Symmetric External Diffie-Hellman (SXDH)* problem is assumed to be hard. The SXDH assumption in short allows for the existence of a bilinear pairing, but assumes that the Decisional Diffie-Hellman problem is hard in both $\mathbb{G}_1$ and $\mathbb{G}_2$ and was used e.g. in [1].

We recall that a bilinear map satisfies the following three properties:

- Bilinear: for $g \in \mathbb{G}_1$, $h \in \mathbb{G}_2$ and for $a, b \in \mathbb{Z}_p^*$

$$\hat{e}(g^a, h^b) = \hat{e}(g, h)^{ab}$$

- Non-degenerate: $\hat{e}(g, h) \neq 1$ is a generator of $\mathbb{G}_T$
- Computable: there exists an efficient algorithm to compute $\hat{e}(g, h)$ for all $g \in \mathbb{G}_1$ and $h \in \mathbb{G}_2$

4.1 Identity-Based Encryption

We capitalize from Waters' [20] and Boneh Boyen Goh's [2] IBE scheme, with some differences. First of all, we modify the scheme so as to include the SXDH assumption, discussed previously. Secondly, we do not adopt Waters' nice hashing scheme but we require random oracles for reasons of our proofs and therefore we use standard hash functions that map strings onto group elements. Note that the random oracle, i.e. the hash function, only operates in one of the two groups of the SXDH assumption.

The IBE scheme has the following algorithms:

Setup(k): Let H be a one way hash function defined from $\{0, 1\}^*$ to $\mathbb{G}_2$. The public parameters are $g \in \mathbb{G}_1$, g^α, $h \in \mathbb{G}_2$. Messages need to be encoded in group $\mathbb{G}_T$ The secret parameter is α. We denote the identity id.

Encrypt(id, m): Choose $s \xleftarrow{R} \mathbb{Z}_p^*$.

$$C = \langle g^s, H(id)^s, \hat{e}(g^\alpha, h)^s m \rangle$$

GetPrivateKey(id, α): Choose $r \xleftarrow{R} \mathbb{Z}_p^*$.

$$k_{id} = \langle g^r, h^\alpha H(id)^r \rangle$$

Decrypt(C, k_{id}):

$$\hat{e}(g^\alpha, h)^s m \frac{\hat{e}(g^r, H(id)^s)}{\hat{e}(g^s, h^\alpha H(id)^r)} = m$$

5   Our SEODA Scheme

For simplicity of the exposition we construct a SEODA scheme for 1-dimensional tuples $t = \langle c \rangle$ in this section. Multi-dimensional tuple definitions are covered in an extended version of the paper.

Let $\mathbb{D} = [d_1, d_2]$ be the domain of c. Let us first explain how we represent ranges in $\mathbb{D}$. We organize all the elements of $\mathbb{D}$ in ascending order as the leaves of a binary tree. Figure 2 shows the tree that is created when $\mathbb{D} = [1, 8]$. Each element is labeled with an identity. This way we have identified $O(|\mathbb{D}|)$ intervals, where each node defines an interval comprised of all the elements of $\mathbb{D}$ that are the leaves of the subtree rooted at the node itself. For instance, with reference

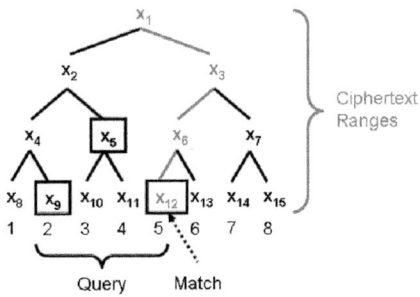

Fig. 2. Representing ranges on a binary tree

to Figure 2, x_2 identifies the interval $[1, 4]$. With combinations of such intervals, we can identify any range in the domain $\mathbb{D}$. For instance the interval $[2, 5]$ is identified by the union of x_9, x_5 and x_{12}. We require the data analyst to query each interval in a separate protocol and later compose the result with an $\wedge$ join.

With this in mind, let us see how we build our scheme.

Setup(k, Γ)

The data owner (DO) sets up the IBE scheme defined in the previous Section. DO also picks $t_{DO} \xleftarrow{R} \mathbb{Z}_p^*$ and publishes $h^{t_{DO}}$. Finally, DO creates a binary tree $T_{\mathbb{D}}$ for the domain $\mathbb{D}$ and makes the identifiers of each node public.

Encrypt(K_{DO}, t)

DO picks $s \xleftarrow{R} \mathbb{Z}_p^*$ and computes the equality token

$$ID_t = \langle g^s, H(t)^{st_{DO}} \rangle$$

DO then selects from $T_{\mathbb{D}}$ the $O(\log n)$ identities $X_t = \{x_i : \text{node } i \text{ is in the path from } t \text{ to the root}\}$ for all ranges from the leaf corresponding to t up to the top of the tree. With reference to Figure 2 once more, if $t = 5$, the considered identities would be x_{12}, x_6, x_3 and x_1. Note that in case of a match between range query and plaintext, there is one and only one range (equality) in common between query and ciphertext. Then, DO IBE-encrypts ID_t under all the identities in X_t. Since ID_t's encoding in $\mathbb{G}_T$ is longer than a single group element, the data owner DO should pick a fresh random key k for a symmetric encryption scheme and encrypt k using the identities. DO can then encrypt ID_t and a checksum for integrity verification using this key k in the symmetric cipher.

After the encryption, DO returns ID_t along with its $\log n$ IBE encryptions.

PrepareIdentityQuery[(c_{id}), (K_{DO})]

DA wants to request an equality token for a value $c_{id} \in \mathbb{D}$. He picks $r \xleftarrow{R} \mathbb{Z}_p^*$, and sends $H(c_{id})^r$ to DO.

DO picks $s \xleftarrow{R} \mathbb{Z}_p^*$ and replies with $(H(c_{id})^r)^{st_{DO}}$, g^s.

DA computes $(H(c_{id})^{rst_{DO}})^{r^{-1}}$, thus obtaining the equality token for c_{id}

$$ID_{c_{id}} = \langle g^s, H(c_{id})^{st_{DO}} \rangle$$

PrepareRangeQuery$[(c_{range}, c'_{range}), (K_{DO})]$

The data analyst DA wants to obtain a range query token for a single range $[c_{range}, c'_{range}]$ within the binary tree of ranges. DA consequently chooses the identity x_r that represents such a range. DA chooses one $r \xleftarrow{R} \mathbb{Z}_p^*$ and sends $H(x_r)^r$ and h^r to the data owner DO. We emphasize that both, $H(x_r)^r$ and h^r, are elements of $\mathbb{G}_2$ and due to the SXDH assumption no efficient linear map $f() : \mathbb{G}_2 \to \mathbb{G}_1$ can exist, such that computing $\hat{e}(f(h^r), H(x_r)) = \hat{e}(f(h), H(x_r)^r)$ is infeasible.

After receiving the identity, DO picks $s \xleftarrow{R} \mathbb{Z}_p^*$. Then DO returns to DA

$$\langle g^s, h^{r\alpha} H(x_r)^{rs} \rangle$$

Upon receipt, DA raises the first term to the multiplicative inverse of r, thus obtaining the following IBE decryption key for identity $H(x_r)$:

$$k_{x_r} = \langle g^s, h^{\alpha} H(x_r)^s \rangle$$

The resulting complexity for a single range is $O(\log \mathbb{D})$. For complex range queries DA must request each range individually and combine the results by himself. Note that there are at most $O(\log \mathbb{D})$ ranges that need to be combined resulting in a complex range query complexity $O(\log^2 \mathbb{D})$.

Analyze$(C, \mathbb{Q}_{range}, \mathbb{Q}_{id}, e)$

For range queries, DA decrypts each IBE encryption of ID_t with each IBE decryption key received from DO upon his query. If any combination decrypts to ID_t, the match was successful.

For equality queries, DA owns (a set of) ID_y for some queried value y. He can check for equality of any tuple t, disposing of $ID_t = \langle g^s, H(t)^{st_{DO}} \rangle$ and $ID_y = < H(y)^{rt_{DO}}, g^r >$ by checking whether

$$\hat{e}(g^r, H(t)^{st_{DO}}) = \hat{e}(g^s, H(y)^{rt_{DO}})$$

holds. If it does, DA concludes that the match was successful.

6 Security

6.1 Symmetric External Diffie Hellman Assumption

Definition 3. *We say that the SXDH assumption holds if, given values $y, y_1, y_2, y_3 \in \mathbb{G}_1$, it is not computationally feasible to decide if there is an integer $a \in \mathbb{Z}_p^*$ such that $y_1 = y^a$ and $y_3 = y_2^a$, i.e., $\mathbb{G}_1$ is a DDH-hard group. The same requirement must hold for $\mathbb{G}_2$, i.e., it is also a DDH-hard group.*

6.2 Bilinear Decisional Diffie Hellman Assumption

Definition 4. *We say that the BDDH assumption holds if, given values $g, g^a, \in \mathbb{G}_1, h, h^b, h^c \in \mathbb{G}_2, \hat{e}(g, h)^x \in \mathbb{G}_T$ it is not computationally feasible to decide if $x = abc$.*

6.3 Protocol Security

We define security of the protocols for PrepareRangeQuery and PrepareIdentity-
Query as semi-honest security for secure two-party computation protocols [14],
i.e. we assume that all parties follow the protocol as described, but try to break
its confidentiality (and therefore the confidentiality of the encryption scheme).
The view of a party (data owner or data analyst) during a protocol is his input,
his coin tosses and the messages he receives. The output is implicit in the view.

Definition 5. *The view of a party $X \in \{A, B\}$ during an execution of a protocol
Ψ between A and B on inputs (ω_A, ω_B) is denoted*

$$VIEW_X^\Psi = \{\omega_X, r, m_1, \ldots, m_\phi\}$$

*where r represents the outcome of X's internal coin tosses, and m_i represents
the i-th message it has received.*

We define the security of a protocol Ψ

Definition 6. *Let $f^\Psi(\omega_A, \omega_B) : (\{0,1\}^*)^2 \mapsto (\{0,1\}^*)^2$ be the (ideal) functionality implemented by protocol Ψ. The protocol Ψ is secure in the semi-honest
model, if there exists a polynomial-time simulator, denoted S, such that for any
probabilistic polynomial-time algorithm $\mathcal{A}$, $S(\omega_X, f^\Psi(\omega_A, \omega_B))$ is computationally indistinguishable from $VIEW_X^\Psi$:*

$$S(\omega_X, f^\Psi(\omega_A, \omega_B)) \overset{c}{=} VIEW_X^\Psi$$

We propose the following theorems for the security of the PrepareRangeQuery
and PrepareIdentityQuery protocols.

Theorem 1. *In our SEODA scheme, the PrepareRangeQuery protocol is secure
in the semi-honest model.*

Theorem 2. *In our SEODA scheme, the PrepareIdentityQuery protocol is secure in the semi-honest model.*

Proof. We prove Theorems 1 and 2 by the simulators $S_{PrepareRangeQuery}$ and
$S_{PrepareIdentityQuery}$.

For the data owner's view simulator $S_{PrepareRangeQuery}$ outputs 2 uniform
random elements from $\mathbb{G}_2$. Simulator $S_{PrepareIdentityQuery}$ outputs 1 uniform
random elements from $\mathbb{G}_2$ for its data owner's view.

Furthermore we need to show that the views are indeed computationally indistinguishable. First, note that the view of the data owner in the PrepareRange-
Query protocol is clearly a superset of its view in the PrepareIdentityQuery
protocol. We therefore conclude that if an algorithm is unable to distinguish the
view in the PrepareRangeQuery protocol, it is unable to do so in the Prepare-
IdentityQuery protocol.

We define a game $Game_{DO}$ for an adversary acting as the data owner. In this
game the data owner is given one range query and then asked to tell whether it

corresponds to a valid range or it is chosen randomly as by the simulator. The security defined by Game $Game_{DO}$ even holds for a binary domain, i.e. there are only two possible values for the range.

We modify the setup of the encryption scheme in the setup of $Game_{DO}$, such that the challenger, i.e. the data analyst, gets to pick the groups the operations are performed in. Note that this does not break the security of the encryption scheme, since the data owner DO can still choose its secret key t_{DO} and the secret parameter of the IBE scheme, as long as the SXDH assumption holds. A query phase in $Game_{DO}$ has been omitted, since the input in a real attack is entirely under control of the data analyst.

$Game_{DO}$ is defined as follows:

- **Setup:** The simulator chooses the initial public parameter P' of Setup(k, Γ) and passes it to the data owner. The data owner completes Setup(k, Γ) by choosing the secret keys and passes the dependent public parameter P'' to the simulator ($P = P' \cup P''$).
- **Challenge:** The simulator sends the data owner one range query request. Note that our reduction would still work, if the simulator also passes the corresponding plaintext range x, which underpins our security against known plaintext-like attacks. The simulator challenges the data owner to tell whether the request is valid or randomly chosen numbers.
- **Guess:** The data owner outputs a guess b ($b = 0$ for a valid request, $b = 1$ for randomly chosen numbers).

A data owner $\mathcal{A}$'s advantage in the above game is defined as

$$Adv_{\mathcal{A}} = |Pr[\mathcal{A}[b] - \frac{1}{2}|$$

Lemma 1. *Suppose there is a data owner $\mathcal{A}$ that has an advantage ϵ in breaking game $Game_{DO}$. Then there exists an algorithm $\mathcal{B}$ that solves DDH in $\mathbb{G}_2$ with advantage at least:*

$$Adv_{\mathcal{B}} \geq \frac{1}{2} + \epsilon$$

Its running is $O(time(\mathcal{A}))$.

A proof of Lemma 1 can be found in an extended version of the paper.

It remains to show that the data analyst's view in the protocols Prepare-RangeQuery and PrepareIdentityQuery can be simulated by $S_{PrepareRangeQuery}$ and $S_{PrepareIdentityQuery}$, respectively. In fact this is simple, since in both cases the view is identical to the output. The simulators which have access to the output can therefore simulate the data analyst's views by simply copying the output.

6.4   Ciphertext Indistinguishability

Theorem 3. *Suppose the hash function H is a random oracle. Then an attacker $\mathcal{A}$ has a negligible advantage in winning the security game $Game_{DA}$ assuming the BDDH assumption holds.*

We prove Theorem 3 by reducing an attacker in game $Game_{DA}$ to an attacker of the BDDH challenge.

Lemma 2. *Suppose there is a data analyst $\mathcal{A}$ that has an advantage ϵ in breaking game $Game_{DA}$. Suppose $\mathcal{A}$ makes at most q_H hash queries to H, at most q_E encryption requests and engages in at most q_I PrepareIdentityQuery protocols. Then there exists an algorithm $\mathcal{B}$ that solves BDDH with advantage at least:*

$$Adv_{\mathcal{B}} \geq \frac{\epsilon}{2e(1 + q_E + q_I)}$$

Its running is $O(time(\mathcal{A}) + (q_H + q_E)q_I)$.

The proof of Lemma 2 is in Appendix A of this paper. Its main idea is adapted from [4].

7 Related Work

A first SEODA scheme has been presented in [16], but it neither enjoyed semantic security relying on the discrete logarithm assumption which does not result in bit security nor was it practically efficient with an encryption time of $O(\mathbb{D}|t|^2)$ per tuple. The scheme in this paper enjoys stronger security relying only on Diffie-Hellman assumptions and reduces the time for range queries to $O(\log^2 \mathbb{D})$ per tuple.

Other examples of such searchable encryption schemes are [9,11,12,13,21]. All these schemes allow searching for keywords on a secret-key encrypted database without revealing the keyword. Note that for efficiency all schemes leak the *access pattern*, i.e. the documents (or tuples) matching the query. Stronger security requires less efficient solutions, such as oblivious RAM [15].

Public-key encrypted, oblivious, keyword search was introduced in [8]. We use the same notion of obliviousness (i.e. privacy of the query), but extend by range queries and query-result reusability. Our construction is more efficient and the generation of the public parameters is significantly simplified, since we do not need to combine homomorphic encryption and bilinear maps.

Keyword searches are important, but to be useful in practice, range queries are indispensable. The problem of range queries has been addressed in [6,18]. Searchable encryption with range queries is presented in [6,18]. Both schemes present efficiency improvements for range queries in searchable encryption, but both reveal at least partially the query to the service provider. Therefore a different application than DAS is suggested in [18] where the database owner publishes his data, but only gives decryption keys (for certain ranges) to qualified users. An example is log data for network traceback.

The first schemes to extend searchable encryption to public key encryption are [3,5]. This is useful for an outsourced e-mail service where the user receives documents (or tuples) from other users, but still has the same security requirements as in the DAS model. Keyword searches are described in [3] and private index queries are described in [5].

Private information retrieval (PIR) [7,10,17] allows a querier to ask for an entry in a remote database without revealing the index of this entry. PIR fully hides the access pattern, i.e. the service provider (database) is not aware which document (tuple) was chosen. This can be done with polylogarithmic communication complexity [7], i.e. without transferring the entire database. Using PIR on encrypted data is significantly less efficient than our approach. It requires processing each tuple for each query on the service providers' side which is less practical than transferring the entire database [19].

8   Conclusion

We considered the problem of outsourcing data analytics, a special case of outsourced auditing. In a such scenario the privacy requirements of data analyst and data owner must be fulfilled and neither the data nor the queries may be revealed.

We present an efficient solution with polylogarithmic range query and polynomial encryption time. We allow range and equality queries and results of those queries can be re-used in subsequent queries as equality query tokens. We proved our scheme and its associated protocols secure under the Bilinear Decisional Diffie-Hellman and the Symmetric External Diffie-Hellman assumption.

Acknowledgements

We would like to thank Julien Vayssiere for initializing discussions on the topic and the reviewers for their insightful comments. This work has been partially financed by the European Commission through the ICT Programme under the Seventh Framework Programme IST Project "Secure Supply Chain Management" (SecureSCM), grant agreement number 213531.

References

1. Ateniese, G., Blanton, M., Kirsch, J.: Secret Handshakes with Dynamic and Fuzzy Matching. In: Proceedings of Network and Distributed System Security Symposium (2007)
2. Boneh, D., Goh, E., Boyen, X.: Hierarchical Identity Based Encryption with Constant Size Ciphertext. In: Cramer, R. (ed.) EUROCRYPT 2005. LNCS, vol. 3494, pp. 440–456. Springer, Heidelberg (2005)
3. Boneh, D., Di Crescenzo, G., Ostrovsky, R., Persiano, G.: Public-key Encryption with Keyword Search. In: Cachin, C., Camenisch, J.L. (eds.) EUROCRYPT 2004. LNCS, vol. 3027, pp. 506–522. Springer, Heidelberg (2004)
4. Boneh, D., Franklin, M.: Identity-based Encryption from the Weil Paring. SIAM Journal of Computing 32(3) (2003)
5. Boneh, D., Kushilevitz, E., Ostrovsky, R., Skeith, W.: Public Key Encryption That Allows PIR Queries. In: Menezes, A. (ed.) CRYPTO 2007. LNCS, vol. 4622, pp. 50–67. Springer, Heidelberg (2007)
6. Boneh, D., Waters, B.: Conjunctive, Subset, and Range Queries on Encrypted Data. In: Vadhan, S.P. (ed.) TCC 2007. LNCS, vol. 4392, pp. 535–554. Springer, Heidelberg (2007)

7. Cachin, C., Micali, S., Stadler, M.: Computationally Private Information Retrieval with Polylogarithmic Communication. In: Stern, J. (ed.) EUROCRYPT 1999. LNCS, vol. 1592, p. 402. Springer, Heidelberg (1999)
8. Camenisch, J., Kohlweiss, M., Rial, A., Sheedy, C.: Blind and Anonymous Identity-Based Encryption and Authorised Private Searches on Public Key Encrypted Data. In: Jarecki, S., Tsudik, G. (eds.) PKC 2009. LNCS, vol. 5443, pp. 196–214. Springer, Heidelberg (2009)
9. Chang, Y., Mitzenmacher, M.: Privacy Preserving Keyword Searches on Remote Encrypted Data. In: Ioannidis, J., Keromytis, A.D., Yung, M. (eds.) ACNS 2005. LNCS, vol. 3531, pp. 442–455. Springer, Heidelberg (2005)
10. Chor, B., Goldreich, O., Kushilevitz, E., Sudan, M.: Private Information Retrieval. In: Proceedings of the 36th IEEE Symposium on Foundations of Computer Science (1995)
11. Curtmola, R., Garay, J., Kamara, S., Ostrovsky, R.: Searchable Symmetric Encryption: Improved Definitions and Efficient Constructions. In: Proceedings of ACM Conference on Computer and Communications Security (2006)
12. Evdokimov, S., Günther, O.: Encryption Techniques for Secure Database Outsourcing. In: Biskup, J., López, J. (eds.) ESORICS 2007. LNCS, vol. 4734, pp. 327–342. Springer, Heidelberg (2007)
13. Goh, E.: Secure Indexes. Cryptology ePrint Archive: Report 2003/216 (2003), http://eprint.iacr.org/2003/216/
14. Goldreich, O.: Secure Multi-party Computation (2002), http://www.wisdom.weizmann.ac.il/~oded/pp.html
15. Goldreich, O., Ostrovsky, R.: Software Protection and Simulation on Oblivious RAMs. Journal of ACM 43(3) (1996)
16. Kerschbaum, F., Vayssiere, J.: Privacy-Preserving Data Analytics as an Outsourced Service. In: Proceedings of the ACM Secure Web Services Workshop (2008)
17. Kushilevitz, E., Ostrovsky, R.: Replication is not needed: Single Database Computationally Private Information Retrieval. In: Proceedings of the 38th IEEE Symposium on Foundations of Computer Science (1997)
18. Shi, E., Bethencourt, J., Chan, H., Song, D., Perrig, A.: Multi-Dimensional Range Query over Encrypted Data. In: Proceedings of IEEE Symposium on Security and Privacy (2007)
19. Sion, R., Carbunar, B.: On the Computational Practicality of Private Information Retrieval. In: Proceedings of Network and Distributed System Security Symposium (2007)
20. Waters, B.: Efficient Identity-Based Encryption Without Random Oracles. In: Cramer, R. (ed.) EUROCRYPT 2005. LNCS, vol. 3494, pp. 114–127. Springer, Heidelberg (2005)
21. Yang, Z., Zhong, S., Wright, R.: Privacy-Preserving Queries on Encrypted Data. In: Gollmann, D., Meier, J., Sabelfeld, A. (eds.) ESORICS 2006. LNCS, vol. 4189, pp. 479–495. Springer, Heidelberg (2006)

A   Proof of Lemma 2

Proof. We show how to construct an adversary $\mathcal{B}$ that uses $\mathcal{A}$ to gain advantage $\frac{\epsilon}{2e(q_E+q_I+1)}$ against our security game. Algorithm $\mathcal{B}$ is given an instance $A = g^a, B = h^b, C = h^c, Z$ of the BDDH problem. It needs to output a guess whether $Z = h^{abc}$.

Note, that we chose challenge elements from $\mathbb{G}_1$ and $\mathbb{G}_2$, but even given an efficient isomorphism $\xi : \mathbb{G}_1 \to \mathbb{G}_2$ our problem remains hard and we even ruled out the existence of such an isomorphism by the SXDH assumption.

The challenge in constructing $\mathcal{B}$ is to be able to answer to the secret Prepare-IdentityQuery protocol request. We do this by using the information in the random oracle and therefore answer H queries as follows. In this proof the random oracle is under the control of the data owner (albeit also algorithm $\mathcal{B}$). We adopted this idea from the proof of the Boneh-Franklin identity-based encryption system [4]:

H queries: At any time algorithm $\mathcal{A}$ can query the random oracle H. In order to respond to these queries the algorithm $\mathcal{B}$ maintains a list of tuples $\langle x, hash, y, coin \rangle$ as explained below. We refer to this list as the $H_{DO} - list$. The list is initially empty. When $\mathcal{A}$ queries the oracle H with a bit-sequence $x \in \mathbb{D}$ algorithm $\mathcal{B}$ responds as follows.

1. If the query sequence x appears on the $H_{DO}-list$ in a tuple $\langle x, hash, y, coin \rangle$, then algorithm $\mathcal{B}$ responds with $H(x) = hash$.
2. Otherwise, $\mathcal{B}$ flips a random coin $coin' \in \{0, 1\}$ so that $Pr[coin' = 0] = \delta$ for some δ that will be determined later.
3. Algorithm $\mathcal{B}$ picks a random y' in $\mathbb{Z}_p^*$. If $coin' = 0$ $\mathcal{B}$ computes $hash' = h^{y'}$, else if $coin' = 1$ $\mathcal{B}$ sets $hash' = B$.
4. Algorithm $\mathcal{B}$ adds the tuple $\langle x, hash', y', coin' \rangle$ to the $H_{DO} - list$ and responds to $\mathcal{A}$ with $H(x) = hash'$. Note that $hash'$ is uniform in $\mathbb{G}_2$ and independent of $\mathcal{A}$'s current view.

Setup: Algorithm $\mathcal{B}$ creates the IBE scheme and gives $\mathcal{A}$ the following parameters $\mathbb{G}_1$, $\mathbb{G}_2$, g, g^α, h, H. Let H be a random oracle controlled by $\mathcal{B}$ as described above. Furthermore $\mathcal{B}$ sets $h^{t_{DO}} = C$.

Query Phase 1: Algorithm $\mathcal{A}$ may now send plaintexts, range query requests and equality query requests. We show how $\mathcal{B}$ answers those.

Encryption Requests: Algorithm $\mathcal{A}$ sends plaintext t. $\mathcal{B}$ invokes the random oracle H. It retrieves the tuple $\langle t, hash, y, coin \rangle$ from the $H_{DO} - list$. If the coin flip $coin$ is 1, then $\mathcal{B}$ aborts. We now know that $coin = 0$ and therefore $H(t) = h^y$. $\mathcal{B}$ chooses $s \xleftarrow{R} \mathbb{Z}_p^*$ and computes

$$ID_t = C^{sy} = H(t)^{st_{DO}}$$

It sends ID_t, g^s to algorithm $\mathcal{A}$.

Range Query Requests: Algorithm $\mathcal{A}$ chooses a range and its corresponding identity x_r. It also chooses a random number r and sends $H(x_r)^r$ and h^r to algorithm $\mathcal{B}$.

$\mathcal{B}$ chooses a random number $s \xleftarrow{R} \mathbb{Z}_p^*$. It returns $h^{r\alpha} H(x_r)^{rs}, g^s$.

Identity Query Requests: Algorithm $\mathcal{A}$ chooses the value t, chooses $r \xleftarrow{R} \mathbb{Z}_p^*$ and sends $H(t)^r, h^r$ to $\mathcal{B}$. Note, that $\mathcal{A}$ must have invoked H for t.

Algorithm $\mathcal{B}$ retrieves all tuples $t, hash, y, coin$ from the $H_{DO} - list$ where $coin = 0$. For each tuple it checks whether $(h^r)^y = H(t)^r$. If it finds such a tuple, it takes note of y, else if it does not find such a tuple, $\mathcal{B}$ aborts. We now know again that $coin = 0$ and that $H(t) = h^y$. $\mathcal{B}$ picks $s \xleftarrow{R} ZZ$ and returns $C^{sy} = H(t)^{st_{DO}}, g^s$.

Challenge: Once algorithm $\mathcal{A}$ decides that the first phase is over it sends two plaintexts $t_0^\star$ and $t_1^\star$ to $\mathcal{B}$.

$\mathcal{B}$ flips a random coin b and chooses $t_b^\star$. It invokes the random oracle H with $t_b^\star$ and retrieves its tuple $t_b^\star, hash, y, coin$ from the $H_{DO} - list$. If $coin = 0$, $\mathcal{B}$ reports failure and aborts. We now know that $coin = 1$ and $H(t) = B$.

$\mathcal{B}$ sets $ID_t = Z$ and $g^s = A$. Note that, since $h^{t_{DO}} = C$, ID_t is a valid ciphertext for t if $Z = h^{abc}$.

It then furthermore selects the identities $x_1, \ldots, x_l$ in T_B according to $t_b^\star$. It encrypts ID_t under each identity x_i. Finally it returns the IBE encryptions and ID_t to $\mathcal{A}$.

Query Phase 2: Algorithm $\mathcal{B}$ responds to $\mathcal{A}$'s queries as in query phase 1.

Guess: Algorithm $\mathcal{A}$ eventually outputs its guess b'. $\mathcal{B}$ outputs b' as its guess.

Claim: If algorithm $\mathcal{B}$ does not abort during the simulation $\mathcal{A}$'s view is identical to its view in a real attack. The responses to H queries are as in a real attack, since each is uniformly and independently distributed in $\mathbb{G}_2$.

According to the rules, no range or equality query can distinguish the challenge plaintext. The only information about plaintexts must stem from the ciphertexts. If $Z = h^{abc}$, then $\mathcal{A}$ has advantage $Adv_{\mathcal{A}} \geq \epsilon$ in breaking game $Game_{DA}$, since its receives a valid ciphertext. If Z is a random number, then the message part $H(t)^{st_{DO}}$ of the equality query token is randomly distributed in $\mathbb{G}_2$ and contains no information to distinguish $t_0^\star$ and $t_1^\star$. Therefore if $\mathcal{B}$ does not abort, $|Pr[b = b'] - \frac{1}{2}| \geq \frac{1}{2}\epsilon$.

To complete the proof of Lemma 2 we need to calculate the probability that algorithm $\mathcal{B}$ aborts during the simulation. Suppose $\mathcal{A}$ makes q_E encryption requests and q_I equality query token requests. Then the probability that $\mathcal{B}$ does not abort in query phases 1 or 2 is $\delta^{q_E+q_I}$. The probability that it does not abort during the challenge step is $1 - \delta$ which results in an overall probability that $\mathcal{B}$ does not abort is $\delta^{q_E+q_I}(1 - \delta)$. This value is maximized at $\delta_{opt} = 1 - \frac{1}{q_E+q_I+1}$. Using δ_{opt} the probability that $\mathcal{B}$ does not abort is at least $\frac{1}{e(q_E+q_I+1)}$ where e is Euler's constant (the base of the natural logarithm). Then $\mathcal{B}$'s advantage in breaking $BDDH$ is at least $\frac{\epsilon}{2e(q_E+q_I+1)}$.

The running time of algorithm $\mathcal{B}$ is the running time of algorithm $\mathcal{A}$ plus the searches in the $H_{DO} - list$ for equality query token requests. Suppose $\mathcal{A}$ makes q_I equality query requests, then there are at most q_I searches in a $H_{DO} - list$ of length at most $q_H + q_E$. The resulting running time is $O(time(\mathcal{A}) + q_I(q_H + q_E))$.

An Identity-Based Proxy Re-Encryption Scheme with Source Hiding Property, and its Application to a Mailing-List System

Keita Emura[1], Atsuko Miyaji[2], and Kazumasa Omote[2]

[1] Center for Highly Dependable Embedded Systems Technology
[2] School of Information Science
Japan Advanced Institute of Science and Technology, 1-1, Asahidai,
Nomi, Ishikawa, 923-1292, Japan
{k-emura,miyaji,omote}@jaist.ac.jp

Abstract. Identity-Based Proxy Re-Encryption (IB-PRE) has been proposed by Green and Ateniese (ACNS2007), where the proxy transforms a source ciphertext encrypted by a delegator's identity into a destination ciphertext that can be decrypted using a delegatee's secret key corresponding to the delegatee's identity. By using IB-PRE, we expect that mailing-list systems can be constructed without public key certificates. However, in all previous IB-PRE, information about whether a source ciphertext (encrypted by a mailing-list address) is the source of a destination ciphertext (encrypted by an e-mail address) or not, is revealed from both the source ciphertext and the destination ciphertext. In this paper, for the first time we propose an IB-PRE scheme with source hiding property, where no information about source identity is revealed from the destination ciphertext. Our work is the valuable and important milestone for establishing the secure PRE-based mailing-list system without public key certificates.

1 Introduction

Proxy Re-Encryption (PRE) was proposed in [4] by Blaze, Bleumer, and Strauss (and more [2, 18, 20]), where a semi-trusted[1] proxy transforms a source ciphertext encrypted by a delegator Alice's public key into a destination ciphertext that can be decrypted using a delegatee Bob's secret key. Applications of PRE schemes such as e-mail systems based on PRE have been proposed [5, 15–17]. Since these e-mail systems apply ElGamal encryption based PRE, public key certificates are necessary in these systems. Identity-Based Proxy Re-Encryption (IB-PRE) has also been proposed [8, 11–13, 19, 22], where the proxy transforms a source ciphertext encrypted by a delegator Alice's identity into a destination ciphertext that can be decrypted using a delegatee Bob's secret key

---

[1] We assume that not only the proxy follows the protocol but also the proxy will not collude with re-encrypt ciphertext receivers, since the proxy and a receiver can decrypt any ciphertext using both a re-encryption key and a receiver secret key as in [8, 11].

J. Camenisch and C. Lambrinoudakis (Eds.): EuroPKI 2010, LNCS 6711, pp. 77–92, 2011.
© Springer-Verlag Berlin Heidelberg 2011

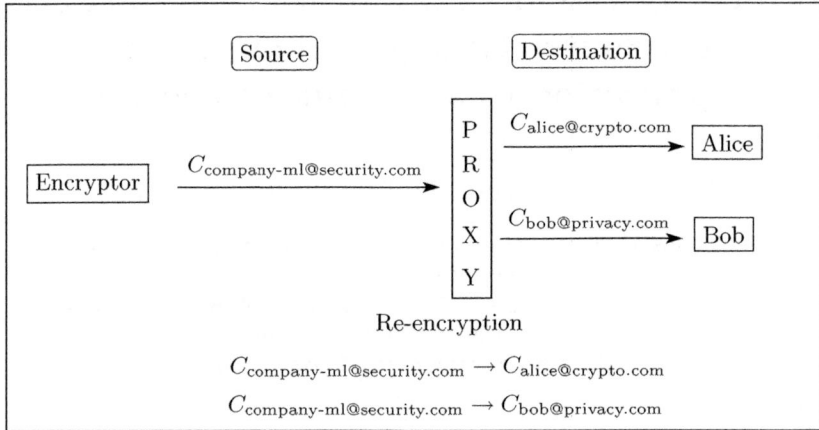

Fig. 1. Mailing-list system based on IB-PRE

corresponding to Bob's identity. By using IB-PRE, we expect that e-mail systems can be constructed without public key certificates. In fact, Green and Ateniese [11] have already introduced secure e-mail forwarding systems as an application of IB-PRE schemes. For example, a source ciphertext under "alice@crypto.com" can be translated by the proxy into a destination ciphertext under "bob@privacy.com". However, they do not consider a mailing-list system. Mailing-list systems are commonly used (using well-known software, e.g., Mailman [14] and Majordomo [3]) in real environments. A mailing-list system based on IB-PRE is shown in Fig.1.

Some may think that this mailing-list system can be constructed easily, by using previous IB-PRE schemes. However, in a mailing-list system, a new security requirement appears, as follows:

- Relationship between a source ciphertext (encrypted by a mailing-list address) and a destination ciphertext (encrypted by an e-mail address) must not be revealed from the destination ciphertext (i.e., whether a source ciphertext is the source of a destination ciphertext or not).

  • If this information is revealed, then the fact that Alice (or Bob) is a member of the mailing-list "company-ml@security.com", is also revealed.

A Naive Approach. To hide the identity assigned with a ciphertext, anonymous Identity-Based Encryption (IBE) is nominated. Especially, anonymous Hierarchical IBE (HIBE) [7] is suitable to handle plural identities. However, HIBE cannot be applied to construct the mailing-list system above, since a mailing-list address and an e-mail address are usually independent of each other (i.e., there are no hierarchical structural relations).

Our Contribution. In this paper, for the first time we propose an IB-PRE scheme with source hiding property, where no information about source identity is revealed from destination ciphertext. Intuitively, an adversary cannot identify whether $C_{\text{company-ml@security.com}}$ is the source of $C_{\text{alice@crypto.com}}$ or not. Source hiding property can positively solve the problem caused by the previous IB-PRE scheme. Our schemes are based on the Green-Ateniese IB-PRE scheme, which is based on the Boneh-Franklin IBE scheme [6]. We apply the homomorphic property of the Boneh-Franklin IBE scheme to hide the source identity.

Mailing-list systems in business environments are more important than one-to-one e-mail systems. If a member of a mailing-list is revealed, it might cause serious information exposure incidents such as exposures of client ID lists. Source hiding property should be encured when applying IB-PRE to Mailing-list systems, and therefore our work captures a risk of the real environments which has not been considered before.

Related Work. There are PRE schemes which achieve proxy invisibility (such as [2]), where they do not require a delegator who sends message to a delegatee to be aware of the existence of the proxy. Although proxy invisibility implies source hiding property, however, no previous IB-PRE scheme achieves proxy invisibility to the best of our knowledge (See Section 4 for details). In addition, proxy invisibility may spoil important information. For example, an e-mail receiver usually wants to know whether the e-mail was sent for him/her only or not. From the viewpoint of the information sharing, it is important in business environments to facilitate an employee with the information of the other receivers of that e-mail. If proxy invisibility is achieved, a receiver cannot distinguish whether a ciphertext was re-encrypted or not. So, an additional part (e.g., encrypted mailing-list address) must be added to the actual ciphertext, and then proxy invisibility does not hold. Thus, proxy invisibility is too strong for Mailing-list systems. On the other hand, Source hiding property can suitably handle this requirement (See Section 7 for details), and therefore our IB-PRE scheme is better than PRE schemes with proxy invisibility in the mailing-list applications.

2   Bilinear Groups and Complexity Assumption

$x \xleftarrow{\$} S$ means that x is chosen uniformly from a set S. $y \leftarrow A(x)$ means that y is an output of an algorithm A under an input x.

Definition 1 (Bilinear Groups). *Bilinear groups and a bilinear map are defined as follows: $\mathbb{G}_1$ and $\mathbb{G}_T$ are cyclic groups of prime order p. g is a generator of $\mathbb{G}_1$. e is an efficiently computable bilinear map $e : \mathbb{G}_1 \times \mathbb{G}_1 \to \mathbb{G}_T$ with Bilinearity: for all $u, u', v, v' \in \mathbb{G}_1$, $e(uu', v) = e(u, v)e(u', v)$ and $e(u, vv') = e(u, v)e(u, v')$, and Non-degeneracy: $e(g, g) \neq 1_{\mathbb{G}_T}$ ($1_{\mathbb{G}_T}$ is the $\mathbb{G}_T$'s unit).*

Definition 2 (Bilinear Diffie-Hellman (BDH) assumption). *The BDH problem in $\mathbb{G}_1$ is a problem, for input of a tuple $(g, g^a, g^b, g^c, \in \mathbb{G}_1^3$ to compute $e(g, g)^{abc}$. An algorithm A has advantage ϵ in solving BDH problem in $\mathbb{G}_1$ if $Adv_{BDH}(A) := \Pr[A(g, g^a, g^b, g^c) = e(g, g)^{abc}] \geq \epsilon(k)$. We say that the BDH assumption holds in $\mathbb{G}_1$ if no Probabilistic Polynomial-Time (PPT) algorithm has an advantage of at least ϵ in solving the BDH problem in $\mathbb{G}_1$.*

Definition 3 (Decision Bilinear Diffie-Hellman (DBDH) assumption).
The DBDH problem in $\mathbb{G}_1$ is a problem, for input of a tuple $(g, g^a, g^b, g^c, Z) \in \mathbb{G}_1^4 \times \mathbb{G}_T$ to decide whether $Z = e(g,g)^{abc}$ or not. An algorithm $\mathcal{A}$ has advantage ϵ in solving DBDH problem in $\mathbb{G}_1$ if $Adv_{DBDH}(\mathcal{A}) := |\Pr[\mathcal{A}(g, g^a, g^b, g^c, e(g,g)^{abc}) = 0] - \Pr[\mathcal{A}(g, g^a, g^b, g^c, e(g,g)^z) = 0]| \geq \epsilon(k)$, where $e(g,g)^z \in \mathbb{G}_T \setminus \{e(g,g)^{abc}\}$. We say that the DBDH assumption holds in $\mathbb{G}_1$ if no PPT algorithm has an advantage of at least ϵ in solving the DBDH problem in $\mathbb{G}_1$.

3 Definitions of IB-PRE

3.1 System Operations of IB-PRE

Here, we show the system operation and security requirements of IB-PRE. First, we define encryption levels as follows: A "level 1" ciphertext is a ciphertext generated directly by the Encrypt algorithm. A "level $(\ell + 1)$" ciphertext is a ciphertext that is a re-encryption result of a "level ℓ" ciphertext by using the Re-Encrypt algorithm. Let MaxLevels be the highest-possible encryption level (for a single-hop scheme, MaxLevels=2, and in this paper, we set 2 for this value). Note that this encryption level notations (defined in [11]) are different from the "first/second level" notations [2]. We use the encryption level notations defined by Green and Ateniese [11], since our scheme is based on the Green-Ateniese IB-PRE scheme.

Definition 4 (System operations of IB-PRE). *An IB-PRE scheme Π consists of six algorithms (*Setup, KeyGen, Encrypt, RKGen, Re-Encrypt, Decrypt*):*

Setup(1^k, MaxLevels) : *This algorithm takes as input the security parameter k and the highest-possible encryption level* MaxLevels *(we set 2 for this value), and returns the master public parameters params and the master secret key msk.*

KeyGen($params, msk, ID$) : *This algorithm takes as input params, msk, and an identity ID, and returns a decryption key sk_{ID} corresponding to that ID.*

Encrypt($params, ID, M$) : *This algorithm takes as input params, ID, and a plaintext M and returns a level 1 ciphertext C_{ID}.*

RKGen($params, sk_{ID_1}, ID_1, ID_2$) : *This algorithm takes as input params, sk_{ID_1}, and identities (ID_1, ID_2), and returns a re-encryption key $rk_{ID_1 \to ID_2}$.*

Re-Encrypt($params, rk_{ID_1 \to ID_2}, C_{ID_1}$) : *This algorithm takes as input params, $rk_{ID_1 \to ID_2}$, and a level ℓ source ciphertext C_{ID_1}, and returns a level $(\ell + 1)$ destination ciphertext C_{ID_2}. If a level* MaxLevels *ciphertext is used in input, then return $\perp$.*

Decrypt($params, sk_{ID}, C_{ID}$) : *This algorithm takes as input params, sk_{ID}, and C_{ID}, and returns M or $\perp$.*

For $C_{ID_2} \leftarrow$ Re-Encrypt$(params, rk_{ID_1 \rightarrow ID_2}, C_{ID_1})$, we call ID_1 (resp. ID_2) a source identity (resp. a destination identity). In addition, we call a source ciphertext C_{ID_1}, and call a destination ciphertext C_{ID_2}, if ID_1 and ID_2 are a source identity and a destination identity, respectively.

A secret key of the source identity (e.g., sk_{ID_1}) is required to compute a re-encryption key (e.g., $rk_{ID_1 \rightarrow ID_2}$) in the RKGen algorithm. There is no guarantee that an encryptor knows sk_{ID_1}. So, we assume that the corresponding re-encryption key has already been preserved in the proxy before the proxy executes the Re-Encrypt algorithm. This procedure is done by a user who has sk_{ID_1} or a key generation center that has msk.

3.2 Security Requirements

First, we define correctness of IB-PRE. C_{ID_1} is defined as a properly-generated ciphertext if C_{ID_2} is generated by Re-Encrypt$^n(\cdots, $ Encrypt$(params, *, M))$ with valid re-encryption keys, where $n \leq$ MaxLevels $- 1$. For $\forall M$, $\forall ID_1$, and $\forall ID_2$, an IB-PRE scheme is *correct* if the following properties hold:

- Decrypt$(params, sk_{ID_1}, C_{ID_1}) = M$
- Decrypt$(params, sk_{ID_2}, $ Re-Encrypt$(params, rk_{ID_1 \rightarrow ID_2}, C_{ID_1})) = M$

where $sk_{ID_1} \leftarrow$ KeyGen$(params, msk, ID_1)$, $sk_{ID_2} \leftarrow$ KeyGen$(params, msk, ID_2)$, and $rk_{ID_1 \rightarrow ID_2} \leftarrow$ RKGen$(params, sk_{ID_1}, ID_1, ID_2)$.

Next, we define the indistinguishability of messages (IND-PrID-CCA). In IND-PrID-CCA experiment, an adversary is assumed to be an eavesdropper or recipients with $ID \neq ID^*$. As in [8, 11], we assume that the proxy will not collude with re-encrypt ciphertext receivers, since the proxy and a receiver can decrypt any ciphertext using both a re-encryption key and a receiver secret key. Instead of colluding with the proxy, an adversary can access the re-encryption oracle $\mathcal{O}_{RE\text{-}ENC}$ and the re-encryption key extraction oracle $\mathcal{O}_{RE\text{-}EXT}$. For (C_{ID_1}, ID_1, ID_2), $\mathcal{O}_{RE\text{-}ENC}$ returns $C_{ID_2} \leftarrow$ Re-Encrypt$(params, rk_{ID_1 \rightarrow ID_2}, C_{ID_1})$. For (ID_1, ID_2), $\mathcal{O}_{RE\text{-}EXT}$ returns $rk_{ID_1 \rightarrow ID_2} \leftarrow$ RKGen$(params, sk_{ID_1}, ID_1, ID_2)$. Other oracles are defined as follows: Let $\mathcal{O}_{EXT}$ be an extraction oracle, for ID, which returns $sk_{ID} \leftarrow$ KeyGen$(params, msk, ID)$. Let $\mathcal{O}_{DEC}$ be a decryption oracle, for (C_{ID}, ID), which returns $M \leftarrow$ Decrypt$(params, sk_{ID}, C_{ID})$. An adversary $\mathcal{A}$ can access these oracles, *except* for the following queries: For the challenge identity ID^* and the challenge ciphertext C^*,

- $\mathcal{O}_{EXT}(ID^*)$
- For all ID, $\mathcal{O}_{EXT}(ID)$ if there exists a path $(ID^*, ID_i, ID_j, \ldots, ID_k, ID)$ such that $\mathcal{O}_{RE\text{-}EXT}(ID^*, ID_i)$, $\mathcal{O}_{RE\text{-}EXT}(ID_i, ID_j)$, ...,$\mathcal{O}_{RE\text{-}EXT}(ID_k, ID)$.
- For all ID and C_{ID}, $\mathcal{O}_{RE\text{-}EXT}(ID^*, ID)$ and $\mathcal{O}_{DEC}(C_{ID}, ID)$
- For all ID, $\mathcal{O}_{RE\text{-}ENC}(C^*, ID^*, ID)$ and $\mathcal{O}_{EXT}(ID)$
- $\mathcal{O}_{DEC}(C^*, ID^*)$
- For all ID, $C_{ID} \leftarrow \mathcal{O}_{RE\text{-}ENC}(C^*, ID^*, ID)$ and $\mathcal{O}_{DEC}(C_{ID}, ID)$

An IB-PRE scheme Π is said to be IND-PrID-CCA-secure if the advantage is negligible for any polynomial-time PPT $\mathcal{A}$ in the following experiment.

Definition 5. *IND-PrID-CCA*

$$Adv_{\Pi,\mathcal{A}}^{IND-PrID-CCA}(k) = \Big| \Pr\Big[\mu \xleftarrow{\$} \{0,1\}; (params, msk) \leftarrow \mathsf{Setup}(1^k);$$

$$(M_0^*, M_1^*, ID^*, State) \leftarrow \mathcal{A}^{\mathcal{O}_{EXT}, \mathcal{O}_{RE-EXT}, \mathcal{O}_{DEC}, \mathcal{O}_{RE-ENC}}(params);$$

$$C^* \leftarrow \mathsf{Encrypt}(params, ID^*, M_\mu^*);$$

$$\mu' \leftarrow \mathcal{A}^{\mathcal{O}_{EXT}, \mathcal{O}_{RE-EXT}, \mathcal{O}_{DEC}, \mathcal{O}_{RE-ENC}}(params, C^*, State); \mu = \mu'\Big] - 1/2\Big|$$

We simply define the IND-PrID-CPA security with $\mathcal{O}_{RE-ENC}$ and $\mathcal{O}_{DEC}$ removed from the above experiment.

Next, we newly define source hiding property of IB-PRE (IND-SH-PrID-CCA). IND-SH-PrID-CCA guarantees that *even if an encryptor (or an eavesdropper) knows a mailing-list address and a mailing-list member address included in the mailing-list, the encryptor (or the eavesdropper) cannot identify whether a source ciphertext (encrypted by the mailing-list address) is the source of a destination ciphertext or not.* Thus, the adversary can be an insider or an eavesdropper.

We allow an adversary to select the challenge source identities (ID_0^*, ID_1^*) and the challenge destination identity ID^*, and guarantee the above requirement. In the IND-SH-PrID-CCA experiment, $\mathcal{A}$ chooses two challenge identities (ID_0^*, ID_1^*) and a challenge plaintext M^*, computes

$$C_0^* \leftarrow \mathsf{Encrypt}(params, ID_0^*, M^*), \text{ and}$$
$$C_1^* \leftarrow \mathsf{Encrypt}(params, ID_1^*, M^*),$$

and obtains the challenge ciphertext C^* which is derived from C_0^* or C_1^*. Even if $\mathcal{A}$ can decrypt the challenge ciphertext C^* (which can be decrypted by sk_{ID^*}), $\mathcal{A}$ only knows that (1) C^* is encrypted by ID^*, and (2) the decryption result is M^*. $\mathcal{A}$ has already known this information. Therefore, $\mathcal{A}$ is admitted to access $\mathcal{O}_{EXT}$, $\mathcal{O}_{RE-EXT}$, $\mathcal{O}_{DEC}$, and $\mathcal{O}_{RE-ENC}$ without any restriction. An IB-PRE scheme Π is said to be IND-SH-PrID-CCA-secure if the advantage is negligible for any polynomial-time PPT $\mathcal{A}$ in the following experiment.

Definition 6. *IND-SH-PrID-CCA*

$$Adv_{\Pi,\mathcal{A}}^{IND-SU-PrID-CCA}(k) = \Big| \Pr\Big[\mu \xleftarrow{\$} \{0,1\}; (params, msk) \leftarrow \mathsf{Setup}(1^k);$$

$$(ID_0^*, ID_1^*, C_0^*, C_1^*, ID^*, State) \leftarrow \mathcal{A}^{\mathcal{O}_{EXT}, \mathcal{O}_{RE-EXT}, \mathcal{O}_{DEC}, \mathcal{O}_{RE-ENC}}(params);$$

$$C^* \leftarrow \mathsf{Re\text{-}Encrypt}(params, rk_{ID_\mu^* \rightarrow ID^*}, C_\mu^*);$$

$$\mu' \leftarrow \mathcal{A}^{\mathcal{O}_{EXT}, \mathcal{O}_{RE-EXT}, \mathcal{O}_{DEC}, \mathcal{O}_{RE-ENC}}(params, C^*, State); \mu = \mu'\Big] - 1/2\Big|$$

We simply define the IND-SH-PrID-CPA security with $\mathcal{O}_{RE-ENC}$ and $\mathcal{O}_{DEC}$ removed from the above experiment.

If an adversary can decide whether two destination ciphertext were derived from the same source ciphertext or not, then the adversary can break the IND-SH-PrID-CCA (IND-SH-PrID-CPA also) security. More precisely, the adversary can send C_0^* to $\mathcal{O}_{RE-ENC}$, obtains the result ciphertext (say C_0'), and can decide whether C'_0 and C^* were derived from C^*_0 or not. Therefore, in the mailing-list usage, the above IND-SH-PrID definitions also guarantee that an adversary cannot decide whether two mailing addresses are included in the same mailing-list or not.

Notice that the source hiding requirement is different from "anonymity" (in the IBE context [7]) and "key privacy" (in the PRE context [1]). More precisely, in the typical ID-based encryption setting, anonymity requires that an identity used for encryption is not revealed from the corresponding ciphertext. In a key-private PRE scheme, a source identity and a destination identity are not revealed from a re-encryption key rk. So, key privacy protects the information on the identity of the actual source/destination users from the proxy's point of view.

4   Previous IB-PRE Schemes

There have been many proposed IB-PRE schemes [8, 11–13, 19, 22]. In previous IB-PRE schemes [8, 11–13, 19], at least one source ciphertext is included in a destination ciphertext. We illustrate this situation in Fig.2 in the case of the Green-Ateniese scheme [11]. An eavesdropper can identify whether $C_{\text{company-ml@security.com}}$ is the source ciphertext of a destination ciphertext $C_{\text{alice@crypto.com}}$ or not.

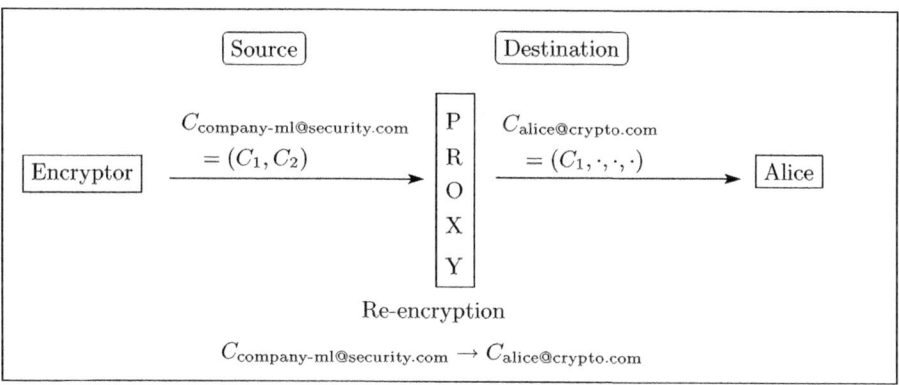

Fig. 2. Linking between a source and a destination ciphertext

Tang et al. [22] proposed an IB-PRE scheme with the inter-domain setting, where a source user and a destination user are from different key generation centers. Although no source identity is directly included in a destination ciphertext, Tang et al.'s scheme does not satisfy proxy invisibility. In addition, this scheme is CPA secure only. A construction of CCA-secure scheme is indicated as the open problem in [22].

5   Proposed IB-PRE Schemes

In this section, we propose two IB-PRE schemes (respectively CPA and CCA secure) with source hiding property.

Protocol 1.   *The proposed CPA-secure IB-PRE scheme with source hiding property*

Setup$(1^k, 2)$: *Let $(\mathbb{G}_1, \mathbb{G}_T)$ be a bilinear group with prime order p, $e : \mathbb{G}_1 \times \mathbb{G}_1 \to \mathbb{G}_T$ a bilinear map, and $g \in \mathbb{G}_1$ a generator. Select $s \xleftarrow{\$} \mathbb{Z}_p$, compute g^s, and output $msk = s$ and $params = (g, g^s, H_1, H_2)$, where $H_1 : \{0,1\}^* \to \mathbb{G}_1$ and $H_2 : \mathbb{G}_T \to \mathbb{G}_1$ are hash functions.*

KeyGen$(params, msk, ID)$: *For $ID \in \{0,1\}^*$, output $sk_{ID} = H_1(ID)^s$.*

Encrypt$(params, ID, M)$: *Choose $r \xleftarrow{\$} \mathbb{Z}_p$, compute $(C_1, C_2) = (g^r, M \cdot e(g^s, H_1(ID)^r))$, and output $C = (C_1, C_2)$.*

RKGen$(params, sk_{ID_1}, ID_1, ID_2)$: *Choose $X \xleftarrow{\$} \mathbb{G}_T$, compute $(R_1, R_2) =$ Encrypt$(params, ID_2, X)$ and $R_3 = sk_{ID_1}^{-1} \cdot H_2(X) = H_1(ID_1)^{-s} \cdot H_2(X)$, and output $rk_{ID_1 \to ID_2} = (R_1, R_2, R_3)$.*

Re-Encrypt$(params, rk_{ID_1 \to ID_2}, C_{ID_1})$: *From a level 1 ciphertext C_{ID_1}, a level 2 ciphertext C_{ID_2} is computed as follows: Let $C_{ID_1} = (C_1, C_2)$ and $rk_{ID_1 \to ID_2} = (R_1, R_2, R_3)$. Choose $t, t' \xleftarrow{\$} \mathbb{Z}_p$, compute $C'_1 = C_1 \cdot g^t$, $C'_2 = C_2 \cdot e(g^s, H_1(ID_1)^t) \cdot e(C'_1, R_3)$, $R'_1 = R_1 \cdot g^{t'}$, and $R'_2 = R_2 \cdot e(g^s, H_1(ID_2)^{t'})$, and output $C_{ID_2} = (C'_1, C'_2, R'_1, R'_2)$.*

Decrypt$(params, sk_{ID}, C_{ID})$: *Let $C_{ID} = (C_1, C_2, \ldots, C_{2\ell})$ be a level ℓ ($\ell \in \{1, 2\}$) ciphertext.*

In the case of $\ell = 1$: *Let (C_1, C_2) be a level 1 ciphertext. Output $C_2/e(C_1, sk_{ID}) = M \cdot e(g^s, H_1(ID)^r)/e(g^r, H_1(ID)^s) = M$.*

In the case of $\ell = 2$: *Let $C_{ID} = (C_1, C_2, C_3, C_4) = (C'_1, C'_2, R'_1, R'_2)$ be a level 2 ciphertext. For the sake of clarity, we describe ID as ID_2, and assume that (C_1, C_2) was computed using ID_1. Let $r, r' \in \mathbb{Z}_p$ be random numbers used in the computation of (C_1, C_2) and (R_1, R_2), respectively, namely $C_1 = g^r$, $C_2 = M \cdot e(g^s, H_1(ID_1)^r)$, $R_1 = g^{r'}$, and $R_2 = X \cdot e(g^s, H_1(ID_2)^{r'})$. Then*

$$C'_1 = C_1 \cdot g^t = g^r \cdot g^t = g^{r+t},$$

$$\begin{aligned}
C'_2 &= C_2 \cdot e(g^s, H_1(ID_1)^t) \cdot e(g^{r+t}, H_1(ID_1)^{-s} \cdot H_2(X)) \\
&= M \cdot e(g^s, H_1(ID_1)^r) \cdot e(g^s, H_1(ID_1)^t) \cdot e(g^{r+t}, H_1(ID_1)^{-s} \cdot H_2(X)) \\
&= M \cdot e(g^s, H_1(ID_1)^r) \cdot e(g^s, H_1(ID_1)^t) \cdot e(g^r, H_1(ID_1)^{-s}) \cdot e(g^r, H_2(X)) \\
&\quad \times e(g^t, H_1(ID_1)^{-s}) \cdot e(g^t, H_2(X)) \\
&= M \cdot e(g^{r+t}, H_2(X)),
\end{aligned}$$

$$R'_1 = R_1 \cdot g^{t'} = g^{r'} \cdot g^{t'} = g^{r'+t'},$$

$$\begin{aligned}
R'_2 &= R_2 \cdot e(g^s, H_1(ID_2)^{t'}) = X \cdot e(g^s, H_1(ID_2)^{r'}) \cdot e(g^s, H_1(ID_2)^{t'}) \\
&= X \cdot e(g^s, H_1(ID_2)^{r'+t'}).
\end{aligned}$$

Given $sk_{ID_2} = H_1(ID_2)^s$, (C'_1, C'_2, R'_1, R'_2) can be decrypted as:

1. Compute $R_2'/e(R_1', sk_{ID_2})$ $\qquad$ = $\qquad$ X $\quad\cdot$
   $e(g^s, H_1(ID_2)^{r'+t'})/e(g^{r'+t'}, H_1(ID_2)^s)$ $\qquad$ = $\qquad$ X $\quad\cdot$
   $e(g, H_1(ID_2))^{s(r'+t')}/e(g, H_1(ID_2))^{s(r'+t')} = X.$

2. Compute $H_2(X)$ $\quad$ and $\quad$ $C_2'/e(C_1', H_2(X))$ $\qquad$ = $\qquad$ M $\quad\cdot$
   $e(g^{r+t}, H_2(X))/e(g^{r+t}, H_2(X)) = M.$

From the above considerations, output $\dfrac{C_2'}{e\Big(C_1', H_2\big(R_2'/e(R_1', sk_{ID_2})\big)\Big)} = M.$

We apply the homomorphic property of the Boneh-Franklin IBE scheme to randomize both the source ciphertext and the re-encryption key included in the destination ciphertext, i.e., for a random value t and $C_{ID} = (C_1, C_2)$, $(C_1 \cdot g^t, C_2 \cdot e(g^s, H_1(ID)^t))$ is also a valid ciphertext under ID.

Next, we propose a CCA-secure IB-PRE scheme with source hiding property. In the Green-Ateniese IND-Pr-ID-CCA-secure scheme, not only a source ciphertext, but also a source identity is included in a destination ciphertext. Therefore, we need a new strategy to construct IND-Pr-ID-CCA-secure scheme with source hiding property. Our scheme is based on the IND-ID-CCA-secure Boneh-Franklin IBE scheme, which applies the Fujisaki-Okamoto transformation [10]. We show the intuition of our construction as follows: note that undefined notations are defined in the following protocol. For a ciphertext $(C_1, C_2, C_3) = (g^r, \sigma \cdot e(g^s, H_1(ID)^r), M \oplus H_5(\sigma))$, where $r = H_4(\sigma, M)$, (C_1, C_2) can be randomized such that $C_1 \cdot g^t$ and $C_2 \cdot e(g^s, H_1(ID)^t)$, where $t \in \mathbb{Z}_p$. However, C_3 cannot be randomized directly (due to bitwise exclusive-or operation). Therefore, we prepare another ciphertext $(C_1', C_2') = (g^{r'}, X \cdot e(g^s, H_1(ID)^{r'})$ for some $X \in \mathbb{G}_T$ and $r' \in \mathbb{Z}_p$, and randomize C_3 to $C_3 \oplus H_5(X)$.

Protocol 2. *The proposed CCA-secure IB-PRE scheme with source hiding property*

Setup$(1^k, 2)$: *Let $(\mathbb{G}_1, \mathbb{G}_T)$ be a bilinear group with prime order p, $e : \mathbb{G}_1 \times \mathbb{G}_1 \rightarrow \mathbb{G}_T$ a bilinear map, and $g \in \mathbb{G}_1$ a generator. Choose $s \xleftarrow{\$} \mathbb{Z}_p$, compute g^s, and output $msk = s$ and $params = (g, g^s, \{H_i\}_{i=1}^5)$, where each H_i is a hash function defined as: $H_1 : \{0,1\}^* \rightarrow \mathbb{G}_1$, $H_2 : \{0,1\}^* \rightarrow \mathbb{G}_1$, $H_3 : \{0,1\}^* \rightarrow \mathbb{G}_1$, $H_4 : \mathbb{G}_T \times \{0,1\}^n \rightarrow \mathbb{Z}_p$, and $H_5 : \mathbb{G}_T \rightarrow \{0,1\}^n$.*

KeyGen$(params, msk, ID)$: *For $ID \in \{0,1\}^*$, output $sk_{ID} = H_1(ID)^s$.*

Encrypt$(params, ID, M \in \{0,1\}^n)$: *Choose $\sigma \xleftarrow{\$} \mathbb{G}_T$, set $r = H_4(\sigma, M)$, compute $(C_1, C_2, C_3) = (g^r, \sigma \cdot e(g^s, H_1(ID)^r), M \oplus H_5(\sigma))$, and output $C = (C_1, C_2, C_3)$.*

RKGen$(params, sk_{ID_1}, ID_1, ID_2)$: *Choose $X_1 \xleftarrow{\$} \mathbb{G}_T$ and $X_2 \xleftarrow{\$} \{0,1\}^n$, set $r' = H_4(X_1, X_2)$, compute $R_1 = g^{r'}$, $R_2 = X_1 \cdot e(g^s, H_1(ID_2)^{r'})$, $R_3 = X_2 \oplus H_5(X_1)$, $R_4 = H_2(X_2) \cdot sk_{ID_1}$, and output $rk_{ID_1 \rightarrow ID_2} = (R_1, R_2, R_3, R_4)$.*

Re-Encrypt$(params, rk_{ID_1 \rightarrow ID_2}, C_{ID_1})$: *From a level 1 ciphertext C_{ID_1}, a level 2 ciphertext C_{ID_2} is computed as follows: Let $C_{ID_1} = (C_1, C_2, C_3)$ and $rk_{ID_1 \rightarrow ID_2} = (R_1, R_2, R_3, R_4)$.*

Choose $X_1', X_2' \overset{\$}{\leftarrow} \mathbb{G}_T$, *set* $t = H_4(C_3, R_3)$, $t' = H_4(X_1', C_3)$, $s' = H_4(X_1', X_2')$, *and* $s'' = H_4(X_2', R_3)$, *compute* $H_1(ID_1)$, $C_1' = C_1 \cdot g^t$, $C_2' = C_2 \cdot e(g^s, H_1(ID_1)^t)/e(C_1', R_4)$, $C_3' = C_3 \oplus H_5(X_1')$, $C_4' = g^{t'}$, $C_5' = X_1' \cdot e(g^s, H_1(ID_2)^{t'})$, $R_1' = R_1 \cdot g^{s'}$, $R_2' = R_2 \cdot e(g^s, H_1(ID_2)^{s'})$, $R_3' = R_3 \oplus H_5(X_2')$, $C_6' = g^{s''}$, $C_7' = X_2' \cdot e(g^s, H_1(ID_2)^{s''})$, $S_1' = H_3(C_1', C_2')^t$, *and* $S_2' = H_3(R_1', R_2')^{s'}$, *and output* $(C_1', \ldots, C_7', S_1', S_2', R_1', R_2', R_3')$.

Decrypt$(params, sk_{ID}, C_{ID})$: *Let* C_{ID} *be a level* ℓ ($\ell \in \{1, 2\}$) *ciphertext.*

In the case of $\ell = 1$ **:** *Let* (C_1, C_2, C_3) *be a level 1 ciphertext. Compute* $C_2/e(C_1, sk_{ID}) = \sigma$, *and* $C_3 \oplus H_5(\sigma) = M$. *Check* $C_1 \overset{?}{=} g^r$, *where* $r = H_4(\sigma, M)$. *If the checking condition does not hold, then output* $\perp$. *Otherwise, output* M.

In the case of $\ell = 2$ **:** *Let* $C_{ID} = (C_1', \ldots, C_7', S_1', S_2', R_1', R_2', R_3')$ *be a level 2 ciphertext. For the sake of clarity, we describe ID as* ID_2, *and assume that* (C_1, C_2, C_3) *was computed using* ID_1. *Let* $r, r' \in \mathbb{Z}_p$ *be random numbers used in the computation of* (C_1, C_2, C_3) *and* (R_1, R_2, R_3, R_4), *respectively, namely* $C_1 = g^r$, $C_2 = \sigma \cdot e(g^s, H_1(ID_1)^r)$, $C_3 = M \oplus H_5(\sigma)$, *where* $r = H_4(\sigma, M)$, $R_1 = g^{r'}$, $R_2 = X_1 \cdot e(g^s, H_1(ID_2)^{r'})$, $R_3 = X_2 \oplus H_5(X_1)$, *and* $R_4 = H_5(X_2) \cdot H_1(ID_1)^s$. *Then*

$$C_1' = C_1 \cdot g^t = g^r \cdot g^t = g^{r+t},$$

$$C_2' = C_2 \cdot e(g^s, H_1(ID_1)^t)/e(C_1', R_4)$$
$$= \sigma \cdot e(g^s, H_1(ID_1)^r) \cdot e(g^s, H_1(ID_1)^t)/\{e(g^{r+t}, H_2(X_2) \cdot H_1(ID_1)^s)\}$$
$$= \sigma \cdot e(g^s, H_1(ID_1)^{r+t})/\{e(g^{r+t}, H_2(X_2)) \cdot e(g^{r+t}, H_1(ID_1)^s)\}$$
$$= \sigma/e(g^{r+t}, H_2(X_2)),$$

$$R_1' = R_1 \cdot g^{s'} = g^{r'} \cdot g^{s'} = g^{r'+s'},$$

$$R_2' = R_2 \cdot e(g^s, H_1(ID_2)^{s'}) = X_1 \cdot e(g^s, H_1(ID_2)^{r'+s'}).$$

Given $sk_{ID_2} = H_1(ID_2)^s$, $(C_1', \ldots, C_7', S_1', S_2', R_1', R_2', R_3')$ *can be decrypted as:*

1. *Compute* $C_5'/e(C_4', sk_{ID_2}) = X_1'$, $C_3' \oplus H_5(X_1') = C_3 \oplus H_5(X_1') \oplus H_5(X_1') = C_3$, *and* $t' = H_4(X_1', C_3)$, *and check* $g^{t'} \overset{?}{=} C_4'$.

2. *Compute* $C_7'/e(C_6', sk_{ID_2}) = X_2'$, $H_5(X_2')$, $R_3' \oplus H_5(X_2') = R_3 \oplus H_5(X_2') \oplus H_5(X_2') = R_3$, *and* $s'' = H_4(X_2', R_3)$, *and check* $g^{s''} \overset{?}{=} C_6'$.

3. *Compute* $s' = H_4(X_1', X_2')$, *and check* $S_2' \overset{?}{=} H_3(R_1', R_2')^{s'}$. *Compute* $R_2'/e(R_1', sk_{ID_2}) = X_1$, $H_5(X_1)$, $R_3 \oplus H_5(X_1) = X_2 \oplus H_5(X_1) \oplus H_5(X_1) = X_2$, *and* $r' = H_4(X_1, X_2)$, *and check* $R_1' \cdot g^{-s'} \overset{?}{=} g^{r'}$.

4. *Compute* $t = H_4(C_3, R_3)$, *and check* $S_1' \overset{?}{=} H_3(C_1', C_2')^t$. *Compute* $C_2' \cdot e(C_1', H_2(X_2)) = \sigma$, $C_3 \oplus H_5(\sigma) = M \oplus H_5(\sigma) \oplus H_5(\sigma) = M$, *and* $r = H_4(\sigma, M)$, *and check* $C_1' \cdot g^{-t} \overset{?}{=} g^r$.

If all checking condition holds, then output M, *and* $\perp$, *otherwise.*

6 Security Analysis

In this section, we show our schemes satisfy the required security notions.

Theorem 1. *Our proposed scheme 1 is IND-PrID-CPA-secure under the BDH assumption in the random oracle model.*

We omit the detailed proof, since it is done with the same manner of the proof of Theorem 3.

Theorem 2. *Our proposed scheme 1 is IND-SH-PrID-CPA-secure in the information theoretic sense.*

Proof. This theorem is clearly satisfied, since a source identity ID_1 is not included in a destination ciphertext (C'_1, C'_2, R'_1, R'_2) as $C'_1 = g^{r+t}$, $C'_2 = M \cdot e(g^{r+t}, H_2(X))$, $R'_1 = g^{r'+t'}$, and $R'_2 = X \cdot e(g^s, H_1(ID_2)^{r'+t'})$, where ID_2 is a destination identity. In addition, no source ciphertext is directly included in a destination ciphertext, namely a part of source ciphertext C_1 is randomized using a random value t. More precisely, for $C_{ID_2} = (C'_1, C'_2, R'_1, R'_2)$ and all identity ID, there exists a ciphertext $C_{ID} = (g^r, M \cdot e(g^s, H_1(ID)^r))$ which can be a source ciphertext of C_{ID_2}. □

Theorem 3. *Our proposed scheme 2 is IND-PrID-CCA-secure under the BDH assumption in the random oracle model.*

Proof. We construct an algorithm $\mathcal{B}$ that breaks IND-ID-CCA security of the Boneh-Franklin IBE [6] by using an adversary $\mathcal{A}$ who breaks IND-Pr-ID-CCA security of our scheme with the non-negligible probability ϵ. Let $\mathcal{C}$ be the challenger of the Boneh-Franklin IBE in the IND-ID-CCA experiment. Note that $\mathcal{B}$ maintains a table (α, ID_1, ID_2, rk), where rk is a re-encryption key, to decide whether $\mathcal{B}$ returns a correct (or an incorrect) secret key or not. Let $*$ be the wildcard on a table managed by $\mathcal{B}$. First, $\mathcal{C}$ sends $param = (g, g^s, H_1, H_4, H_5)$ to $\mathcal{B}$. $\mathcal{B}$ adds H_2 and H_3 into $param$, and forwards $param$ to $\mathcal{A}$.

Phase 1:

- When $\mathcal{A}$ calls $\mathcal{O}_{EXT}(ID)$, then $\mathcal{B}$ flips a weighted coin to set $\alpha = 1$ with probability δ. If $\alpha = 0$, or $(0, ID, *, *)$ or $(0, *, ID, *)$ already exists in the table, $\mathcal{B}$ outputs a random bit and aborts. Otherwise, if $\alpha = 1$, then $\mathcal{B}$ issues $\mathcal{EXTRACT}(ID)$ (which is defined in the IND-ID-CCA experiment), obtains sk_{ID}, records $(1, ID, ID, \bot)$, and returns sk_{ID} to $\mathcal{A}$.

- When $\mathcal{A}$ calls $\mathcal{O}_{RE\text{-}EXT}(ID_1, ID_2)$, then $\mathcal{B}$ flips a weighted coin as in $\mathcal{O}_{EXT}(ID)$. If $\alpha = 1$, or $(1, ID_1, ID_1, *)$ or $(1, ID_2, ID_2, *)$ already exists in the table, $\mathcal{B}$ issues $\mathcal{EXTRACT}(ID_1)$, obtains sk_{ID_1}, runs $rk_{ID_1 \to ID_2} \gets$ RKGen$(params, sk_{ID_1}, ID_1, ID_2)$, and returns $rk_{ID_1 \to ID_2}$ to $\mathcal{A}$. $\mathcal{B}$ records $(1, ID_1, ID_2, rk_{ID_1 \to ID_2})$ in the table. Otherwise, $\mathcal{B}$ returns an invalid re-encryption key $rk_{ID_1 \to ID_2} = (R_1, R_2, R_3, R_4)$ as follows: Choose $X_1 \xleftarrow{\$} \mathbb{G}_T$

and $X_2 \xleftarrow{\$} \{0,1\}^n$, set $r' = H_4(X_1, X_2)$, compute $R_1 = g^{r'}$, $R_2 = X_1 \cdot e(g^s, H_1(ID_2)^{r'})$, $R_3 = X_2 \oplus H_5(X_1)$, and $R_4 := x \xleftarrow{\$} \mathbb{G}_1$, and output $rk_{ID_1 \to ID_2} = (R_1, R_2, R_3, R_4)$. $\mathcal{B}$ records $(0, ID_1, ID_2, rk_{ID_1 \to ID_2})$ in the table. Note that this x can be expressed as $(H_1(ID_2)^s \cdot y)$ for an unknown $y \in \mathbb{G}_1$. An adversary who can distinguish invalid re-encryption keys in this simulation must be able to determine that (R_1, R_2, R_3) do not encrypt a value $Y \in \mathbb{G}_T$ such that $H_2(Y) = y$. Therefore, we can construct an algorithm $\mathcal{B}'$ that can solve the DBDH problem by using an adversary $\mathcal{A}'$ who can distinguish an incorrect simulation (including invalid re-encryption keys) from a correct simulation (in which all values are correctly formed).

- When $\mathcal{A}$ calls $\mathcal{O}_{RE\text{-}ENC}(C_{ID_1}, ID_1, ID_2)$, if $(*, ID_1, ID_2, *)$ does not exist in the table, $\mathcal{B}$ performs $\mathcal{O}_{RE\text{-}EXT}(ID_1, ID_2)$ simulation, obtains $rk_{ID_1 \to ID_2}$, and runs Re-Encrypt$(params, rk_{ID_1 \to ID_2}, C_{ID_1})$.

- When $\mathcal{A}$ calls $\mathcal{O}_{DEC}(C_{ID}, ID)$, if $C_{ID} = (C_1, C_2, C_3)$ is a level 1 ciphertext, then $\mathcal{B}$ issues $\mathcal{DECRYPT}((C_1, C_2, C_3), ID)$ (which is defined in the IND-ID-CCA experiment), obtains M, and returns M to $\mathcal{A}$. Otherwise, there are only three ways for $\mathcal{A}$ to obtain a valid level 2 ciphertext $C_{ID} = (C'_1, \ldots, C'_7, S'_1, S'_2, R'_1, R'_2, R'_3)$: (Case-1) $\mathcal{A}$ issues $\mathcal{O}_{RE\text{-}EXT}(*, ID)$, and applies the Re-Encrypt algorithm, (Case-2) $\mathcal{A}$ issues $\mathcal{O}_{RE\text{-}ENC}$, and (Case-3) $\mathcal{A}$ computes the RKGen algorithm with sk_{ID}, and computes the Re-Encrypt algorithm.

  • In cases 1 and 2, there exists $(*, *, ID, rk_{* \to ID})$ in the table. If $(1, *, ID, rk_{* \to ID})$ exists in the table, then $\mathcal{B}$ obtains sk_{ID} (from $\mathcal{EXTRACT}(ID)$), decrypts C_{ID} using sk_{ID}, and returns M. Else if $(0, *, ID, rk_{* \to ID})$ exists in the table, $\mathcal{B}$ returns M as follows:

    1. $\mathcal{B}$ issues $\mathcal{DECRYPT}((C'_3, C'_4, C'_5), ID)$ and obtains C_3 or $\perp$.
    2. $\mathcal{B}$ issues $\mathcal{DECRYPT}((C'_6, C'_7, R'_3), ID)$ and obtains R_3 or $\perp$.
    3. $\mathcal{B}$ computes $t = H_4(C_3, R_3)$, and checks $S'_1 \stackrel{?}{=} H_3(C'_1, C'_2)^t$.
    4. $\mathcal{B}$ computes $C_1 = C'_1 \cdot g^{-t}$.
    5. For all ID' in $(0, ID', ID, rk_{ID' \to ID})$, $\mathcal{B}$ executes the following procedure until either M can be computed or there is no remaining entry in the table.
       (a) Let $rk_{ID' \to ID} = (*, *, *, x)$. Then $C'_2 = C_2/e(C'_1, x)$. $\mathcal{B}$ computes $C_2 = C'_2 \cdot e(C'_1, x)$ using x.
       (b) $\mathcal{B}$ issues $\mathcal{DECRYPT}((C_1, C_2, C_3), ID')$ and obtains M or $\perp$.
    6. If all checking condition holds (incl. there is no $\perp$ result), then $\mathcal{B}$ returns M to $\mathcal{A}$. Otherwise, $\mathcal{B}$ returns $\perp$.

  • In case 3, there exists $(1, ID, ID, \perp)$ in the table. $\mathcal{B}$ decrypts C_{ID} using sk_{ID}, and returns M.

Challenge: $\mathcal{A}$ sends (M_0, M_1, ID^*) to $\mathcal{B}$ as the challenge message. For any ID, if $(1, ID^*, ID, *)$ exists in the table, then $\mathcal{B}$ outputs a random bit and aborts. Otherwise, $\mathcal{B}$ sends (M_0, M_1, ID^*) to $\mathcal{C}$ as the challenge message, obtains the challenge ciphertext $C^* = (C_1^*, C_2^*, C_3^*)$ from $\mathcal{C}$, and returns C^* to $\mathcal{A}$.

Phase 2:

- When $\mathcal{A}$ calls $\mathcal{O}_{EXT}(ID)$, then $\mathcal{B}$ answers as in Phase 1.
- When $\mathcal{A}$ calls $\mathcal{O}_{RE\text{-}EXT}(ID_1, ID_2)$, if $ID_1 \neq ID^*$, then $\mathcal{B}$ answers as in Phase 1. If $ID_1 = ID^*$, then $\mathcal{B}$ returns a random re-encryption key as in Phase 1, and records $(0, ID_1, ID_2, rk_{ID_1 \to ID_2})$ in the table.
- When $\mathcal{A}$ calls $\mathcal{O}_{RE\text{-}ENC}(C_{ID_1}, ID_1, ID_2)$, then $\mathcal{B}$ answers as in Phase 1.
- When $\mathcal{A}$ calls $\mathcal{O}_{DEC}(C_{ID}, ID)$, then $\mathcal{B}$ answers as in Phase 1.

Guess: $\mathcal{B}$ outputs 1 if $\mu' = \mu$, and 0, otherwise.

If $\mathcal{B}$ does not abort during the simulation, then $\mathcal{A}$'s view is identical to a real attack except for invalid re-encryption keys. We already showed that we can construct an algorithm $\mathcal{B}'$ that can solve the DBDH problem by using an adversary $\mathcal{A}'$ who can distinguish an incorrect simulation (including invalid re-encryption keys) from a correct simulation (in which all values are correctly-formed). Therefore, we just estimate the probability that $\mathcal{B}$ does not abort.

In Phase 1 or 2, $\mathcal{B}$ does not abort with the probability δ^{q_E}, where q_E is the number of queries issued by $\mathcal{A}$. In addition, $\mathcal{B}$ does not abort with the probability $(1 - \delta)$ in the challenge phase. To sum up, $\mathcal{B}$ does not abort with the probability $\delta^{q_E}(1 - \delta)$, and this value is maximized at $\delta_{opt} = 1 - 1/(q_E + 1)$. Therefore, $\mathcal{B}$'s advantage is at least $\epsilon/\hat{e}(q_E + 1)$, where $\hat{e} \approx 2.718$ is the base of the natural logarithm. $\qquad\square$

Theorem 4. *Our proposed scheme 2 is IND-SH-PrID-CCA-secure in the information theoretic sense.*

Proof. This theorem is clearly satisfied, since a source identity ID_1 is not included in a destination ciphertext $(C_1', \ldots, C_7', S_1', S_2', R_1', R_2', R_3')$ as $C_1' = g^{r+t}$, $C_2' = \sigma/e(g^{r+t}, H_2(X_2))$, $C_3' = C_3 \oplus H_5(X_1')$, $C_4' = g^{t'}$, $C_5' = X_1' \cdot e(g^s, H_1(ID_2)^{t'})$, $C_6' = g^{s''}$, $C_7' = X_2' \cdot e(g^s, H_1(ID_2)^{s''})$, $R_1' = g^{r'+s'}$, $R_2' = X_1 \cdot e(g^s, H_1(ID_2)^{r'+s'})$, $R_3' = R_3 \oplus H_5(X_2')$, $S_1' = H_3(C_1', C_2')^t$, and $S_2' = H_3(R_1', R_2')^{s'}$. In addition, no source ciphertext is directly included in a destination ciphertext, namely a part of source ciphertext C_1 is randomized using random values t, t', s', and s''. More precisely, for $C_{ID_2} = (C_1', \ldots, C_7', S_1', S_2', R_1', R_2', R_3')$ and all identity ID, there exists a ciphertext $C_{ID} = (g^r, \sigma \cdot e(g^s, H_1(ID)^r), M \oplus H_5(\sigma))$, where $r = H_4(M, \sigma)$, which can be a source ciphertext of C_{ID_2}. $\qquad\square$

7 A Mailing-List System Based on IB-PRE with Source Hiding Property

In this section, we consider a mailing-list system (without public key certificates) based on IB-PRE with source hiding property. First, we assume that a trusted mailing-list manager stores re-encryption keys $\{rk_{\text{company-ml@security.com} \to U_i@*.*}\}_{U_i \in List}$ to the proxy server, where $List$ is the member list of company-ml@security.com. The proxy translates a source ciphertext $C_{\text{company-ml@security.com}}$ into a destination ciphertext $\{C_{U_i@*.*}\}_{U_i \in List}$.

Here, we should consider how a receiver knows whether the e-mail was sent for him/her only or not. To achieve this requirement, the proxy server encrypts the source identity "company-ml@security.com" as a plaintext by using each member's public key, and adds this additional ciphertext in the re-encrypted ciphertext. In addition, the proxy computes a signature (by using its signing key sk_p) for re-encrypted and additional ciphertexts to bind these ciphertexts such as $\sigma_A = Sign(sk_p, (C_{\text{alice@crypto.com}}, Enc(PK_A, \text{company-ml@security.com})))$.

The proxy has to identify the source identity "company-ml@security.com" from the source ciphertext, since the proxy needs to decide which re-encryption keys are to be used in the Re-Encrypt algorithm. In addition, our randomization procedure needs corresponding source identity. However, a source identity is not revealed from the corresponding source ciphertext, since the Boneh-Franklin IBE is anonymous [7]. As a simple solution, a source identity is added into a source ciphertext. Note that, in the security definition of source hiding property, an adversary $\mathcal{A}$ knows (ID_0^*, ID_1^*, ID^*). This suggests that even if $\mathcal{A}$ knows source and destination identities, no information about the source identity "company-ml@security.com" is revealed from the destination ciphertext. Therefore, there is no problem to add a source identity into the corresponding ciphertext from the viewpoint of source hiding property. A mailing-list system based on our IB-PRE is shown in Fig.3.

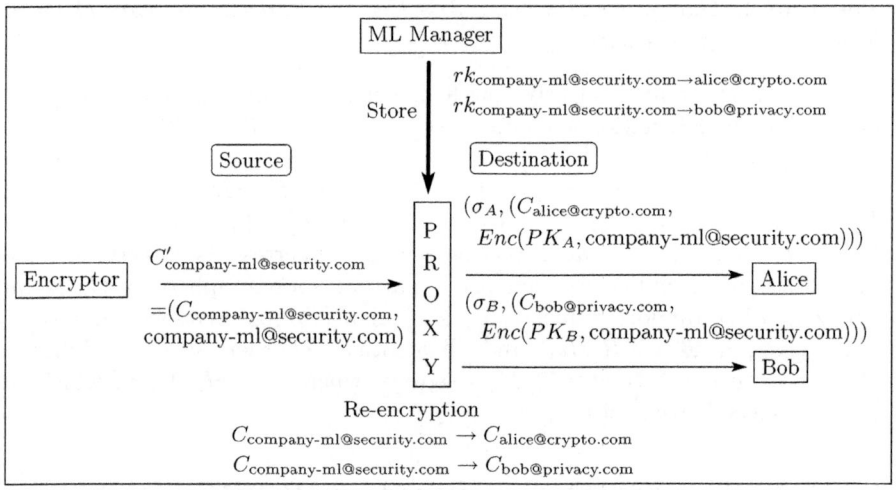

Fig. 3. Mailing-list system based on our IB-PRE

8 Conclusion

In this paper, we propose IB-PRE schemes with source hiding property, where no information about a source identity is revealed from a destination ciphertext. We insist that our work is the valuable and important milestone for establishing the secure PRE-based mailing-list system without public key certificates.

By regarding this paper as the starter, there will be interesting tasks which should be solved as follows: First of all, we need to consider how to reduce the computational costs of our CCA-secure IB-PRE scheme (in this paper, we mainly focus on how to achieve the security requirements). In addition, IB-PRE with source hiding property in the standard model is also an important task. Our scheme may be improved for the level of privacy by applying the following PRE: Anonymous conditional PRE [9], where a source ciphertext satisfying a condition set by a delegator can be transformed by the proxy and then decrypted by a delegatee without revealing the condition. Key-private PRE [1], where a source identity and destination identity are not revealed from a re-encryption key rk. Especially, PRE with collusion attack resistance [2, 18, 20, 21, 23] should be considered, since a delegator's secret key is revealed if the proxy and a delegatee collude with each other in our schemes. There is space for arguement on these points.

Acknowledgements

The authors would like to thank the anonymous reviewers of EuroPKI 2010 for their invaluable comments, and also would like to thank the participants of our presentation in Athens for their invaluable comments and questions. The first author Keita Emura is supported by the Center for Highly Dependable Embedded Systems Technology as a Postdoc researcher.

References

1. Ateniese, G., Benson, K., Hohenberger, S.: Key-private proxy re-encryption. In: Fischlin, M. (ed.) CT-RSA 2009. LNCS, vol. 5473, pp. 279–294. Springer, Heidelberg (2009)
2. Ateniese, G., Fu, K., Green, M., Hohenberger, S.: Improved proxy re-encryption schemes with applications to secure distributed storage. ACM Trans. Inf. Syst. Secur. 9(1), 1–30 (2006)
3. Barr, D.: Majordomo, http://www.greatcircle.com/majordomo/
4. Blaze, M., Bleumer, G., Strauss, M.: Divertible protocols and atomic proxy cryptography. In: Nyberg, K. (ed.) EUROCRYPT 1998. LNCS, vol. 1403, pp. 127–144. Springer, Heidelberg (1998)
5. Bobba, R., Muggli, J., Pant, M., Basney, J., Khurana, H.: Usable secure mailing lists with untrusted servers. In: IDtrust, pp. 103–116 (2009)
6. Boneh, D., Franklin, M.K.: Identity-based encryption from the weil pairing. SIAM J. Comput. 32(3), 586–615 (2003)
7. Boyen, X., Waters, B.: Anonymous hierarchical identity-based encryption (Without random oracles). In: Dwork, C. (ed.) CRYPTO 2006. LNCS, vol. 4117, pp. 290–307. Springer, Heidelberg (2006)
8. Chu, C.-K., Tzeng, W.-G.: Identity-based proxy re-encryption without random oracles. In: Garay, J.A., Lenstra, A.K., Mambo, M., Peralta, R. (eds.) ISC 2007. LNCS, vol. 4779, pp. 189–202. Springer, Heidelberg (2007)
9. Fang, L., Susilo, W., Wang, J.: Anonymous conditional proxy re-encryption without random oracle. In: Pieprzyk, J., Zhang, F. (eds.) ProvSec 2009. LNCS, vol. 5848, pp. 47–60. Springer, Heidelberg (2009)

10. Fujisaki, E., Okamoto, T.: Secure integration of asymmetric and symmetric encryption schemes. In: Wiener, M. (ed.) CRYPTO 1999. LNCS, vol. 1666, pp. 537–554. Springer, Heidelberg (1999)
11. Green, M., Ateniese, G.: Identity-based proxy re-encryption. In: Katz, J., Yung, M. (eds.) ACNS 2007. LNCS, vol. 4521, pp. 288–306. Springer, Heidelberg (2007)
12. Hu, X., Chen, X., Huang, S.: Fully secure identity based proxy re-encryption schemes in the standard model. In: ICCSIT 2008: Proceedings of the 2008 International Conference on Computer Science and Information Technology, pp. 53–57. IEEE Computer Society, Washington, DC, USA (2008)
13. Ibraimi, L., Tang, Q., Hartel, P.H., Jonker, W.: A type-and-identity-based proxy re-encryption scheme and its application in healthcare. In: Jonker, W., Petković, M. (eds.) SDM 2008. LNCS, vol. 5159, pp. 185–198. Springer, Heidelberg (2008)
14. Free Software Foundation Inc. Mailman, the GNU Mailing List Manager, http://www.list.org/
15. Khurana, H., Hahm, H.-S.: Certified mailing lists. In: ASIACCS, pp. 46–58 (2006)
16. Khurana, H., Heo, J., Pant, M.: From proxy encryption primitives to a deployable secure-mailing-list solution. In: Ning, P., Qing, S., Li, N. (eds.) ICICS 2006. LNCS, vol. 4307, pp. 260–281. Springer, Heidelberg (2006)
17. Khurana, H., Slagell, A.J., Bonilla, R.: SELS: a secure e-mail list service. In: SAC, pp. 306–313 (2005)
18. Libert, B., Vergnaud, D.: Unidirectional chosen-ciphertext secure proxy re-encryption. In: Cramer, R. (ed.) PKC 2008. LNCS, vol. 4939, pp. 360–379. Springer, Heidelberg (2008)
19. Matsuo, T.: Proxy re-encryption systems for identity-based encryption. In: Takagi, T., Okamoto, T., Okamoto, E., Okamoto, T. (eds.) Pairing 2007. LNCS, vol. 4575, pp. 247–267. Springer, Heidelberg (2007)
20. Shao, J., Cao, Z.: CCA-secure proxy re-encryption without pairings. In: Jarecki, S., Tsudik, G. (eds.) PKC 2009. LNCS, vol. 5443, pp. 357–376. Springer, Heidelberg (2009)
21. Shao, J., Cao, Z., Liu, P.: SCCR: a generic approach to simultaneously achieve CCA security and collusion-resistance in proxy re-encryption. Security and Communication Networks (2), 1–16 (2009)
22. Tang, Q., Hartel, P.H., Jonker, W.: Inter-domain identity-based proxy re-encryption. In: Yung, M., Liu, P., Lin, D. (eds.) Inscrypt 2008. LNCS, vol. 5487, pp. 332–347. Springer, Heidelberg (2009)
23. Wang, L., Wang, L., Mambo, M., Okamoto, E.: New identity-based proxy re-encryption schemes to prevent collusion attacks. In: Joye, M., Miyaji, A., Otsuka, A. (eds.) Pairing 2010. LNCS, vol. 6487, pp. 327–346. Springer, Heidelberg (2010)

E-Voting: A New Approach Using Double-Blind Identity-Based Encryption*

David Gray and Caroline Sheedy

School of Computing, Dublin City University,
Glasnevin, Dublin 9, Ireland
{dgray,csheedy}@computing.dcu.ie

Abstract. We present a new cryptographic construction, double-blind identity-based encryption (DB-IBE). In standard IBE, the identity string that is passed to a key generation centre ($\mathcal{KGC}$) during the key extraction phase is visible to the $\mathcal{KGC}$. Recent work introduced the idea of blinding the identity string, resulting in a blind IBE scheme which obscures the identity string from a $\mathcal{KGC}$. Double-blind IBE schemes, which are extensions of blind IBE schemes, allow a user to construct an identity string that is partially obscured from the $\mathcal{KGC}$, while also facilitating the $\mathcal{KGC}$ adding elements to the identity string which are obscured from the user. Using DB-IBE, we present an e-voting scheme with desirable features such as universal verifiability, voter verifiability and receipt-freeness.

Keywords: identity-based encryption, electronic voting, blind identity-based encryption, double-blind identity-based encryption, designated confirmer signatures, voter verifiability, receipt-freeness.

1 Introduction

Democratic governments face the challenge of holding elections to appoint successors. Voting is a complex task, made more so by the conflict between the requirements of verifiability and secrecy. Voters and independent observers want to verify that the election process occurred correctly, and individual votes were recorded accurately. However, an individual must not be able to prove to a third party that she voted in a particular way.

A cryptographic voting scheme is an election system that provides mathematical proofs of the election results, with the aim of producing a secure and verifiable election. Electronic voting refers to both on-line voting, such as remote internet voting, and physical voting. Physical voting incorporates the use of direct recording electronic machines (DREs) in polling stations [22], and paper-based systems such as Scratch & Vote and Three Ballot [2,27]. E-voting has the potential to increase efficiency and accuracy of voting, and provide transparency in the voting process.

1.1 Desirable Properties

Elections are bound by criteria that reflect the characteristics required by legal principles. They must be universal and equal. Universal elections provide equal suffrage,

---

* The authors thank Science Foundation Ireland (SFI) for support under grant 08/RFP/CMS1347.

J. Camenisch and C. Lambrinoudakis (Eds.): EuroPKI 2010, LNCS 6711, pp. 93–108, 2011.

which is tantamount to access to voting for all. Equal elections count all ballots as having commensurate influence on the final election outcome. An e-voting scheme is also expected to satisfy a number of commonly accepted security criteria [2,3,15,14]. Typically, e-voting schemes should aspire to the following properties.

1. **Secrecy.** The way in which a voter casts her vote should not be revealed to the election authorities or any other party.
2. **Eligibility.** Every eligible voter should be able to vote, but at most, only once.
3. **Receipt-Freeness (Coercion Resistance).** A voter should not be able prove to a third party how she cast her vote.
4. **Voter Verifiability (Ballot Casting Assurance).** Each voter should be able to verify that her vote has been accurately cast and recorded.
5. **Universal Verifiability.** Any observer should be able to verify that the recorded tally of an election matches the published tally.
6. **Fairness**. No partial tally of results should be available during the election so as not to bias the election outcome.

In addition to these requirements, we assume that voting is to be carried out in a 'vote and go' manner. We also accept that vote manipulation [19] is part of an election process, and no attempt is made to prevent it.

1.2   Our Contribution

In this paper, we introduce a universally verifiable e-voting scheme that allows voter verifiability. Our system is auditable, and produces a paper receipt that allows a voter to check that their vote has been recorded accurately, while maintaining the property of receipt-freeness. *Note that we use the term "receipt-freeness" in its technical sense (see above) and not to mean that the voter does not obtain a receipt.*

Our scheme is intuitive for voters, as it mimics the traditional voting experience. Voters cast their ballots in the privacy of a voting booth. In place of a traditional ballot box, the booth contains a Ballot Construction Machine (BCM) for constructing a ballot paper and a Ballot Box Machine (BXM) for casting a ballot. The BCM accepts the voter's choice, constructs a ballot paper which is accepted by the voter and printed. The voter then casts her ballot paper by presenting it to the BXM. The BXM records the vote by appending it to a bulletin board, retains part of the ballot paper for auditing purposes and writes a receipt to the other part of the ballot paper, which is then returned to the voter.

Voter verifiability is achieved by having voters compare printed strings on their ballot paper when it is cast, and later by checking that printed strings on their receipt appear on a web site. We do not require voters to perform complex calculations, and the paper receipt allows a voter, but no one else, to verify that her vote has been correctly cast.

Our scheme relies on a novel cryptographic construction (*double-blind IBE*) which combines properties of blind signatures [7] with those of undeniable signatures [11]. In addition to these properties, our construction allows the key generating party to embed elements into the identity string, which distinguishes it from existing partially blind schemes. We use this construction as a signature scheme for our e-voting scheme to achieve the desired properties.

2   Preliminaries

2.1   Identity-Based Encryption

IBE was introduced by Shamir [30] in 1984 to allow some publicly known identity id of a recipient to be used as their public key. This allows anyone to encrypt a message for the recipient once they know this identity. The corresponding private key is generated by a trusted key generation centre ($\mathcal{KGC}$) who is given the identity string during a key extraction phase.

An IBE scheme consists of four polynomial time algorithms: Setup, Extract, Encrypt and Decrypt. Setup takes a security parameter k, and generates the $\mathcal{KGC}$'s public system parameters $params$ and a master secret key sk_m. Extract takes sk_m and an identity id, and generates the private key pk_{id} corresponding to id. Encrypt takes id, $params$ and a message m, and generates the ciphertext ct for the m. Decrypt takes the private key pk_{id} and a ciphertext ct, and decrypts ct using pk_{id} to retrieve the m. The majority of IBE schemes use groups with efficiently computable bilinear maps [5].

Definition 1. *Let $\mathbb{G}$ and $\mathbb{G}_T$ be groups of prime order p. A bilinear map $e : \mathbb{G} \times \mathbb{G} \rightarrow \mathbb{G}_T$ satisfies the following properties:*

(a) Bilinearity: *The map $e : \mathbb{G} \times \mathbb{G} \rightarrow \mathbb{G}_T$ is bilinear if $e(a^x, b^y) = e(a, b)^{xy}$.*
(b) Non-degeneracy: *for all generators $g \in \mathbb{G}$, e is non degenerate, that is $e(g, g) \neq 1$.*
(c) Efficiency: *e is efficiently computable.*

Definition 2 (Decisional BDH Problem (DBDH)). *Consider $g, g^a, g^b, g^c \in \mathbb{G}$, where g is a generator of $\mathbb{G}$, $a, b, c \in \mathbb{Z}_p$ and a value β is selected at random from $\{0, 1\}$. Let $z = e(g, g)^{abc}$ if $\beta = 1$ and let z be a random element from $\mathbb{G}_T$ otherwise. Given g, g^a, g^b, g^c, z output a guess β' of β. An algorithm has an advantage ϵ in solving DBDH if $\left| Pr[\beta' = \beta] - \frac{1}{2} \right| \geq \epsilon$.*

The security of our scheme is based on the assumption that the DBDH problem is hard.

3   Double-Blind Identity-Based Encryption

The property of *blinding* is most commonly associated with digital signature schemes where a signature for a message can be obtained without revealing the message to the signer. Recent work [6,20] has focused on blinding the key extraction protocol of IBE schemes. This allows a user to obtain a private key for an identity without revealing the identity or this private key to the $\mathcal{KGC}$. We propose using double-blind IBE (DB-IBE) as a means of achieving privacy for a user's id and public key pk_{id}, while still allowing the $\mathcal{KGC}$ to enforce certain restrictions on the public key id.

With a standard IBE scheme, a user $\mathcal{U}$ supplies the $\mathcal{KGC}$ with its identity id over an authenticated and confidential connection. The $\mathcal{KGC}$ generates the private key pk_{id} and returns it to $\mathcal{U}$. At the end of the key extraction, the $\mathcal{KGC}$ knows $\mathcal{U}$'s key-pair (id, pk_{id}), and $\mathcal{U}$ can check that the validity of pk_{id} by encrypting and decrypting some test message m.

With a blind IBE scheme [6,20], $\mathcal{U}$ sends $\overline{id}$ (a blinded version of id) to the $\mathcal{KGC}$ which then generates $\overline{pk_{id}}$ (a blinded version of pk_{id}) and returns it to $\mathcal{U}$. $\mathcal{U}$ can unblind this result to recover pk_{id} and can validate pk_{id} as with the standard IBE. However, at the end of the key extraction, the $\mathcal{KGC}$ does not know either id or pk_{id}, and cannot associate id or pk_{id} with this instance of the key extraction protocol should either become known to the $\mathcal{KGC}$ at a later stage. Of course, blind IBE cannot be used for normal public-key cryptography as a user can obtain the private key for any id of its choice.

With a double-blind IBE scheme, an id consists of the concatenation of three components id_1, id_2 and id_3, i.e., $id = id_1|id_2|id_3$. $\mathcal{U}$ selects id_1 and id_2, and sends $id_1, \overline{id_2}$ to the $\mathcal{KGC}$. The $\mathcal{KGC}$ selects id_3 and generates a blinded key $\overline{sk}_{id_1|id_2|id_3}$ which is returned to $\mathcal{U}$. $\mathcal{U}$ can unblind this result and recover the key $sk_{id_1|id_2|id_3}$. At the end of key extraction, the $\mathcal{KGC}$ knows id_1 and id_3, but not id_2 or $sk_{id_1|id_2|id_3}$. $\mathcal{U}$ knows id_1, id_2 and $sk_{id_1|id_2|id_3}$, but not id_3.

If required, during key extraction, the $\mathcal{KGC}$ can ensure that id_1 conforms to some specific format. Also, by using different values for id_3 for each key extraction, the $\mathcal{KGC}$ can associate $id = id_1|id_2|id_3$ and $sk_{id_1|id_2|id_3}$ with this instance of the key extraction protocol. However, if the same id_1 and id_3 are used for all extractions, then this association cannot be established.

At the end of key extraction, $\mathcal{U}$ does not know the complete id, and cannot check that $sk_{id_1|id_2|id_3}$ is a valid key by performing encryption and decryption. This problem can be overcome in our concrete scheme (see section 3.1), but since such a test is unnecessary with our proposed e-voting scheme, we do not present a solution here.

After key extraction, assuming that id_2 and id_3 cannot be guessed (e.g., they are large randomly selected values), it is computationally infeasible for anyone to perform encryption for the identity id. However, $\mathcal{U}$ and the $\mathcal{KGC}$ can selectively release id_2 and id_3 over time to allow encryption and decryption to be performed.

3.1   Our Concrete DB-IBE Scheme

Our DB-IBE scheme is based on the IBE scheme due to Naccache [23], which is an adaptation of a scheme due to Waters [31]. We follow the approach taken by Camenisch et al [6] and replace the Extract algorithm with an interactive key issuing protocol between $\mathcal{U}$ and the $\mathcal{KGC}$ as follows:

$$\mathsf{DoubleBlindExtract}(\mathcal{U}(params, id_1, id_2), \mathcal{KGC}(params, sk_m, id_3)) \rightarrow (pk_{id}, id_1)$$

where $\mathcal{U}$ has inputs $params$, id_1 and id_2 and receives output pk_{id}, and the $\mathcal{KGC}$ has inputs $params$, sk_m and id_3 and receives output id_1. Neither party receives or can compute any other new information. Our DB-IBE scheme uses the same Setup, Encrypt and Decrypt algorithms as Naccache's scheme, but to aid understanding we reproduce Naccache's Setup and Extract algorithms here.

Let $\mathbb{G}$ and $\mathbb{G}_T$ be groups of prime order p, and $e : \mathbb{G} \times \mathbb{G} \to \mathbb{G}_T$ be a bilinear map. Let g be a generator of $\mathbb{G}$. Identities are represented as n dimensional vectors $v = (v_1, \ldots, v_n)$ where each v_i is an ℓ-bit integer. Note that the components v_i can be obtained by using a collision-resistant hash function on longer bit strings.

Setup: Pick $\alpha \in \mathbb{Z}_p$ and $g \in \mathbb{G}$ at random, and let $g_1 = g^\alpha$. Pick $u' \in \mathbb{G}$ and the n dimensional vector $U = (u_1, \ldots, u_n)$ at random. The public parameters $params$ are g, g_1, g_2, u' and U. The master secret key sk_m is g_2^α, and α is kept secret or destroyed.

Extract: Let id be the vector $v = (v_1, \ldots, v_n) \in (\{0,1\}^\ell)^n$. Pick $r \in \mathbb{Z}_p$ at random. The private key pk_{id} is d_{id} given by:

$$d_{id} = \left(g_2^\alpha \left(u' \prod_{i=1}^{n} u_i^{v_i}\right)^r, g^r\right) \tag{1}$$

The expression $\prod_{i=1}^{n} u_i^{v_i}$ is essentially a hash function that maps the id to an element of $\mathbb{G}$. We will call this the Waters' hash function. Note that, as expected, the Waters' hash function is also used in the encryption algorithm [23].

Our DB-IBE scheme is identical to Naccache's scheme, except that we divide the vector v into three parts corresponding to id_1, id_2 and id_3. Given l and m such that $1 \leq l < m < n$, then id_1 is encoded as $v_1, \ldots, v_l$, id_2 as $v_{l+1}, \ldots, v_m$ and id_3 as $v_{m+1}, \ldots, v_n$. It is easy to show that

$$\prod_{i=1}^{n} u_i^{v_i} = \left(\prod_{i=1}^{l} u_i^{v_i}\right) \left(\prod_{i=l+1}^{m} u_i^{v_i}\right) \left(\prod_{i=m+1}^{n} u_i^{v_i}\right)$$

and thus it is possible to compute the Waters' hash of id from the hashes of its individual components.

Using this split representation, we can implement DoubleBlindExtract to generate keys that are compatible with Naccache's scheme.

DoubleBlindExtract:

1. Given id_1 and id_2, $\mathcal{U}$ constructs an m dimensional vector $v = (v_1, \ldots, v_m)$ using the representation given above. $\mathcal{U}$ picks $\beta, y \in \mathbb{Z}_p$ uniformly at random and constructs the n dimensional vector $\overrightarrow{v}$ such that:

$$\overrightarrow{v} = \begin{cases} (u_i^\beta, v_i) & \text{if } 1 \leq i \leq l \\ \perp & \text{if } l < i \leq m \\ u_i^\beta & \text{if } m < i \leq n \end{cases}$$

$\mathcal{U}$ computes $X = (g^{\beta y} u'^\beta \prod_{i=l+1}^{m} u_i^{\beta v_i})$ and sends $(X, \overrightarrow{v}, g^\beta, u'^\beta)$ to $\mathcal{KGC}$. $\mathcal{U}$ can prove to the $\mathcal{KGC}$ that it knows y, β and $v_{l+1}, \ldots, v_m$ using zero-knowledge proofs as outlined in [25].

2. The $\mathcal{KGC}$ chooses random $r \in \mathbb{Z}_p$ and constructs $d'_{id} = (d'_1, d'_2)$ as

$$d'_{id} = \left(g_2^\alpha \left(\prod_{i=1}^{l} u_i^{\beta v_i}\right)^r X^r \left(\prod_{i=m+1}^{n} u_i^{\beta v_i}\right)^r, g^{\beta r}\right)$$

$$= \left(g_2^\alpha g^{\beta y r} \left(u' \prod_{i=1}^{n} u_i^{v_i}\right)^{\beta r}, g^{\beta r}\right)$$

The $\mathcal{KGC}$ also computes $f = \left(\prod_{i=m+1}^{n} u_i^{v_i}\right)^r$ and passes d'_{id} and f to $\mathcal{U}$. The value f allows $\mathcal{U}$ to check that the key is correctly constructed by performing the test:

$$e(g_1, g_2) \cdot e\left(d'_2, g^y u' \prod_{i=1}^{m} u_i^{v_i}\right) \cdot e(g^\beta, f) = e(g, d'_1). \tag{2}$$

3. If the test passes, $\mathcal{U}$ chooses random $z \in \mathbb{Z}_p$ and computes $d_{id} = (d_1, d_2)$ as

$$d_{id} = \left(d_1'/(d_2')^y \cdot (u' \prod_{i=1}^{n} u_i^{v_i})^z, d_1' \cdot g^z\right) \tag{3}$$

$$= \left(g_2^\alpha (u' \prod_{i=1}^{n} u_i^{v_i})^{\beta r + z}, g^{\beta r + z}\right) \tag{4}$$

If the test fails, $\mathcal{U}$ outputs $\bot$ and aborts. Note that the structure of the LHS of equation (1) is the same as a (4) with r replaced by $\beta r + z$. Also note that the $\mathcal{KGC}$ does not know d_1 or d_2.

3.2 Security

Naccache's IBE scheme [23] is semantically secure against passive adversaries (IND-ID-CPA) [5]. This remains the case with our DB-IBE scheme provided the double-blind key extraction protocol is secure.

Following the work of Green and Hohenberger [20], given an IBE scheme with a blinded extraction protocol, secure blindness is achieved by satisfying two properties: *leak-freeness* and *selective-failure blindness*.

1. **Leak-freeness** requires that DoubleBlindExtract is a secure two-party computation that does not leak any more information to $\mathcal{U}$ than Extract.
2. **Selective-failure blindness** requires that a potentially malicious authority does not learn anything about the user's identity during the DoubleBlindExtract protocol. Also, the authority cannot cause the algorithm DoubleBlindExtract to selectively fail depending on the user's choice of identity.

Double-blind IBE schemes require that the user applying for a private key does not know the full corresponding public key $id = id_1|id_2|id_3$. We capture this requirement by introducing the concept of Ciphertext Awareness (CTA).

3. **Ciphertext Awareness** is a requirement that a decrypting entity can only produce a *valid* plaintext by applying the decryption algorithm with her private key to a ciphertext encrypted using the corresponding public key.

Definition 3 (Secure Double-Blinded IBE).
A DB-IBE scheme is secure if and only if: (1) the underlying IBE scheme is secure, (2) DoubleBlindExtract is leak-free and selective-failure double-blind, and (3) the resulting scheme is ciphertext aware.

3.3 Convertible, Designated Confirmer Signature Scheme Using DB-IBE

Undeniable signatures, proposed by Chaum and van Antwerpen [11], are digital signatures that cannot be verified without interacting with the signer. This property is useful in situations such as e-voting, where the ease of copying and universal verification of traditional signatures is not desirable. A verifier must be unable to distinguish between a valid and an invalid signature without entering into the verifying protocol with the signer. Numerous undeniable signature schemes have been presented [8,17,18].

In certain applications, a signer can also specify by whom his signatures may be verified. This concept is known as *designated confirmer signatures* [9]. Such schemes address a potential weakness of undeniable signature schemes which are not verifiable if the signer becomes unavailable for some reason, or refuses to cooperate. A *convertible undeniable signature* scheme is one in which the signer can convert an undeniable signature into a universally verifiable signature.

Using the double-blind IBE scheme presented above, we describe a new convertible, designated confirmer signature scheme. Here, the $\mathcal{KGC}$ acts as the signer, $\mathcal{U}$ as the signature recipient and the verifier $\mathcal{V}$ as a designated third party.

Our signature scheme is based on Naor's observation that any IBE scheme can be converted into a signature scheme. In the resulting signature scheme, the master secret key sk_m of the IBE scheme is used as the private key and the global system parameters *params* as the public key. To sign a message m, we treat m as an identity string and m's signature σ is the IBE private key for this identity. To verify a signature, we choose a random m' and encrypt m' with the IBE scheme using m as the public key. Then we attempt to decrypt using the signature σ, and if the decryption computes correctly, the signature is valid; otherwise the signature is invalid.

Our signature scheme consists of three polynomial time algorithms: Setup, Sign and Verify.

Setup: The $\mathcal{KGC}$ executes the DB-IBE Setup algorithm and publishes the public parameters *params* as its public key.

Sign: To sign a message m, $\mathcal{U}$ first represents m as id_1 and id_2. Depending on the context, one or other of id_1 and id_2 may be null. This allows $\mathcal{U}$ to reveal some, all or none of m to the $\mathcal{KGC}$. $\mathcal{U}$ then uses the DB-IBE DoubleBlindExtract protocol to obtain the DB-IBE private key pk_{id} for the identity $id = id_1|id_2|id_3$. This key is now the signature σ for the message m. Note that $\mathcal{U}$ does not know id_3 and cannot determine if σ is a signature for m, as without knowledge of the full $id = id_1|id_2|id_3$, it is impossible to construct a ciphertext to verify the signature.

Verify: To verify that σ is a valid signature for m, $\mathcal{U}$ passes id_2, σ and m to $\mathcal{V}$, who has received id_3 from the $\mathcal{KGC}$. $\mathcal{V}$ constructs the full identity $id = id_1|id_2|id_3$ and using the DB-IBE Encrypt algorithm, produces ciphertext ct for some random message m'. Using the DB-IBE Decrypt algorithm with σ as the private key, $\mathcal{V}$ checks that ct decrypts to m'. Note that while the $\mathcal{KGC}$ can act as a verifier, this would require $\mathcal{U}$ to reveal id_2 to the $\mathcal{KGC}$. Also note that the $\mathcal{KGC}$ can convert a signature σ into a universally verifiable signature by making id_3 public.

4   Our E-Voting Scheme

In the following discussion we assume that there are n candidates, that each candidate will receive N *dummy votes* (see below) and that the total number of cast votes on the bulletin board at the end of the election is M.

4.1 The Principals

Our e-voting scheme has five principals: the Voting Authority (VA), the Ballot Constructor (BC), the Ballot Box (BX), the bulletin board Operator (BD) and the Vote Seeder
(VS). Each principal is an independent, trusted party.

VA: The rôle of the voting authority is to sign ballots on behalf of the BC and VS, and
therefore, it performs the rôle of the signer ($\mathcal{KGC}$) in our designated confirmer signature
scheme. Before the election, the VA performs Setup and publishes $params$ as its public
key. A ballot will consist of three components corresponding to id_1, id_2 and id_3 of our
designated confirmer signature scheme. The name of the election will be represented as
id_1, and id_3 will be a secret value selected by the VA. It is possible to have multiple
names (e.g., one per polling station), but in our description we will assume there is only
one name used for all ballots. A voters choice $\mathcal{V}$ will be concatenated with a random
value $\mathcal{R}$ to produce the value $id_2 = \mathcal{V}|\mathcal{R}$.

The VA will make id_3 available to the BX and BD at the start of the election, and at the
end of the election the VA will publish id_3.

BC: The ballot constructor interacts with voters to elicit their votes and have their ballots signed by the VA. After obtaining a voters choice $\mathcal{V}$, the BC selects $\mathcal{R}$ at random to
construct $id_2 = \mathcal{V}|\mathcal{R}$ and obtains a signature $\sigma_{id_1|id_2|id_3}$ for $id_1|id_2|id_3$ from the VA.
We will represent a *ballot* as a tuple $(id_1, id_2, \sigma_{id_1|id_2|id_3})$, or simply as (id_1, id_2, σ).
A ballot is *valid* if the signature σ is valid. Note that a ballot can only be validated by
entities knowing id_3.

BX: The ballot box checks that ballots produced by the BC are valid and passes them
to the BD to be recorded, i.e., when a voter supplies a ballot $(id_1, \mathcal{V}|\mathcal{R}, \sigma)$, the BX val-
idates the signature σ, and if it is valid, sends the ballot to the BD to be recorded.

The BX is also responsible for supplying each voter with a list containing one valid
ballot for each candidate in the election. Once a voter's ballot has been validated and
recorded, the BD supplies the BX with a list $(b_1, \ldots, b_{n-1})$ of ballots picked uniformly
at random from its database, one for each candidate not chosen by the voter. The BX
checks that this list is correctly structured and that each ballot is valid. The ballots are
then supplied to the voter; see section 4.4 for more details on how this information is
presented to the voter.

BD: The bulletin board operator is responsible for maintaining a database of valid ballots and publishing these ballots (in random order) at the end of the election.

Before the election starts, the VA, VS and BD interact to create N valid *dummy ballots*
for each candidate in the election and place them in the BD's database; see section 4.3.
These dummy ballots are used to bootstrap the process of supplying valid ballots to the
BX as described above. Dummy ballots and real ballots are both published at the end of
the election, but the tally for a candidate is the number of valid ballots on the bulletin

board for that candidate minus N. The BD makes no distinction between dummy and real ballots.

The BD ensures that all ballots placed in the database are valid.

VS: Before the election starts, the vote seeder creates N dummy ballots for each candidate and submits them to the BD to be recorded. Each ballot is signed by the VA; see section 4.3.

4.2   Hardware and Software

The VA and BD are implemented as centralized servers, and the VS as an application that communicates with both the VA and BD over the Internet. The BC and BX are implemented as multiple *ballot construction machines* (BCMs) and *ballot box machines* (BXMs) which are located in polling stations. The BCMs communicate with the VA over the Internet and have a one-way, paper-based communication with BXMs using ballot papers. The BXMs communicate with the BD over the Internet.

The VA distributes id_3 to the BD and BXMs using a one-way communication, possibly over the Internet.

The implementations of the VA, BD, VS, BC and BX are owned, developed and deployed by different trusted parties. All Internet connections are authenticated and confidential based on standard technology such as TSL/SSL.

4.3   Initialization and Vote Seeding

Before an election starts, the VA must generate its key-pair and the BD's database must be seeded with N dummy ballots per candidate. This is achieved by the VA, VS and BD interacting as follows:

1. The VA performs the Setup of our designator confirmer signature scheme and publishes *params* as its public key.
2. The VA picks a value for id_3 and shares it with the BD.
3. The VA is setup to sign at most $n \times N$ ballots from the VS.
4. The VS generates N ballots for each of the n candidates and obtains $n \times N$ signatures from the VA.
5. The VS sends the $n \times N$ ballots to the BD.
6. The BD ensures that each ballot is valid and that there are N ballots for each candidate.
7. The BD initializes its database with these $n \times N$ ballots.
8. The VA confirms that $n \times N$ signatures were produced for the VS and the BD confirms that its database was correctly initialized.
9. If the seeding process fails for any reason, the process is re-run from step 2.

4.4   The Voter Experience

To vote, a voter follows the following steps at a polling station.

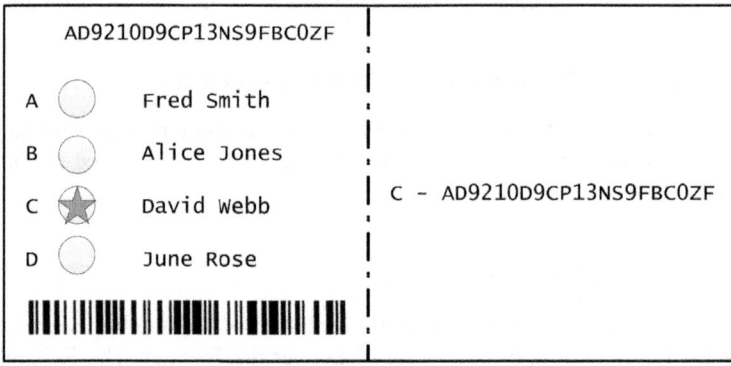

Fig. 1. Ballot Paper Construction

1. The voter presents her credentials to an official, and if they are acceptable, she is given a blank ballot paper and allowed access to a BCM. The blank ballot paper has no markings that would identify the voter.
2. Using the BCM, she enters her choice of candidate. This process will allow the voter time to look at her vote on a display and if necessary, allow her to change her choice.
3. Once the voter is satisfied with her displayed choice, she gives the BCM permission to generate a ballot and have it signed by the VA. This results in a ballot $(id_1, \mathcal{V}|\mathcal{R}, \sigma)$.
4. The BCM then prints a copy of the voter's ballot onto her ballot paper; see Figure 1. This ballot paper is in two halves separated by vertical perforations. On the LHS, from top to bottom the following are printed:
   (a) The signature σ.
   (b) A list of candidates labelled A, B,. . . with the voter's selection marked.
   (c) The random value $\mathcal{R}$ encoded using a barcode to prevent the voter from memorizing some or all of the value.
   On the RHS the letter corresponding to the voters choice and the signature σ are printed.
5. The voter examines the ballot, checking that the signatures σ is the same on both sides and that the correct candidate has been marked.
6. If the voter is unhappy with the ballot paper, she can take it to an official who will put into a sealed *discarded ballot papers* box. The voter can return to step 2 and repeat the process.
7. The voter is now given access to the BXM to cast her vote.
8. The BXM reads the two copies of the signature σ, the random value $\mathcal{R}$, the voters choice $\mathcal{V}$ and the list of candidates. The BXM ensures that the two copies of the signature match and that the candidates appear in the correct order. This requires optical character recognition. The BXM then reconstructs the ballot $(id_1, \mathcal{V}|\mathcal{R}, \sigma)$ and validates its signature. If there are any problems the BXM rejects the ballot paper. Again, an official places the problem ballot paper into the *discarded ballot papers* box, and the voter returns to step 2.

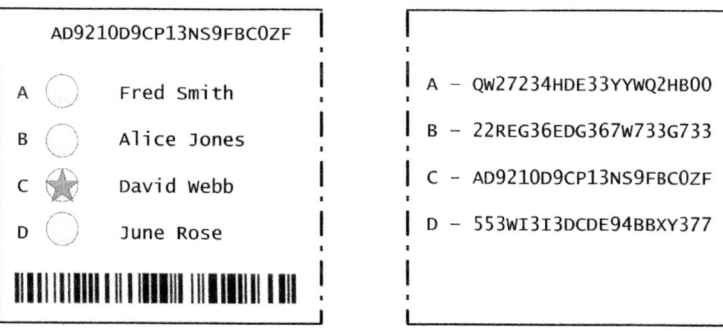

Fig. 2. Cast Ballot Paper

9. The BXM submits the ballot to the BD and in return, gets a list of valid ballots for the other candidates. The signatures for these ballots are printed on the RHS of the ballot paper as shown in Figure 2.
10. The BXM divides the ballot paper into its two parts. The RHS is returned to the voter as a receipt and the LHS is retained for auditing purposes.

4.5   Timeline for an Election

The security of our voting system requires certain information to be kept secret; either for all time or for some period of time during the election.

The VA should keep its private key secret for all time. In addition, while it must share the secret value id_3 with the BD and BX at the start of the election, id_3 must otherwise be kept secret while polling stations remain open. However, after the polling stations have closed and no more voting is allowed, id_3 must be made public so that cast ballots can be validated.

Neither the VS nor BD should ever reveal which ballots are dummies.

The BD must keep its database of cast votes secret during the election. When the polling stations are closed, the BD must publish all valid ballots (in random order) on a publicly accessible bulletin board. While the BD does not publish the entire database while polling is still active, it does release the signatures of ballots so that they can be printed on receipts given to voters. If an attacker is able to gather a sufficient number of receipts, then he may be able estimate the number of ballots cast for each candidate by counting signatures that are repeated on receipts. It is unlikely that such an attack would be any more accurate than exit polls at predicting the outcome of the election. However, the probability of this attack succeeding can be reduced by increasing N, the number of dummy ballots issued for each candidate. In fact, we can always make N sufficiently large so that each receipt links to n unique votes.

4.6   Post-Election Verification and Auditing

The following verification steps and auditing can be performed after the list of cast ballots has been published on the bulletin board.

1. Anyone with access to the bulletin board can check that all published ballots are valid and they can tally the ballots to compute the outcome of the election.

2. A voter can check that her vote has been correctly recorded on the bulletin board by searching for her ballot using its signature on her receipt. However, since all signatures on her receipt will have corresponding ballots on the bulletin board, there is no way that she can prove to a third party which way she voted.

3. The VS can check that all the dummy ballots generated during initialization have been included on the bulletin board.

4. Each polling station keeps a record of the number of ballot papers issued to voters and the number of ballot papers rejected. The difference between these counts gives the number of valid votes for the polling station and summing the number of valid votes over all polling stations should give a value approximately equal to $M-n \times N$. This test is only approximate, as a certain level of human error can be expected.

5. Each discarded ballot paper can be inspected to determine if it was arbitrarily discarded by the voter or if it is evidence of fraud.

6. The BX will have the LHS of every ballot paper cast during the election. A count of these ballot papers should (very accurately) approximate $M- n \times N$. A selection, or all of these ballot papers can be checked to ensure that they are correctly recorded on the bulletin board. If necessary, it would be possible to recompute the outcome of the election from these receipts. Note however, that they cannot be used to reconstruct the bulletin board as they do not contain the dummy votes.

4.7 Security Properties

In section 1.1 we introduce desirable security properties for an e-voting scheme. In this section we give informal justifications for claiming that our e-voting scheme has these properties.

1. **Secrecy**. The voter's identity and credentials are verified outside of the voting booth, and once inside the booth, the voter is anonymous as nothing is required by the BCM or BXM that distinguishes one individual voter from another.

2. **Eligibility**. As with traditional elections, a voter gains access to the voting booth only once and as each booth may record only one vote per reset by an election official, a voter will have at most one vote.

3. **Receipt-Freeness (Coercion Resistance).** Despite holding a receipt with sufficient information to convince herself that her vote was correctly cast, a voter does not hold sufficient information to prove to a third party how she voted as the receipt contains one valid vote per candidate. Of course, if the order in which the ballots on her receipt were cast can be determined, then with a high probability, the last ballot cast would be her vote. This attack is prevented by only publishing the bulletin board (in random order) at the end of the election.

4. **Voter Verifiability (Ballot Casting Assurance).** After the polling stations close, a voter can use her receipt to verify that the unique signature for her ballot appears on the bulletin board and that the ballot is for the candidate of her choice.

5. **Universal Verifiability**. After the election, using the bulletin board, an observer can be assured that all ballots are valid and the published tally equates to the votes as recorded on the bulletin board.

6. **Fairness.** The property of fairness is achieved by ensuring the bulletin board is not published until the end of the election.

Of course, the security of our scheme depends on the principals behaving properly. While we assume that the VA, VS, BC, BX and BD are trusted parties, we still have security mechanisms and checks in place to prevent or detect errant behaviour. Space does not permit all of these checks and mechanisms to be described, but the following are some examples.

1. The VA signs ballots in which the chosen candidate is blinded. So the VA cannot produce information on the numbers of votes for each candidate before the bulletin board is published. The VA could construct and sign its own ballots, but would need to collude with another principal to (for example) have these placed on the bulletin board. However, this would be detected as the number of physical ballot papers would not be consistent with the final tally.
2. The VA ensures that the VS can only sign $n \times N$ ballots and the BD ensures that its database is seeded with exactly N ballots for each candidate. After the bulletin board has been published, the VS can check that all of its $n \times N$ ballots appear on the bulletin board. In addition, since the VS is restricted to obtaining exactly $n \times N$ signatures, it does not have any additional signed ballots that could be used to prove that the BD did not publish one of the dummy ballots. In fact, the only other source of signed ballots for VS is the bulletin board and these cannot be used to discredit the BD.
3. The BC can request and obtain as many signed ballots as it desires, but is constrained, by the number of physical ballot papers, to use only signed ballots approved by a voter. In particular, since it cannot communicate directly over the Internet with the BX or BD, there is no way other signed ballots can reach the bulletin board. If the BC colludes with the BX or BD by sending other votes by another channel, this will be detected by the discrepancy between the number of ballots on the bulletin board and the number of physical ballot papers.
4. For the BX the only source of signed ballots are the physical ballot papers, and for the BD the only sources are the VS and BX. Any attempt by the BX or BD to discard signed ballots will be detectable by the verification performed by voters and the VS.

5   Conclusion

There are many secure e-voting schemes based on blind signatures [16,29,24], homomorphic encryption [4,13] or anonymous channels, such as mixnets [12,21]. To address the apparent contradiction between secrecy and transparency, some authors [10,28,27,2,26] have included voter verifiability (ballot casting assurance) [1] by introducing a physical ballot paper, part or all of which can be used as a receipt. With these schemes, the voter leaves the polling station with a paper receipt that she can use to check that her vote has been properly cast and recorded. Of course, to maintain receipt-freeness (coercion resistance), this receipt should not allow the voter to prove to a third party how she voted.

In [10], Chaum uses visual cryptography to print a ballot on two layers of transparent material such that the natural language text of the vote is visible if these two layers are aligned and viewed in front of a light source. However, when separated, each layer contains a random pattern of dots that reveals no information about the vote cast. After voting, the voter takes one of these layers as a receipt and the other is destroyed. With Prêt à Voter [28], Scratch& Vote [2] and PunchScan [26], a ballot paper also consists of two parts; either two columns [28,2] or two layers [26]. Together, these parts contain all the information about the vote cast, but when the ballot paper is cast, the voter only retains one part, which by itself, does not reveal her vote. For example, with Prêt à Voter a ballot paper has two aligned columns, the LHS being the list of candidates in random order and the RHS a mark indicating the voter's choice. The RHS acts as a receipt, but without the corresponding LHS, the voter's choice cannot be determined. After an election a voter can check that her vote has been correctly cast by checking that her receipt appears on a bulletin board.

With these schemes, tallying is performed using mixnets in which the individual receipts are decrypted and shuffled via a number of mixes. The result is a list of plaintext votes that can be published and tallied. While this process may be provably secure, the voter is given no direct assurance that her vote has been counted as cast.

Like Prêt à Voter, our scheme uses a two column ballot paper and the RHS is used as a receipt. However, rather than having a receipt that reveals nothing about the vote cast, we have a receipt that links to one plaintext ballot per candidate on the bulletin board. This gives the voter direct assurance that her vote has been tallied as cast.

We have presented a new e-voting scheme that provides a familiar experience for voters. We believe that our scheme adheres to commonly accepted security criteria for electronic elections, as well as ballot casting assurance, but more work is needed to formally verify the security of our scheme. A novel contribution is the recording of the votes cast on a public bulletin board in plaintext which provides a simple, direct method for voter verification.

As a receipt must contain an example of every possible vote, our scheme is only suitable for *first past the post* elections. More work is required to adapt our scheme to other voting systems such as proportional representation.

References

1. Adida, B., Neff, C.A.: Ballot casting assurance. In: EVT 2006, Proceedings of the First Usenix/ACCURATE Electronic Voting Technology Workshop, Vancouver, BC, Canada, August 1 (2006)
2. Adida, B., Rivest, R.L.: Scratch & vote: self-contained paper-based cryptographic voting. In: Proceedings of the 5th ACM Workshop on Privacy in Electronic Society, pp. 29–40. ACM, New York (2006)
3. Anane, R., Freeland, R., Theodoropoulos, G.: e-Voting Requirements and Implementation. In: The 9th IEEE International Conference on E-Commerce Technology and the 4th IEEE International Conference on Enterprise Computing, E-Commerce, and E-Services, CEC/EEE 2007, pp. 382–392 (2007)
4. Benaloh, J., Tuinstra, D.: Receipt-free secret-ballot elections (extended abstract). In: Proceedings of the Twenty-Sixth Annual ACM Symposium on Theory of Computing, pp. 544–553. ACM, New York (1994)
5. Boneh, D., Franklin, M.: Identity-based encryption from the weil pairing. In: Kilian, J. (ed.) CRYPTO 2001. LNCS, vol. 2139, pp. 213–229. Springer, Heidelberg (2001)

6. Camenisch, J., Kohlweiss, M., Rial, A., Sheedy, C.: Blind and anonymous identity-based encryption and authorised private searches on public key encrypted data. In: Jarecki, S., Tsudik, G. (eds.) PKC 2009. LNCS, vol. 5443, pp. 196–214. Springer, Heidelberg (2009)

7. Chaum, D.: Blind signatures for untraceable payments. In: Proceedings of Advances in Cryptology (CRYPTO 1983). LNCS, vol. 82, pp. 23–25 (1982)

8. Chaum, D.: Zero-knowledge undeniable signatures. In: Damgård, I.B. (ed.) EUROCRYPT 1990. LNCS, vol. 473, pp. 458–464. Springer, Heidelberg (1991)

9. Chaum, D.: Designated confirmer signatures. In: De Santis, A. (ed.) EUROCRYPT 1994. LNCS, vol. 950, pp. 86–91. Springer, Heidelberg (1995)

10. Chaum, D.: Secret-ballot receipts: True voter-verifiable elections. IEEE Security & Privacy Magazine 2(1), 38–47 (2004)

11. Chaum, D., van Antwerpen, H.: Undeniable signatures. In: Brassard, G. (ed.) CRYPTO 1989. LNCS, vol. 435, pp. 212–216. Springer, Heidelberg (1990)

12. Chaum, D.L.: Untraceable electronic mail, return addresses, and digital pseudonyms. Communications of the ACM 24(2), 84–90 (1981)

13. Cramer, R., Gennaro, R., Schoenmakers, B.: A secure and optimally efficient multi-authority election scheme. In: Fumy, W. (ed.) EUROCRYPT 1997. LNCS, vol. 1233, pp. 103–118. Springer, Heidelberg (1997)

14. Delaune, S., Kremer, S., Ryan, M.: Verifying Properties of Electronic-Voting Protocols. In: Proceedings of the IAVoSS Workshop On Trustworthy Elections (WOTE 2006), pp. 45–52 (2006)

15. Dini, G.: A secure and available electronic voting service for a large-scale distributed system. Future Generation Computer Systems 19(1), 69–85 (2003)

16. Fujioka, A., Okamoto, T., Ohta, K.: A practical secret voting scheme for large scale elections. In: Zheng, Y., Seberry, J. (eds.) AUSCRYPT 1992. LNCS, vol. 718, pp. 244–251. Springer, Heidelberg (1993)

17. Galbraith, S., Mao, W., Paterson, K.G.: RSA-based undeniable signatures for general moduli. In: Preneel, B. (ed.) CT-RSA 2002. LNCS, vol. 2271, pp. 200–217. Springer, Heidelberg (2002)

18. Gennaro, R., Krawczyk, H., Rabin, T.: RSA-Based Undeniable Signatures. In: Kaliski Jr., B.S. (ed.) CRYPTO 1997. LNCS, vol. 1294, pp. 132–149. Springer, Heidelberg (1997)

19. Gibbard, A.: Manipulation of Voting Schemes: A General Result. Econometrica 41(4), 587–601 (1973)

20. Green, M., Hohenberger, S.: Blind identity-based encryption and simulatable oblivious transfer. In: Kurosawa, K. (ed.) ASIACRYPT 2007. LNCS, vol. 4833, pp. 265–282. Springer, Heidelberg (2007)

21. Hirt, M., Sako, K.: Efficient receipt-free voting based on homomorphic encryption. In: Preneel, B. (ed.) EUROCRYPT 2000. LNCS, vol. 1807, pp. 539–556. Springer, Heidelberg (2000)

22. Moynihan, D.P.: Building Secure Elections: E-Voting, Security, and Systems Theory. Public Administration Review 64(5), 515–528 (2004)

23. Naccache, D.: Secure and practical identity-based encryption. IET Image Processing 1(2), 59–64 (2007)

24. Okamoto, T.: Receipt-free electronic voting schemes for large scale elections. In: Christianson, B., Lomas, M. (eds.) Security Protocols 1997. LNCS, vol. 1361, pp. 25–35. Springer, Heidelberg (1998)

25. Okamoto, T.: Efficient blind and partially blind signatures without random oracles. In: Halevi, S., Rabin, T. (eds.) TCC 2006. LNCS, vol. 3876, pp. 80–99. Springer, Heidelberg (2006)

26. Popoveniuc, S., Hosp, B.: An Introduction to Punchscan (2006) (unpublished draft),
    `http://punchscan.org/papers/`
    `popoveniuc_hosp_punchscan_introduction.pdf`
27. Rivest, R.L.: The ThreeBallot voting system (2006) (unpublished draft),
    `http://theory.lcs.mit.edu/ rivest/`
    `Rivest-TheThreeBallotVotingSystem.pdf`
28. Ryan, P.Y.A., Bismark, D., Heather, J., Schneider, S., Xia, Z.: Prêt à Voter: a Voter-Verifiable
    Voting System. Trans. Info. For. Sec. 4(4), 662–673 (2009)
29. Sako, K.: Electronic voting scheme allowing open objection to the tally. IEICE Transactions on Fundamentals of Electronics, Communications and Computer Sciences 77(1), 24–30 (1994)
30. Shamir, A.: Identity-based cryptosystems and signature schemes. In: Blakely, G.R., Chaum, D. (eds.) CRYPTO 1984. LNCS, vol. 196, pp. 47–53. Springer, Heidelberg (1985)
31. Waters, B.: Efficient identity-based encryption without random oracles. In: Cramer, R. (ed.) EUROCRYPT 2005. LNCS, vol. 3494, pp. 114–127. Springer, Heidelberg (2005)

BBox: A Distributed Secure Log Architecture

Rafael Accorsi

Department of Telematics
University of Freiburg, Germany
accorsi@iig.uni-freiburg.de

Abstract. This paper presents BBox, a digital black box to provide for authentic archiving in distributed systems. Based upon public key cryptography and trusted computing platforms, the BBox employs standard primitives to ensure the authenticity of records during the transmission from devices to the collector, as well as during their storage on the collector and retrieval by auditors. Besides presenting the technical underpinnings of the BBox, this paper demonstrates the authenticity guarantees it ensures and reports on the preliminary deployment figures.

Keywords: Distributed log architecture, public key cryptography.

1 Introduction

The growing number of national and international compliance requirements emphasizes the importance archiving of business processes transactions, where records are analyzed as part of an audit to corroborate or refute potential violations of compliance rules [7]. To this end, authentic records are essential to guarantee reliable accountability and non-repudiation of actions [19].

While the demand for digital black boxes as a means to guarantee the authenticity of records is evident [21], to-date this is realized with ordinary logging services that record log file entries for the events happening in the system. These services alone are not sufficient for sound authenticity guarantees [20]. Although several proposals for secure logging services exist, none of them ensures sufficient authenticity guarantees for both log data in transit and at rest and, at the same time, allow the selective disclosure of records to auditors [5].

This paper presents BBox, a digital black box to provide for authentic system records in distributed systems. Authenticity means on the one hand the *integrity* of records and, on the other, their *confidentiality*. While integrity is an indisputable requirement, the importance of confidentiality stems largely from the context within which the BBox is employed. Generally, it is simply unreasonable to store entries in clear, even though this complicates the log files search [28]. For these requirements, the BBox addresses the collection, the transmission, the storage and the retrieval of records. Among others, the BBox guarantees:

- *Reliable data origin.* Only events sent by authorized devices are recorded in log files. Provenance information is stored in log entries for further investigation as a kind of hearsay statement, ensuring liability and accountability.

J. Camenisch and C. Lambrinoudakis (Eds.): EuroPKI 2010, LNCS 6711, pp. 109–124, 2011.

- *Tamper-evident storage.* Through the use of hash chains, log entries are stored in a way that tampering attempts, such as adding counterfeit entries or modifying the payload of legitimate entries, can be detected by a verifier.
- *Encrypted records.* Records are not stored in clear-text, but encrypted with a unique, evolving key, thereby providing for *forward secrecy*: if an attacker surreptitiously obtains the key of some entry, this attacker cannot deduce the keys used to encrypt the previous entries [6].
- *Keyword-based retrieval of records.* Despite the encryption of entries, the BBox allows for simple keyword searches for log entries, thereby generating the so-called "log views". In doing so, the retrieval solely requires the decryption of entries matching with the keyword. This not only reduces the cost of log view generation, it also enforces that only the necessary information is disclosed to auditors, acting thereby as an access control mechanism.

The BBox builds upon public key cryptography and trusted computing modules to ensure the authenticity of log records in distributed systems. It is being deployed as a component of a business process management system (BPMS) to guarantee authentic archiving during the workflow execution in a service-oriented architecture. To this end, the workflow specification language is slightly extended with tags to define the service-side devices empowered to communicate events to the BBox (residing at the BPMS). Tis realization of the BBox builds upon standard protocols for web services communication and workflow execution, addressing the criteria in [9]. The following presents the high-level cryptographic building blocks, not their particular implementation details in the BPMS.

This paper is organized as follows. §2 builds the core of the paper, presenting the architecture, components and operation of the BBox. §3 addresses the retrieval of log views. §4 reports on the security analysis of the BBox. §5 concludes the paper and discusses further research topics for digital black boxes.

1.1   Terminology and Related Work

A log architecture consists of subjects that may play one of three roles: *devices* capture events and send them to *collectors* that store the events in log-files. (*Relays* between the devices and the collectors my exist, but are often omitted.) Authorized *auditors* retrieve the collector and obtain portions of the log file. Log messages sent by devices to the collector are *in transit* and messages recorded in the log file are *at rest*. Parts of the log file retrieved by auditors are *in processing*.

Existing secure log services can be categorized in those adding security functionalities to the syslog [26] and those based on the Schneier-Kelsey scheme [24]. Proposals in the former category focus on log data in transit. The "reliable-syslog" improves the transport protocol of syslog from UDP to TCP, thereby ensuring reliable message delivery [22]. The syslog-sign extends syslog with signature blocks preventing tampering of log data in transit [13]. However, since these signature blocks are loosely coupled to the entries and can be deleted after storage, protection for log data at rest is not given. Moreover, the entries are transmitted in clear. Distributions of *nix systems have been equipped with

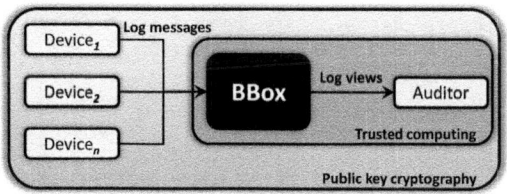

Fig. 1. The high-level architecture of the BBox logging

syslog-ng, the successor of the syslog [27]. Besides reliable transfer over TCP, it also supports IPv6 and encrypted log message transfer using the TLS protocol.

Unlike the extensions of the syslog, proposals based on the Schneier-Kelsey scheme focus rather on log data *at rest*. Accorsi presents a simple extension of this scheme to address distributed storage [1]. Stathopoulos et al. present the application of Schneier-Kelsey's scheme for the telecommunication setting [25] and Chong et al. employ it for DRM [8]. These proposals exhibit a similar vulnerability: the "tail-cut" attack differently reported in [5] and [12]. Logging services based on the Schneier-Kelsey scheme employ hash chains [15] to create dependencies between log entries. Hence, removing one or more log entries from the "chain" makes tampering detectable to verifiers. However, if the attacker removes entries from the end of the log file (i.e. the attacker truncates the log file), the verifier cannot detect the attack unless he is aware of the original length of the hash chain. While employing similar cryptographic primitives as Schneier-Kelsey, the BBox is not susceptible to tail-cut attacks.

Xu et al. propose the SAWS architecture, the secure audit web server [29]. Since no algorithms are provided, only the architectural similarities between the BBox and SAWS can be compared: both employ public key cryptography and trusted computing modules for storage, but transmission and retrieval capabilities are not addressed. Recently, Ma and Tsudik proposed a novel approach to secure logging based on cumulative signatures that replace the use of hash chains [18]. This approach also focuses on data storage and it is currently unclear whether it is susceptible to "tail-cut" attacks. It is, from the performance viewpoint, an approach that clearly succumbs the use of hash chains.

Compared with the aforementioned state of the art, the advantages of the BBox are the simultaneous provision of: first, authenticity protection for both data in motion and at rest, providing for tamper evidence guarantees. Second, keyword search in encrypted log files. Third, during an audit, attestation that the certified algorithms are running, thereby enhancing the probative force of evidence generated using the BBox [14].

2   BBox: Architeture and Logging Algorithms

Fig. 1 depicts the high-level architecture of the BBox. While the BBox cannot check the veracity of the events, i.e. whether these events really correspond to what happens in the system, it ensures that only authorized devices submit *log*

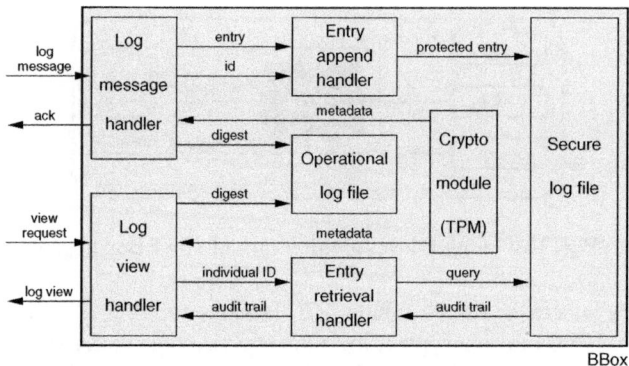

Fig. 2. BBox: Architecture, components and main information flows

messages and that no subject other than the BBox accesses these messages. This is achieved with public key cryptography. Accredited auditors may query the BBox to obtain *log views*, i.e. audit trails containing the all log entries matching the search criteria.[1] Here, a protocol ensures the mutual authentication between collector and auditors, and a trusted computing platform, in particular remote attestation, ensures that the corresponding secure logging protocols are in place.

2.1 BBox Architecture Components

The architecture of the BBox, its components and the information flows happening therein are depicted in Fig. 2. Its functionality can be distinguished in two logical units: the "recording unit" is an input channel for logging communicated events in a secure manner and consists of the log message and the entry append handlers; the "retrieval unit" is an output channel for the generation of log views which encompasses the log view and the entry retrieval handlers. In detail:

– *Log message handler* (LMH). The LMH receives incoming log messages sent by the device and carries out an integrity check to determine (1) whether the contents of the message are eligible to be appended to the secure log file and (2) whether the devices' certificate are legitimate.
– *Entry append handler* (EAH). If a log message passes the integrity test carried out in the LMH, its payload and keyword ID are given to the EAH, which transforms these components in a protected entry for inclusion into the secure log file. To this end, it employs the protocol described in §2.3.
– *Secure log file*. This is the container where events are securely recorded after being prepared by the EAH.
– *Log view handler* (LVH). The LVH controls the disclosure of collected data by receiving view requests, authenticating auditors and passing on the necessary information to the entry retrieval handler.

---

[1] The concrete shape of the keyword depends on the application, e.g. it could be the ID of a particular subject to which the record refers.

- *Entry retrieval handler* (ERH). The ERH receives the keyword ID of the requesting individual and produces a corresponding query over the secure log file. To this end, information in the crypto module is needed in order to allow the decryption of the corresponding log entries.
- *Crypto module.* This is a trusted computing module (TPM) responsible for, among others, storing the cryptographic keys, providing metadata and a basis for remote attestation.
- *Operational log file.* The functioning of the BBox is recorded in a write-once, read-many operational log file. Events recorded in this file include, e.g., the decision whether a log message has passed the integrity test and service disruptions, such as (re-)initialisations and shutdowns.

Notation. The presentation of the BBox employs the following notation: d_i denotes the ith device; P_i refers to the *payload* of the ith log message; K_s stands for the *public key* of a subject s and K_s^{-1} stands for the corresponding *private key*; K_i with $i \in \mathbb{N}$ stands for a *symmetric key* and the *symmetric encryption* of X with K_i is denoted by $\{X\}_{K_i}$; $\{X\}_{K_s}$ denotes the *asymmetric encryption* of message X under the key K_s. $\{X\}_{K_s^{-1}}$ stands for the *signature* of X by s with K_s^{-1}; $Hash(X)$ stands for the *one way hash* of X; X, X' denotes the *juxtaposition* of X and X'; and E_i stands for the ith *log entry*.

The BBox assumes that the cryptographic primitives exhibit the expected properties, e.g., it is infeasible for an attacker to intentionally cause collisions of hash values or calculate the pre-image of hash functions, and that decryption of messages requires the appropriate cryptographic key. A further assumption is that no subject other than s possesses his private key K_s^{-1}.

2.2   BBox Initialization and Incoming Log Messages

Assuming that the BBox is not compromised and initially offline, its initialisation phase encompasses four steps. The first step places the asymmetric key pair K_{BBox} and K_{BBox}^{-1} into the crypto module and synchronizes its internal clock with a reliable clock. (These keys are *not* the same as the attestation key of the crypto module.) Based on these keys, the second step generates the value $G_0 = Hash(K_{\mathsf{BBox}}^{-1})$ which is used as basis for the secure logging service (see §2.3).

The third step at initialising the BBox appends the device authorization and key lookup table (DAKL) to the LMH. This table is necessary to authenticate devices, as they must have been previously authorized to send messages to the BBox. As depicted in Table 1, each entry in the DAKL table contains the identifier of a device expressed by its MAC address, the respective public key and a human readable comment about the particular device. Thus, adding devices to the system on an already online BBox leads to an update of the DAKL and a corresponding entry in the operational log file.

The fourth and final step consists in opening the both the *secure* and the *operational* log files and appending the corresponding initialization entry to them.

Receiving log messages. The communication between the device and the BBox does not require mutual authentication. It only prescribes that events are en-

Table 1. Excerpt of a BBox' DAKL table

Devices' MAC	Public key	Comment
00:C0:9F:30:A6:1B	9TPYHfeWH+Bok5rgMa...	RFID reader #43
00:F0:4A:23:B2:AA	OuanFjE7W4vjo6KLly...	RFID reader #12
00:0B:6A:04:97:20	whbUE3xfIC+JafigeI...	Database server #1

crypted using the public key of BBox and signed by a legitimate device. In detail, the log message communicating the event P sent by a device d_i carrying a keyword I to the BBox at time t is denoted as

$$(Log\ message)\quad d_i \rightarrow \mathsf{BBox} : \{d_i, \{I, P, t\}_{K_{d_i}^{-1}}\}_{K_{\mathsf{BBox}}},$$

where the identity d_i of the device is expressed in terms of its MAC address.

Upon the receipt of a log message the LMH carries out an integrity check whose goal is to assert that: (a) the device d_i is allowed to communicate events to the BBox; (b) the message has not been altered along the way between d_i and the BBox; (c) the received message is not a replay of an expired log message.

The integrity test consists of the following steps. First, BBox decrypts the message using its private key K_{BBox}^{-1} and uses the DAKL table to check whether the sending device d_i is legitimate and, if so, whether its certificate has not been revoked. Second, the signature, and thereby the integrity of the message's payload, is verified. Third, if the checksum is validated, the timestamp is checked to avoid replay attacks. If it has not expired, the event P and the keyword I are passed to the EAH for inclusion in the log file. Messages that fail to comply with the integrity requirements are discarded and the corresponding entry is included in the operational log file.

2.3   Appending Log Entries

The core of the EAH is a secure logging protocol. Parameterized by the keyword and payload of an entry, its goal is to generate a secure log entry by applying a series of cryptographic primitives to them and append it to the secure log file.

Cryptographic building blocks. The cryptographic building blocks used to generate the entries are the *evolving cryptographic key* G used to compute K (see §2.2) and the links of the *hash chain*.

In contrast to usual cryptography, where keys are kept the same over time, in evolving key cryptosystems keys change, or evolve, from time to time, thereby limiting the damage that can result if an attacker learns the current cryptographic key [11]. In the BBox, each payload is encrypted with a unique key K_i derived from an evolving *entry authentication key* G_i and the entry identifier I by hashing these two values. The entry authentication key G evolves for each entry. Hence, the keys $K_i, K_{i+1}, \ldots$ are independent from each other, so that if the attacker obtains a particular K_i, he can neither obtain K_{i-1} nor K_{i+1}. To make it harder for attackers to decrypt the payload of messages, the entry keyword I is stored as a hash value, so that even if the attacker obtains some G, he still has to obtain I to gain access to the payload.

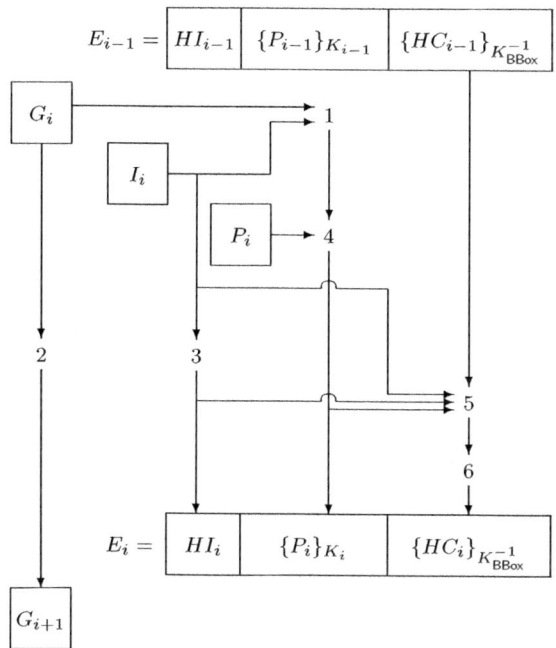

Fig. 3. Appending an entry to the secure log file

A hash chain is a successive application of a cryptographic hash function to a string [15]. By knowing the initial value and the parameters with which the chain is generated, the integrity of an existing hash chain can be checked for broken links by recomputing each element of the chain. (Alternatively, it is also possible to check the integrity of contiguous regions of the chain instead of its whole.) The BBox uses hash chains to create an interdependency between an entry i and its predecessor $i-1$, thereby linking entries to each other. Moreover, since elements of the hash chain can as well be seen as a checksum of the involved parameters, in computing an element of the chain and comparing it with the existing link, the BBox can also assert whether the corresponding entry has been modified or not. Hence, tamper evidence for integrity properties are accounted for.

Format of the entries and secure logging protocol. Fig. 3 depicts the format of the entries E_{i-1} and the steps used to produce the subsequent entry E_i. Each entry consists of the hashed keyword (denoted HI), the payload encrypted under the unique symmetric key (denoted $\{P_i\}_{K_i}$) and the signed link of the hash chain (denoted $\{HC_i\}_{K_{BBox}^{-1}}$).

Assuming that the ith log message has passed the integrity test, the EAH receives the keyword I_i and the payload P_i from the LMH and with the value G_i at hand, performs the following operations:

1. $K_i = Hash(G_i, I_i)$ generates the cryptographic key for the ith log entry.
2. $G_{i+1} = Hash(G_i)$ generates the authentication key for the entry E_{i+1}.

3. $HI_i = Hash(I_i)$ computes the hash of the keyword of the entry E_i.
4. $\{P_i\}_{K_i}$ is payload P_i encrypted with K_i.
5. $HC_i = Hash(I_i, HI_i, \{P_i\}_{K_i}, \{HC_{i-1}\}_{K_{BBox}^{-1}})$ is the ith link of the hash chain.
6. $\{HC_i\}_{K_{BBox}-1}$ is the signed hash chain value for the ith entry.

These operations are depicted as a diagram in Fig. 3, where the numbers labeling the arrows correspond to those in the description of the operation. The labels also encode the order in which the operations are carried out. The resultant log entry, denoted $E_i = (HI_i, \{P_i\}_{K_i}, \{HC_i\}_{K_{BBox}^{-1}})$, consists of the index HI_i, the encrypted log entry $\{P_i\}_{K_i}$ and the signed hash chain value HC_i. The authentication key G_{i+1} is employed to append the next incoming entry.

2.4   Authentication of Secure Log Files

Authenticating secure log files means making tampering evident to a verifier, so that corrective measures can be taken to repair the file, e.g. using a rollback. The BBox employs the hash chain to this end: intermittently or before generating a log view, the secure log file can be authenticated, thereby excluding certain forms of tampering attempts. This is achieved by Alg. 1, which roughly speaking "traverses" the hash-chain seeking for broken links.

Alg. 1 requires a hash table $Hash\_Table$ relating the values HI with the corresponding pre-image values I necessary to compute the links of the hash chain, the file handler/pointer for the secure log file $LogFile$ and the initial entry authentication key G_0 and the current entry authentication key $G_{current}$. It returns the variables $Integrity$ and $Result$: $Integrity$ is a Boolean variable, assuming True if no tampering has been detected in $LogFile$ and False otherwise; $Result$ encodes the kind of tampering found during the authentication, namely: 0 if no tampering is detected; 1 if the initial entry has been tampered with; 2 if the hash chain is broken, i.e. the expected and actual values of a hash chain link diverge; 3 if the hashed index value is not listed in the $Hash\_Table$; 4 if the signature of the hash chain link is invalid; and 5 if the length of the hash chain does not match with the expected length of $LogFile$ (implicitly encoded by current entry authentication key $G_{current}$).

Alg. 1 starts by checking the integrity of the initial entry. (This case must be singled out because E_0 exhibits a special format.) An empty log file indicates a tampering, as well as a flawed initial entry. If testing the initial entry succeeds, the remaining entries of the log file are tested while no tampering is found, i.e. $Integrity$ = True, and the end of file has not been reached (Line 7). This while-loop starts by evolving the entry authentication key (Line 8), overwriting the previous value with the new one. It then checks whether the signature of the ith link of the hash chain is valid (Line 9). If so, the algorithm checks whether the index is listed in the $Hash\_Table$ (Line 11) and, if this is the case, compares the actual value of the hash link with the computed value, i.e. the value obtained by recomputing the HC link (Line 13). If this test succeeds, the algorithm moves to the next entry. If one of these tests fail, the $Integrity$ variable is set to False (Lines 14, 17 and 20) and the tampering attack is encoded in the variable $Result$.

Algorithm 1. Log File Authentication

Require: *Hash_Table, LogFile,* G_0, $G_{current}$
Provide: *Result, Integrity*
1: $G \leftarrow G_0$
2: **if not** EMPTY(*LogFile*) **and** CHECK-FIRST-ENTRY(*LogFile*) **then**
3:      *Integrity* $\leftarrow$ True; *Result* $\leftarrow$ 0
4: **else**
5:      *Integrity* $\leftarrow$ False; *Result* $\leftarrow$ 1
6: **end if**
7: **while** (*Integrity*) **and not** EOF(*LogFile*) **do**
8:      $G \leftarrow$ HASH(G)
9:      **if** CHECK-LINK-SIGNATURE(*Entry.HC*) **then**
10:         $HC \leftarrow$ DECRYPT(*Entry.HC* using K_{BBox}^{-1})
11:         **if** *Entry.HI* $\in$ *Hash_Table* **then**
12:             $I \leftarrow$ LOOKUP-PRE-IMAGE(*Hash_Table, Entry.HI*)
13:             **if** $HC \neq$ HASH(*I, HI, Entry.Payload, PreviousEntry.HC*) **then**
14:                 *Integrity* $\leftarrow$ False; *Result* $\leftarrow$ 2
15:             **end if**
16:         **else**
17:             *Integrity* $\leftarrow$ False; *Result* $\leftarrow$ 3
18:         **end if**
19:     **else**
20:         *Integrity* $\leftarrow$ False; *Result* $\leftarrow$ 4
21:     **end if**
22: **end while**
23: **if** (*Integrity*) **and** (HASH(G) $\neq G_{current}$) **then**
24:     *Integrity* $\leftarrow$ False; *Result* $\leftarrow$ 5
25: **end if**

If no tampering is detected during the while-loop, it traverses the whole log file. In this case, the length of the log file is tested, using to this end the entry authentication key G (Line 23): G is the result of the n iterations of the hash function, where n is the number of entries in the *LogFile*; $G_{current}$ is the result of $m+1$ applications the hash function, where m is the number of appended entries by the EAH. Ideally, $n+1$ and $m+1$ must be equal, otherwise the actual and the expected number of entries do not coincide, indicating tampering. Specifically, this indicates the deletion of entries (Lines 23 and 24).

3 Retrieval of Log Views

The concept of log view bears similarity with its homonymous counterpart in databases, where a view can be thought of as either a virtual table or a stored query, thereby acting as a filter on the underlying tables referenced in the view.

Four components of the BBox are involved in the generation of log views. The LVH is responsible for performing the following protocols:

– *Mutual authentication between the auditor* and the BBox. To ensure that log view is generated for the pertinent auditor, entity authentication. From an

---

Algorithm 2. Entry Selection

Require: I, *LogFile*, *OpLogFile*, G_0, $G_{current}$
Provide: T, Authentcation_Failure
1: *integrity* ← True
2: *keyword* ← HASH(I)
3: G ← G_0
4: **while** (*integrity*) **and not** EOF(*LogFile*) **do**
5:     G ← HASH(G)
6:     **if** CHECK-ENTRY-INTEGRITY **then**
7:         **if** *keyword* = *Entry.HI* **then**
8:             K ← HASH(G, I)
9:             P ← DECRYPT(*Entry.Payload* using K)
10:             APPEND-TO-BUFFER(T, P)
11:         **end if**
12:     **else**
13:         *integrity* ← False
14:     **end if**
15: **end while**
16: **if** (*integrity*) **and** (HASH(G) ≠ $G_{current}$) **then**
17:     **return** T
18: **else**
19:     WRITE(Authentication_Failure in *OpLogFile*)
20:     **return** T, Authentication_Failure
21: **end if**

---

auditor's viewpoint, he must also be aware that they communicated with correct the BBox. Thus, *mutual* authentication between requesting individuals and the BBox is necessary.

– *Remote attestation of the* BBox. Authentication provides no assurance with respect to the configuration of the BBox, e.g. whether the secure log mechanism is in place and the algorithm for retrieving log views is reliable. To achieve such guarantees, the LVH uses remote attestation protocols provided by the crypto module.

If these two protocols run as expected, the ERH receives the keyword I and searches the secure log file for the matching entries. The resultant audit trail T contains all the entries related to I. T is given to the LVH, which is responsible for computing the metadata M (e.g. number of entries in T and generation timestamp) and sending the resultant tuple T, M to the requesting individual.

The following focuses on the selection of entries. Details about the mutual authentication and remote attestation are not given here. Mutual authentication is prototypically achieved with a variant of the Needham-Schroeder protocol and attestation employs the standard primitives.

Selection of log entries. Alg. 2 shows how entries are selected and appended to the audit trail T. It consists of a linear search over the secure log file, where the integrity of hash chain is checked when searching for the matching entries (Line 6). This integrity test consists of checking the signature of the hash chain link, decrypting its contents and checking whether the expected and actual contents correspond. If the integrity test fails, the search is aborted and the failure is recorded in the operational log file *OpLogFile* (Line 19) and reported to the BBox (Line 20). If a matching entry is found (Line 7), i.e. if the keyword searched matches with the keyword of the entry, the corresponding symmetric key K is computed (Line 8). With K, the payload of the entry is decrypted (Line 9) and appended to the buffer T (Line 10).

Provided that the log file has not been tampered with, the search finishes when all the entries of the secure log file are visited, producing the audit trail T. The LVH then encrypts the tuple T, M and sends it to the requesting auditor A.

4   Security Analysis of the BBox

The cryptographic building blocks and protocols provide for authentic and confidential log data in transit and at rest. While the BBox provides for tamper evidence, its design does not account for tamper resistance. To this end, other measures, such as partial confinement, rollbacks and firewalls should be in place.

This section demonstrates the extent to which authenticity is achieved by the BBox and reports on experiments carried out with the prototypical implementation of the BBox. Along with the security analysis, this section discusses the main design decisions and assumptions underlying the BBox.

4.1   Log Data in Transit

Digital signatures are used to sign log messages sent from the devices to the BBox, thereby ensuring that only authorized devices, i.e. those listed in the DAKL, can submit log messages. The one-way authentication protocol (see §2.2) has been verified in the AVISPA tool for authentication and replay-freeness properties. Specifically: the analysis aimed to check whether BBox could be tricked into accepting a log message from an illegal device, or a replayed message. Given a Dolev-Yao attacker model [10], no such attack could be found. Moreover, since the messages are encrypted, confidentiality against an eavesdropper is preserved.

The use of timestamps averts the possibility of replay attacks, provided the replay happens after the specified timespan. Although this timespan is kept short, it could still be exploited to store replicated messages. However, this would be inoffensive for the authenticity of the log file: the replay only leads to identical copies of a legitimate entry in the secure log file and auditors aware of this could simply filter the entries, keeping only their first appearance.

The use of timestamps could be circumvented if the device and the BBox mutually authenticate, guaranteeing the freshness and origin authentication of a message. However, this causes an overhead that cannot be justified in various application scenarios, e.g. pervasive and ubiquitous computing settings [2].

With regard to the communication between auditors requesting log views and the BBox, the prototypical protocol authenticating these peers is based on the Needham-Schroeder public key protocol. This protocol has also been formalized in the AVISPA tool and checked against man-in-the-middle attacks, where no attack could be pinpointed. The protocol for remote attestation is a standard TPM protocol. In particular, we employ the concept of "persistent link" to eliminate one relevant kind of attack in which a corrupted BBox could trick an auditor into accepting a log view generated by a flawed BBox algorithm [17].

4.2   Log Data at Rest

Two security properties are relevant for log data at rest: confidentiality and integrity. The former is achieved by encrypting the payload of the entries with the symmetric key K. This key is generated using the evolving key G (derived form the private key of the BBox) and the keyword for the entry I. Since I is not stored in clear in the BBox and G does not leave the TPM, log data at rest can be considered confidential. If an intruder – by guessing or inference – obtains the some key G_i for the ith entry, it is still impossible to decrypt the contents of the entries appended after E_i, as the intruder does not possess the keyword I. (This confidentiality guarantee is called "I-confidentiality".) Similarly, if the intruder gets aware of some I, all the entries prefixed with the hash of I could be decrypted upon the event of discovering the value G. (This confidentiality guarantee is called "G-confidentiality".) If the intruder knows both I_i and G_i for some entry E_i, then no confidentiality guarantee is provided.

The use of a hash table to relate HI with its pre-image I is a vulnerable spot of the BBox. If an attacker succeeds in obtaining this table, then not only the confidentiality of entries would be harmed, but also, e.g., the privacy of users. In [23], we employ the BBox to store the events of customers in a retailer using different forms of customer communication and ubiquitous computing. Here, I stands for the unique identifier of the customers, so that in case of an attack, the events of the customers could be linked and their identity could be disclosed.

With regard to integrity guarantees, Alg. 1 is responsible for detecting attacks upon log entries, i.e. inclusion, modification and deletion of entries. To demonstrate its correctness, we consider an attacker model in which an intruder can read, (over)write, mode and delete (fields of the) log entries stored in the secure log file. In doing so, the attacker may generate message items from the items he already possesses. However, the attacker can only obtain the plain-text of an encrypted message if he possesses the corresponding decryption key. Moreover, it is also assumed that the attacker is computationally bounded.

Given this attacker, the correctness property of the Alg. 1 is defined as the absence of false negatives: whenever the algorithm decides that a log is authentic, then there was no tampering – modification, appending and removal of entries.

Definition 1. *Alg. 1 is correct iff it does not exhibit false negatives.*   ⊣

Theorem 1. *Alg. 1 is correct with regard to authentication.*   ⊣

To show Theorem 1, every attack tampering attempt on an initially authentic log file must be examined, thereby demonstrating that they are detected. Due to space constraints, below we only demonstrate one case of the proof – for modification attacks. Other attacks are shown in a similar manner [3].

Proof (for modification attacks). Let *LogFile* be an authentic log file consisting of a sequence of entries $E_0, \ldots, E_n$ constructed according to §2.3, where each entry E_j, with $0 \leq j \leq n$, assumes the form $E_j = (HI_j, \{P_j\}_{K_j}, \{HC_j\}_{K_{BBox}^{-1}})$.

Case 1: Modification attacks. Let E_j be an entry of the *LogFile*. The modification of each of the three entry fields (i.e. entry's index, payload and hash chain link) must be analyzed in isolation.

(1.1) Overwriting the index of E_j: the attacker either overwrites the index HI_j of E_j with the index of an existing entry E_k or generates a new index H'_j. For the former case, the algorithm detects a broken hash chain by computing HC'_j and determining that $HC_j \neq HC'_j$ (Line 13). For the latter case, the value H'_j will not be contained in the *Hash_Table*, indicating the violation (Line 11).

(1.2) Overwriting the encrypted payload of E_j: irrespective of whether the attacker reuses the payload field of an existing entry E_k or generates a new payload field from the items he possesses, such an overwriting leads to a broken hash chain, as the expected value for link of the hash chain diverges from the actual value (Line 13).

(1.3) Overwriting the hash chain link of E_j: the attacker either overwrites the link $\{HC_j\}_{K_{BBox}^{-1}}$ with the link of an existing entry E_k or generates a new link. For the former case, the algorithm detects a broken hash chain by computing HC'_j and determining that $HC_j \neq HC'_j$ (Line 13). For the latter case, since the attacker does not possess K_{BBox}^{-1}, he cannot generate a legitimate link that passes the signature check (Line 9). □

The following provides an intuition of how the other violations of integrity properties are detected by the algorithm. *Inclusions* are detected using the signature appended to the link of the hash chain: since the attacker does not possess K_{BBox}^{-1} and since he cannot cause collision of hash links, the attacker cannot produce valid signatures. A broken hash chain or a chain shorter than expected indicates that the some link or part of the log file has been *removed*.

4.3   BBox Prototype

The BBox has been realized as a prototype using the programming language Java and standard protocols for remote attestation found in trusted computing platforms TCB 1.1b. To obtain practical evidence as to whether the proposed algorithms and techniques provide the expected confidentiality and integrity guarantees, we employed ATLIST – a state of the art vulnerability analysis technique [16] – to identify potential vulnerabilities. Moreover, we conducted man-in-the-middle and tampering attacks to observe how the BBox behaves.

Among others, the vulnerability analysis with ATLIST pointed to three weak spots of the BBox: first, the possibility of impersonation attacks, both when attackers impersonate the devices and the auditors. Second, the hash-table linking the hash values to their pre-images. Third, the storage of the credentials used to create and assert the authenticity of the log file. Given that, we extensively tested the BBox for middle-man attacks and impersonation attacks,

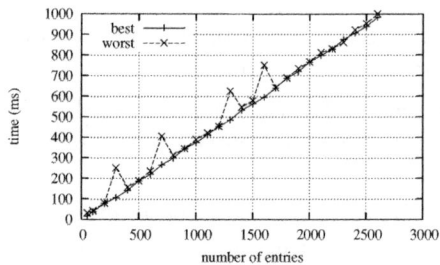

Fig. 4. Time necessary to authenticate a secure log file

demonstrating that such attacks were not possible. The other two weak spots regard tamper-resistance and cannot be tackled with the algorithms implemented in the BBox.

Focusing on tamper evidence, we simulated every possible tampering combination of log files – considering the attacker model mentioned above. The goal was to demonstrate that these attack attempts are detected by the implementation of the algorithm. The BBox succeeded in authenticating the log files and detecting the attack attempts. For illustration, Fig. 4 depicts the runtime necessary to authenticate sample log files. (These runtime figures were obtained in a standard desktop PC with 1.92GHz, 512MB of RAM and 250GB hard disk operating under MS-Windows and Java version 1.6; each entry payload amounts to 50Kb.) While being based on a prototypical implementation, these runtime figures already indicate to one problem of secure logging implementation based on standard libraries: their performance is rather poor for use in large applications. Hence, besides improving the prototypical implementation, we currently investigate the benefits brought by fast hash chains verification techniques, e.g. [30].

Finally, denial of service attacks can be carried out upon the prototypical implementation of the BBox. We simulate these attacks by sending, over a period of five minutes, a constantly raising number of log messages (between 500 and 2500 messages per minute; step 500). Legitimate entries sent after within the third minute were no longer added to the log file. While we currently investigate this issue in more detail, these preliminary figures already indicate that receiving messages is, in practice, not costly. In fact, the process of adding entries to the log file is rather expensive and turns to a bottleneck in the BBox architecture.

5 Summary

The paper introduced the architecture and main components of the BBox, a digital black box to ensure authentic archival of records as a basis for reliable accountability. It is shown that tamper evidence and confidentiality of log data in transit and at rest can be provided and also the limits in which this is possible. Besides the implementation of its components with a business process management system, the algorithms behind the BBox are being further developed to improve performance. In particular, we aim at employing faster algorithms to verify the integrity of log entries and, more importantly, improved methods to search for log entries. As for the latter, we have been testing with (distributed) hash tables, which clearly accelerate the search but introduce a tremendous overhead for creating indexes on-the-fly in settings where a large number of records are transmitted to the collector.

Overall, we identify the need for efficient data-structures in digital black boxes as the main research direction in this setting. Here, tree-structures appear to be more promising then distributed hash tables. Similar to log file audit [4], we have been experimenting with tree-structures to accelerate the retrieval of log entries. A crucial aspect is to decide on the branching criteria. Preliminary tests using object and role hierachies show that fine-grained hierarchies, in this case for objects, lead to more efficient search trees. However, we still have to substantiate with more formal evidence.

References

1. Accorsi, R.: On the relationship of privacy and secure remote logging in dynamic systems. In: Fischer-Hübner, S., et al. (eds.) IFIP Conf. Proceedings, vol. 201, pp. 329–339. Springer, Heidelberg (2006)
2. Accorsi, R., Hohl, A.: Delegating secure logging in pervasive computing systems. In: Clark, J.A., Paige, R.F., Polack, F.A.C., Brooke, P.J. (eds.) SPC 2006. LNCS, vol. 3934, pp. 58–72. Springer, Heidelberg (2006)
3. Accorsi, R.: Automated counterexample-driven audits of authentic system records. Ph.D. dissertation, University of Freiburg (2008)
4. Accorsi, R., Stocker, T.: Automated privacy audits based on pruning of log data. In: IEEE Enterprise Distributed Object Computing Conference, pp. 175–182 (2008)
5. Accorsi, R.: Safe-keeping digital evidence with secure logging protocols: State of the art and challenges. In: Goebel, O., et al. (eds.) Incident Management and Forensics, pp. 94–110. IEEE, Los Alamitos (2009)
6. Bellare, M., Yee, B.: Forward integrity for secure audit logs. Tech. report, U of California, San Diego, Dept. of Computer Science & Engineering (1997)
7. Carlin, A., Gallegos, F.: IT audit: A critical business process. IEEE Computer 40(7), 87–89 (2007)
8. Chong, C., Peng, Z., Hartol, P.: Secure audit logging with tamper-resistant hardware. In: Gritzalis, D., et al. (eds.) IFIP Conf. Proceedings, vol. 250, pp. 73–84. Kluwer, Dordrecht (2003)
9. Chuvakin, A., Peterson, G.: Logging in the age of web services. IEEE Security and Privacy 7(3), 82–85 (2009)
10. Dolev, D., Yao, A.: On the security of public key protocols. IEEE Transactions on Information Theory 2(29), 198–208 (1983)
11. Franklin, M.: A survey of key evolving cryptosystems. International Journal of Security and Networks 1(1-2), 46–53 (2006)
12. Holt, J.: Logcrypt: Forward security and public verification for secure audit logs. In: Buyya, R., et al. (eds.) Australasian Symposium on Grid Computing and e-Research. CRIPT, vol. 54, pp. 203–211 (2006)
13. Kelsey, J., Callas, J.: Signed syslog messages. IETF Internet Draft (2005)
14. Kenneally, E.: Digital logs - Proof matters. Digital Investigation 1(2), 94–101 (2004)

15. Lamport, L.: Password authentication with insecure communication. Commun. ACM 24(11), 770–772 (1981)
16. Lowis, L., Accorsi, R.: Finding vulnerabilities in SOA-based business processes. IEEE Transactions on Services Computing (2010) (to appear)
17. Lowis, L., Hohl, A.: Enabling Persistent Service Links. In: IEEE Conference on E-Commerce Technology, pp. 301–306 (2005)
18. Ma, D., Tsudik, G.: A new approach to secure logging. ACM Transactions on Storage 5(1), 1–21 (2009)
19. Müller, G., Accorsi, R., Höhn, S., Sackmann, S.: Sichere Nutzungskontrolle für mehr Transparenz in Finanzmärkten. Informatik Spektrum 33(1), 3–13 (2010)
20. Mercuri, R.: On auditing audit trails. Commun. ACM 46(1), 17–20 (2003)
21. Oppliger, R., Ritz, R.: Digital evidence: Dream and reality. IEEE Security and Privacy 1(5), 44–48 (2003)
22. Reliable syslog, http://security.sdsc.edu/software/sdsc-syslog/
23. Sackmann, S., Strüker, J., Accorsi, R.: Personalization in privacy-aware highly dynamic systems. Commun. ACM 49(9), 32–38 (2006)
24. Schneier, B., Kelsey, J.: Security audit logs to support computer forensics. ACM Transactions on Information and System Security 2(2), 159–176 (1999)
25. Stathopoulos, V., Kotzanikolaou, P., Magkos, E.: A framework for secure and verifiable logging in public communication networks. In: López, J. (ed.) CRITIS 2006. LNCS, vol. 4347, pp. 273–284. Springer, Heidelberg (2006)
26. Syslog, http://www.syslog.org/
27. Syslog-ng web site, http://www.balabit.com/products/syslog_ng/
28. Waters, B., Balfanz, D., Durfee, G., Smetters, D.: Building an encrypted and searchable audit log. In: Network and Distributed System Security (2004)
29. Xu, W., Chadwick, D., Otenko, S.: A PKI Based Secure Audit Web Server. In: IASTED Communications, Network and Information (2005)
30. Yum, D., Kim, J., Lee, P., Hong, S.: On fast verification of hash chains. In: Pieprzyk, J. (ed.) CT-RSA 2010. LNCS, vol. 5985, pp. 382–396. Springer, Heidelberg (2010)

A Fair and Abuse-Free Contract Signing Protocol from Boneh-Boyen Signature

Somayeh Heidarvand* and Jorge L. Villar**

Universitat Politècnica de Catalunya, Spain
{somayeh,jvillar}@ma4.upc.edu

Abstract. A fair contract signing protocol is used to enable two mistrusted parties to exchange two signatures on a given contract, in such a way that either both of them get the other party's signature, or none of them gets anything. A new signature scheme is presented, which is a variant of Boneh and Boyen's scheme, and building on it, we propose a new signature fair exchange protocol for which all the properties of being optimistic, setup-free and abuse-free can be proved without random oracles, and it is more efficient than the known schemes with comparable properties.

Keywords: optimistic fair exchange, Boneh-Boyen signature, abuse-freeness, standard model.

1 Introduction

Due to the developing of the Internet and other computer networks in all aspects of life, electronic commerce has introduced the new need of being able to sign contracts remotely, especially when two parties A and B do not trust each other. A contract signing protocol is called *fair* if both parties get the desired signatures or none of them gets anything, even in the case they try to cheat each other. In traditional paper-based contract signing, the two parties sign a contract at the same place and time, so fairness can be 'physically' enforced. However, in online contract signing once one party (say B) gets the signature from the other party (say A), nobody can prevent him from immediately leaving the protocol without committing himself to the contract. Fairness in contract signing can be considered in the more general context of *fair exchange of signatures*, that is closely related to some other concepts like certified e-mail systems and non-repudiation protocols.

Many protocols for fair exchange of signatures have been proposed in the literature. The early works on this subject focused on gradual release of two signatures from two parties [17] and [10], but the resulting protocols are very inefficient and they only provide a weak notion of fairness. Hence, most fair exchange

---

* Partially supported by the Spanish CRM.

** Partially supported by the Spanish research project MTM2009-07694, and the European Commission through the ICT programme under contract ICT-2007-216676 ECRYPT II.

J. Camenisch and C. Lambrinoudakis (Eds.): EuroPKI 2010, LNCS 6711, pp. 125–140, 2011.

protocols make use of a trusted third party or arbitrator T. Straightforward yet inefficient protocols can be defined assuming T is available online [4,12]. However, the most interesting protocols are *optimistic* [1,3], that is, T is not invoked in a normal protocol execution but only when one party has to complain against the other. In optimistic fair exchange (OFE) protocols the messages exchanged by the parties are commitments to the signatures, which can be opened by the trusted party in case of conflict. For instance, verifiable escrows are used in [1], while verifiable encryptions are used in [3].

Although some existing OFE protocols use many rounds, here we will restrict ourselves to three-move protocols, in which after setting up the system a signer A sends a commitment of her signature to B, then after some verifications B sends his signature to A, and finally A opens the committed signature to B. If A does not fulfil the third move, then B can ask T for the opening of the committed signature. Notice that in this case, B must provide some information to T so that he can extract and send B's signature to A, thus guaranteeing the protocol fairness.

As well as fairness and optimism, some other desirable properties for a contract signing protocol have been considered in the literature. Nevertheless, *abuse-freeness* [16] seems to be the most important and difficult property among them. In some applications, it is very important to preserve the signers' privacy until the very end of the protocol. Therefore the following attack must be considered: Getting A's commitment to her signature, B could leave the protocol and prove to an external party C that A has committed to a signature on the contract, thus showing A's intention to sign it. Abuse-free optimistic contract signing protocols prevent this and other similar attacks. The main goal in these systems is making the transcript of an unfinished protocol instance completely simulatable by the malicious party alone, and thus non-convincing for an external party. The concept of abuse-freeness is in a very close relation to *designated verifier* signature schemes. Actually some fair exchange protocols make use of designated verifier signatures, which can be turned into universally verifiable by both the signer and T.

Timeliness is a property of an exchange protocol that informally assures that any party will end the protocol execution in a finite bounded time. To address that problem a synchronous network model, which assumes the existence of a network global time, is considered. An interesting discussion about the different approaches to the concept of timeliness can be found in [30], and some results about optimistic contract signing protocols in both the synchronous and asynchronous network models are presented in [29].

Another desirable property of an OFE is *setup-freeness*, which means that no interaction between the signers and the trusted party is required, either during setup or during the normal protocol execution. This property allows the signers to freely designate the trusted party in a system in which more than one are available. Moreover, non setup-free protocols require T to maintain some setup information that grows with the number of potential signers.

1.1   Our Contribution

Our contribution is twofold. On the one hand, we propose a new signature scheme, which is a variant of Boneh-Boyen signature scheme [5], and we show it is strong existentially unforgeable under chosen message attacks in the standard model, under the strong Diffie-Hellman assumption. We also build a convertible signature scheme from it, which we call a *partial signature scheme*. The partial signatures derived from it can be verified or converted into universally verifiable signatures either by the signer or by T. Actually, the conversion is very efficient (compared to other schemes using verifiable encryption) since it involves just one exponentiation, and the partial signatures can be verified in zero-knowledge by either the signer or T by means of the efficient concurrent proof of equality of two discrete logarithms [9,10] (described in Section 3.2).

On the other hand, based on the new signature schemes we propose a new contract signing protocol, which is optimistic, setup-free and abuse-free in the certified key model (*i.e.*, every party registers his public keys by proving the knowledge of the corresponding secret key). Indeed it is the verifiable knowledge of the secret key by B what makes B unable to convince a third party about the information he collects during an unfinished exchange protocol. All the above properties of our scheme hold in the standard model. To the best of our knowledge, our proposal is the most efficient abuse-free optimistic contract signing protocol in the standard model.

The efficiency of the new contract signing scheme is comparable to the existing abuse-free protocols in the random oracle model [16,31]. The proposed scheme works in only five rounds (three rounds correspond to the three-move architecture of the exchange protocol, and the two extra rounds come from the zero-knowledge proof). The communication complexity of our protocol is very small compared to the RSA based schemes: Typically the total length of a partial signature in our scheme is about 480 bits. The ordinary signatures sent by both signers in the last rounds of our protocol have the same length as the partial signature. However, in the last round, the signer can just send one group element (160 bits) instead of a whole signature, which saves 320 bits.

1.2   Related Work

Some practical fair exchange protocols have been recently introduced, but only a few of them address the abuse-free property. In 2001 an efficient protocol is proposed in [25], but abuse-freeness is not addressed. Some protocols for contract signing based on RSA are proposed in [27,31]. However the scheme in [27] is broken and repaired in [14], where it is proved to be secure in the random oracle model. The idea of these two papers is splitting the secret exponent d into two secrets d_1 and d_2 such that $d = d_1 + d_2$, and sending d_2 to T. Then the first signer A gives a partial signature on the contract with the secret key d_1, along with a 5-round zero-knowledge proof of its validity (note that the related 'public' exponents e_1 and e_2 are kept secret here). Abuse-freeness is considered in [31] but only in an informal way. Actually, abuse-freeness could hold in the random oracle model, and under some computational assumption (an adversary capable to solve the DDH problem can easily break the abuse-freeness, in a single instance of the protocol). The protocol in [14] is not setup-free since the first signer must send d_2 to the trusted party before running an instance of the protocol.

In 2006, Lu et al. [24] proposed the first verifiably encrypted signature scheme, provably secure in the standard model. The scheme is based on Waters' signature scheme [32], and it works in the certified key model. In 2008 another proposal [19] is introduced, which works in the more general chosen key model, which means the adversary can choose its public key arbitrarily without requiring it to prove the knowledge of the corresponding secret key. Although both schemes are quite efficient, they do not address the abuse-free property. In a later work [20], the same authors define the notion of *signer-ambiguity*, which is tightly related to abuse-freeness, and they propose a new setup-free optimistic fair exchange protocol that achieves signer-ambiguity. However, the resulting scheme is far from being practical due to the computational cost of the pairing-based non-interactive zero-knowledge proofs by Groth and Sahai [18].

A more general notion of contract signing protocols in the certified key model was proposed in [13], where a generic construction in a multi-user setting based on one-way functions is provided. However, in this paper we focus on the most common scenario of two-party schemes, but we attach the identities of both signers and T to the contract in order to prevent trivial attacks in the multi-user setting.

1.3   Road Map

The rest of the paper is organized as follows: We first recall the formal definition of a fair exchange protocol in Section 2. In Section 3 the basic tools on which our scheme is based are presented. Section 4 introduces the two new signature schemes based on Boneh-Boyen's one. Section 5 gives the description and the security analysis of the proposed contract signing protocol. We conclude the paper with some considerations about efficiency.

2   Model and Definitions

In this section we restrict the definition of an optimistic contract signing protocol to the *three-move* architecture [14] described in the introduction, which is enough for our purposes. For a more general definition, see [16,31].

A contract signing protocol is a protocol in which two parties A and B exchange two signatures σ_A, σ_B on a contract M. We assume in all the paper that A starts the protocol execution. The signatures exchanged, called *ordinary signatures*, are assumed to be existentially unforgeable[1]. Ordinary signatures correspond to a signature scheme, described with the usual subprotocols **KeyGen**, **Sign** and **Ver**, respectively denoting key generation, signing and verification.

---

[1] There is no need to consider the strong unforgeability for the selected signature scheme. Actually once a signer signs a contract, it does not matter if another signature for the same contract be forged under the public key of the signer.

An auxiliary subprotocol called a *partial signature scheme* is needed in the definition of the three-move protocol. It is functionally described as follows:

- **PKeyGen** is the key generation for the signer A, the recipient B and the trusted party T.
- **PSign.** A partial signature on a message m is computed by A. The public key of T is used as an input.
- **PVer** is an interactive verification protocol[2] for a partial signature ρ_A between A and B, which is run immediately after **PSign**.
- **Conv** is a protocol run by T on a partial signature ρ_A to extract the corresponding ordinary signature σ_A.

We assume that T can noninteractively verify the validity of a partial signature ρ_A. A three-move *optimistic contract signing* protocol can be described by the following subprotocols:

- **Setup.** On a common input of some system parameters, during this protocol every signer produces, registers and publishes his signing and verification keys; and T produces, registers and publishes his resolving key, according to **KeyGen** and **PKeyGen**.
- **Exch.** In a first move A runs **PSig** on a contract M (known to both A and B) and sends the resulting partial signature ρ_A to B. Then A and B execute **PVer** so that B can check the validity of ρ_A. In a second move, B runs **Sig** to obtain a signature σ_B on M, and sends it back to A. In the third move, after A verifies σ_B with **Ver**, she sends a signature σ_A on M to B (computed directly with **Sig** or from the output of **Conv** on the input of ρ_A).
- **Res.** A protocol run by B and T, started by B when in the last move of **Exch**, B receives an invalid σ_A or nothing (*i.e.*, A left the protocol). If T accepts (after verifying some information provided by B, which could include ρ_A and a partial signature ρ_B on M) then he extracts σ_A and σ_B from the information received, and sends σ_A to B and σ_B to A.

Notice that we do not allow A to raise any complain to T. Although in a more general definition that possibility exists, in a three move protocol either A receives nothing (and hence B does not come up with a valid signature), or A receives B's signature, either from B or from T.

2.1   Security Notions

We briefly review the security definitions in [14,13] except for abuse-freeness, which is not addressed there. We follow the commonly accepted definition of abuse-freeness in [16], but adapted to the case of three-move protocols.

A secure *abuse-free* optimistic contract signing protocol has to fulfil the following security requirements:

---

[2] **PVer** is defined as an interactive protocol to allow the use of interactive proof systems, like zero-knowledge proofs.

- Correctness. If all the parties behave honestly (and the network works properly) then at the end of **Exch** every signer gets a valid signature on the contract M under the public key of the other signer.
- Ambiguity. Any resolved signature (*i.e.*, resulting from **Res**) is indistinguishable from a signature generated with **Sig**.
- Security Against A. A must not be able to produce a partial signature ρ_A in such a way that convinces B about its correctness, but it cannot be transformed into a valid signature by T during a **Res** subprotocol execution.
- Security Against B. B must not be able to output an ordinary signature σ_A on M, even after executing **PSig**, **PVer** and **Res** for some partial signatures and messages adaptively chosen by B, with the only restriction that **Res** is not executed on any partial signature on M.
- Security against T. Here we assume that T is an honest but curious adversary. Informally, T is prevented from performing any meaningful computation other than **Res**. More precisely, T must not be able to forge a valid ordinary signature σ_A on M, even after eavesdropping at some executions of **Exch** on contracts different from M.
- Abuse-freeness. B does not obtain publicly verifiable information about (honest) A signing the contract until B is also bound by the contract. Observe that A cannot abuse B in a three-move contract signing protocol, since the only information A can receive from an honest B is his ordinary signature (and this happens only when A herself is bound to the contract). Abuse-freeness is equivalent to show the impossibility for an external party to publicly verify a partial signature issued by A (providing him with the information learned by B in the **PVer** execution).

Observe that assuming the unforgeability of the ordinary signatures, the above definitions of security against A and B imply fairness. Indeed, if finally A learns a valid signature σ_B, it must come from B (in the second move) or from T (as a result of **Res**, which means that B also receives σ_A). But the first case means that B receives a valid ρ_A, which allows B to successfully run **Res** with T and get σ_A. Conversely, if B gets σ_A, it must come from A (in the third move, so A also have σ_B) or from T (so A also received σ_B). Otherwise, B forged σ_A perhaps from ρ_A, which is impossible due to the definition of security against B.

To address the *timeliness* property (*i.e.*, the execution of a protocol instance will be terminated by any party in finite bounded time) we assume that the communication of honest parties with T is reliable enough, so that an adversary can only introduce some delay in the delivery of messages (say up to certain limit Δ), but it is not allowed to delete or replace such messages. This allows us to use the deadline technique suggested by Micali in [26]. We also assume that the parties can reliably refer to T's local time. Actually, in any optimistic fair exchange protocol some extra assumption about the availability of the trusted party must be made, since T not being available within a reasonable time implies breaking one of the timeliness or fairness properties.

An optimistic fair exchange protocol is *setup-free* if **Setup** can be run with no interaction between T and the signers, with common input of some trustily generated system parameters. Therefore, setup-freeness is basically depends on the properties of the **PKeyGen** protocol.

3 Basic Tools

3.1 Pairing Systems

Assume that $G_1 = \langle g_1 \rangle$, $G_2 = \langle g_2 \rangle$ and G_T are (multiplicative) groups of prime order p that have a non-degenerate efficiently computable bilinear map $e : G_1 \times G_2 \to G_T$ such that

- (Bilinear) For all $(u, v) \in G_1 \times G_2$, for all $a, b \in \mathbb{Z}, e(u^a, v^b) = e(u, v)^{ab}$.
- (Non-degenerate) $g_T = e(g_1, g_2) \neq 1$, so g_T is a generator of G_T.
- (Efficient) e and the group operations in G_1, G_2 and G_T can be efficiently computed.

It is often assumed that $G_1 = G_2$ but some known pairing systems allows for $G_1 \neq G_2$ and give a more compact representation of elements in G_1, which is interesting for efficiency reasons [15]. Also an efficiently computable isomorphism $\psi : G_2 \to G_1$ could exist in some pairing systems. Notice that we do not require $\psi(g_2) = g_1$ as many papers do. This means that we use randomized generators g_1 and g_2. We say that the pairing system parameters are $\mathsf{psys} = (p, G_1, G_2, G_T, g_1, g_2, e, \psi, g_T)$, and they are hereafter assumed to be known by all the parties in a pairing based cryptographic protocol. It is widely believed that the following two assumptions hold in some pairing systems:

Assumption 1 (Strong Diffie-Hellman (q-SDH)). *[6] Every probabilistic polynomial-time algorithm $\mathcal{A}$ has a negligible success probability in solving the following problem: Given a pairing system psys and the tuple $(g_1^x, g_1^{x^2}, \ldots, g_1^{x^q}, g_2^x)$ for a random $x \in \mathbb{Z}_p^*$ as input, output $(r, g_1^{\frac{1}{x+r}})$ for an arbitrary $r \in \mathbb{Z}_p \setminus \{-x\}$. In [6] the existence of ψ is not required.*

Assumption 2 (Decisional Tripartite Diffie-Hellman (DTDH)). *[22] Every probabilistic polynomial-time algorithm $\mathcal{A}$ has a negligible success probability in telling apart the following two probability distributions D_0 and D_1, for a pairing system psys:*

$D_0 = (g_2^x, g_2^y, g_1^z, g_2^u)$ *for random* $x, y, z, u \in \mathbb{Z}_p^*$
$D_1 = (g_2^x, g_2^y, g_1^z, g_2^{xyz})$ *for random* $x, y, z \in \mathbb{Z}_p^*$. *In [22] it is also required that $\psi(g_2) = g_1$ for technical reasons.*

Boneh-Boyen's (BB) signature scheme [5,6]. The secret and public keys are $sk = (y, s)$ and $pk = (Y = g_2^y, S = g_2^s)$, for random $y, s \in \mathbb{Z}_p^*$. The signature on a message $m \in \mathbb{Z}_p$ is $\sigma = (r, g_1^{\frac{1}{y+m+rs}})$, for a random $r \in \mathbb{Z}_p$. The signature $\sigma = (r, b)$ is verified by checking $e(b, Y g_2^m S^r) = g_T$. Boneh-Boyen's signature scheme is (strong) existentially unforgeable under SDH (which is the asymptotic version of q-SDH, where q is bounded by a polynomial on the security parameter [6]).[3]

3.2   A Concurrent Zero-Knowledge Argument

In this section we describe a concurrent zero-knowledge argument[4], which is an instance of the construction given by Damgård in [11] applied to Chaum and Pedersen's Proof of Knowledge [9] of $\lambda \in \mathbb{Z}_p{}^*$ such that $u_1 = g_1^\lambda$ and $u_2 = g_2^\lambda$, on common input $(g_1, g_2, u_1, u_2, p, G_1, G_2)$, where $g_1, u_1 \in G_1 \setminus \{1\}$ and $g_2, u_2 \in G_2 \setminus \{1\}$ and G_1 and G_2 are groups of prime order p. The proof is used in the design of the new partial signature scheme.

The well-known Chaum-Pedersen proof is a Σ-protocol that works as follows: The prover picks a random $\gamma \in \mathbb{Z}_p{}^*$ and sends $v_1 = g_1^\gamma$ and $v_2 = g_2^\gamma$ to the verifier. Then the verifier sends a challenge $f \in \mathbb{Z}_p$, and the prover responds by sending $s = \gamma + f\lambda$ to the verifier. Finally, the verifier checks the equations $g_1^s = v_1 u_1^f$ and $g_2^s = v_2 u_2^f$. To make the protocol concurrent zero-knowledge, we make use of Pedersen's trapdoor commitments in [28]. To commit to a value $m \in \mathbb{Z}_p$, we choose a random $\alpha \in \mathbb{Z}_p$ and compute the commitment $C(\alpha, m) = g^\alpha h^m$, where g, h are two generators of a group G of prime order p. The trapdoor of the commitment is $t \in \mathbb{Z}_p$ such that $h = g^t$. Obviously, the trapdoor allows to open any commitment c for any m' if we also know one opening $C = C(\alpha, m)$, as $C(\alpha - t(m' - m), m') = C(\alpha, m)$.

The concurrent version of the ZK proof works as follows: On common input $(g_1, g_2, u_1, u_2, p, G, g, h, G_1, G_2, H)$, where (g, h) is the auxiliary string and $\hat{H} : G_1 \times G_2 \to \mathbb{Z}_p$ is a collision resistant hash function, the prover computes γ, v_1, v_2 as in Chaum-Pedersen proof and sends a commitment $C = C(\alpha, \hat{H}(v_1, v_2))$ to the verifier. Then, the verifier sends a challenge f, and the prover responds sending (α, v_1, v_2, s) to the verifier. Finally, the verifier checks the validity of the commitment and the verification equations of Chaum-Pedersen proof.

Notice that the zero-knowledgeness of the proof can be proved without the need of rewinding a dishonest verifier. Indeed, the simulator, knowing the trapdoor of the commitments, just sends a commitment $C = C(\alpha, m)$ that he can open in any possible way. Then, after receiving the challenge, the simulator computes $s, v_1 = g_1^s u_1^{-f}, v_2 = g_2^s u_2^{-f}$ and α' such that the commitment opens correctly to $m' = \hat{H}(v_1, v_2)$. Hence, the verifier is allowed to choose the challenge in the whole set $\mathbb{Z}_p$, and only one round of the protocol suffices to achieve soundness with a negligible probability $1/p$.

Showing a knowledge extractor is not so trivial, but you can find the details in [10]. Basically, after rewinding an honest prover for a polynomial number of times, one can get with high probability two conversations with the same v_1, v_2 but two different challenges f, f'. Then, the extractor computes $\lambda = (s' -$

---

[3] The weaker (deterministic) signature $\sigma = g_1^{\frac{1}{y+m}}$ is also considered in the paper.

[4] Actually, a ZK-argument is enough for the security of the proposed scheme, because all parties are modeled as polynomial-time Turing machines.

$s)/(f' - f)$, where s, s' are the responses given by the prover to the challenges f, f', respectively.

4   The New DBB and PDBB Signature Schemes

Here we give a variation of the signature proposed by Boneh and Boyen, which is still strongly unforgeable under the SDH assumption. For simplicity we refer to it as DBB signature scheme (from *Double* Boneh-Boyen signature). Essentially, the new signature consists of a weak-BB signature b on a random element r, with respect to the base g_1 and signing key x, and another BB signature c on the message m with respect to the base b^u and signing keys y and s.

- **KeyGen.** The signer chooses four random secret elements $x, y, s, u \in \mathbb{Z}_p^*$ and publishes $pk = (X = g_2^x, Y = g_2^y, S = g_2^s, U = g_2^u)$.
- **Sign.** To sign a message $m \in \mathbb{Z}_p$, the signer chooses a random $r \in \mathbb{Z}_p$ and computes $\sigma = (r, g_1^{\frac{1}{x+r}}, g_1^{\frac{u}{(x+r)(y+m+rs)}})$.
- **Ver.** To verify a signature $\sigma = (r, b, c)$, a verifier checks that $e(b, Xg_2^r) = g_T$ and $e(c, Yg_2^m S^r) = e(b, U)$.

To improve the efficiency of the scheme, we can save computing some pairings in the cost of a nonzero but negligible error probability: To verify a signature, a verifier can choose a random $\alpha < 2^t$ and check a single equality $e(b, Xg_2^r U^\alpha) = g_T e(c^\alpha, Yg_2^m S^r)$. Thus the computation of one pairing is replaced by two extra short exponentiations, and the error probability in the verification is 2^{-t}.

Theorem 1. *The DBB signature scheme is strong existentially unforgeable under chosen message attack, assuming that the SDH Assumption holds.*

Proof. Let $\mathcal{F}$ be a forger for the proposed scheme. We will use this forger to make another forger $\mathcal{A}$ that after at most q adaptive queries to a BB signing oracle, it outputs a valid BB message/signature pair, different from the oracle queries, with the same probability.

After receiving the public key of the BB signature instance $(Y = g_2^y, S = g_2^s)$, $\mathcal{A}$ chooses random $x, u \in \mathbb{Z}_p^*$ and lets $X = g_2^x$, $U = g_2^u$. Then $\mathcal{A}$ sends the DBB public key $pk = (X, Y, S, U)$ for the same pairing system to $\mathcal{F}$. Every time that $\mathcal{F}$ asks for a DBB signature on a message m_i, $\mathcal{A}$ forwards the message to the BB oracle and gets the BB signature $(r_i, \gamma_i) = (r_i, g_1^{\frac{1}{y+m_i+r_i s}})$. Then $\mathcal{A}$ computes and forwards $(r_i, g_1^{\frac{1}{x+r_i}}, \gamma_i^{\frac{u}{x+r_i}})$ as a DBB signature on the message m_i to $\mathcal{F}$. If $\mathcal{F}$ succeeds as a forger, then it eventually stops and outputs a valid forgery $(r^*, b^* = g_1^{\frac{1}{x+r^*}}, c^* = g_1^{\frac{u}{(x+r^*)(y+m^*+r^* s)}})$ on the message m^* such that (m^*, r^*) is different from all (m_i, r_i). Raising c^* to the power of $\frac{x+r^*}{u}$, $\mathcal{A}$ will get $g_1^{\frac{1}{y+m^*+r^* s}}$ and outputs it as a valid BB forgery. Clearly, the success probability of $\mathcal{F}$ is not less than the success probability of $\mathcal{A}$. ∎

4.1   The Partial Signature Scheme (PDBB)

In order to get a partial signature scheme (which we call PDBB scheme), in which signatures are not universally verifiable but can only be verified by the Trusted Party or by the signer[5], we build on the previous DBB scheme, introducing the new public keys $(Z_1 = g_1^z, Z_2 = g_2^z)$ generated by the Trusted Party. The signer can convince the recipient of the signature about its validity by means of an interactive zero-knowledge proof. To make this proof non-convincing for an external party, the signer uses a concurrent version of Chaum-Pedersen proof of knowledge [9] combined with Pedersen's trapdoor commitments [28], which is an efficient zero-knowledge argument in the auxiliary string model [11] (as described in Section 3.2). We actually need that both the Trusted Party and the recipient register their keys by proving in zero-knowledge (*e.g.*, to a Certification Authority) the knowledge of the corresponding secret keys (respectively z and the trapdoor of the commitment), so that the recipient cannot later deny his ability to forge a validity proof.[6] The proposed partial signature scheme consists of the following protocols involving a signer A, a recipient B and the Trusted Party:

- **PKeyGen.** As in DBB signatures, A chooses $x, y, s, u \in \mathbb{Z}_p^*$ at random and publishes $pk_A = (X = g_2^x, Y = g_2^y, S = g_2^s, U = g_2^u)$. The Trusted Party chooses $z \in \mathbb{Z}_p^*$ and registers $(Z_1 = g_1^z, Z_2 = g_2^z)$ proving the knowledge of z. B chooses a random $\tau \in \mathbb{Z}_p^*$ and registers $h = g^\tau$ also proving the knowledge of τ, where $G = \langle g \rangle$ is a group of order p. The pair (g, h) is used as the auxiliary string for the concurrent zero-knowledge argument in **PVer**. Observe that no interaction between T and B is required.
- **PSign.** To sign a message $m \in \mathbb{Z}_p$, A chooses a random $r \in \mathbb{Z}_p$ and computes
  $$\rho = (r, Z_1^{\frac{1}{x+r}}, g_1^{\frac{u}{(x+r)(y+m+rs)}}).$$
- **PVer.** Upon reception of a partial signature $\rho = (r, d, c)$ from A, both A and B engage in an interactive verification protocol, firstly checking the equation $e(d, Xg_2^r) = e(g_1, Z_2)$, then running the concurrent zero-knowledge proof that A knows $\lambda = y + m + rs$ such that $Y g_2^m S^r = g_2^\lambda$ and $e(d, U) = e(c, Z_2)^\lambda$. (See Section 3.2.)
- **Conv.** The Trusted Party extracts a DBB signature $\sigma = (r, b, c)$ on m from a PDBB signature $\rho = (r, d, c)$, just by computing $b = d^{1/z}$. Observe that he can also verify the validity of ρ as $e(d, Xg_2^r) = g_T^z$ and $e(d, U) = e(c^z, Y g_2^m S^r)$.

It can be shown that the above scheme is also strong existentially unforgeable (even if z is given to the adversary) under the same assumption as DBB signature. Moreover, an *invisibility* property holds. Namely, no polynomial-time

---

[5] Observe that the partial signature scheme is not a fully-fledged designated verifier scheme, since we do neither require the verifier to prove the validity of a signature in a non-transferable way, nor the signer to verify any previously issued partial signature.

[6] As in most works we are only considering off-line non-transferability. For more details on how to address on-line attacks see [23].

adversary can distinguish a valid PDBB signature on an adversarially chosen message m from a PDBB signature on a random message, under DTDH assumption. Due to the lack of space we decided not to include the proofs in this paper. However, these properties are implicitly used in the design of the contract signing protocol presented in the next section, and the omitted security proofs can be easily inferred from the security analysis of the contract signing protocol.

5   The Proposed Contract Signing Scheme

In this section we describe the proposed contract signing protocol following the description of the three-move architecture instantiated with the signature schemes presented in previous sections.

In order to prevent trivial attacks in the multi-user setting[7], such as the one reported in [13], the partial and ordinary signatures will be computed on the contract digest $m = H(M||ID_A||ID_B||ID_T||t)$ instead of the contract itself, where $H : \{0,1\}^* \to \mathbb{Z}_p$ is a collision-resistant hash function, ID_A and ID_B are the identities of both signers, ID_T is the identity of T, and t is the session deadline for **Exch** and **Res**. In this contract signing protocol, the ordinary signature scheme is DBB, while the partial signature scheme is PDBB, both described in the previous section.

We assume that all the parties are given the following system parameters: a security parameter $\ell \in \mathbb{Z}$, the pairing system parameters $\mathsf{psys} = (p, G_1, G_2, G_T, g_1, g_2, e, \psi, g_T)$, where p is ℓ bits long, the group $G = \langle g \rangle$ for the trapdoor commitments, and the two collision resistant hash functions $H, \hat{H} : \{0,1\}^* \to \mathbb{Z}_p$, respectively for the contract digest and the trapdoor commitments.

- **Setup.** Both signers A, B and T generate and certify their keys as specified in PDBB **PKeyGen**[8]. So we define $sk_A = (x, y, s, u, \tau)$, $pk_A=(X, Y, S, U, h)$, and similarly $sk_B = (x', y', s', u', \tau')$, $pk_B = (X', Y', S', U', h')$, and $sk_T = z$, $pk_T = (Z_1, Z_2)$. We recall T proves the knowledge of z such that $Z_2 = g_2^z$, while A and B respectively prove the knowledge of τ and τ' such that $h = g^\tau$ and $h' = g^{\tau'}$, to a certification authority.
- **Exch.** Once A and B agree on M, the trusted party identity ID_T and a timeout $t > \Delta$, both compute m and run the protocol as specified in Section 2, using **PSig**, **PVer**, **Sig** and **Ver** in PDBB and DBB definitions. Namely, in the first move A runs **PSig** on M and sends ρ_A to B. Then A and B execute **PVer** to check the validity of ρ_A. In case B do not accept, he just leaves the protocol. In the second move, B runs **Sig** on M and sends σ_B to A. In the third move, after A verifies σ_B with **Ver**, she sends a signature σ_A on M to B (computed with **Sig** or directly from ρ_A). After the second move, if the time to the deadline t is less than Δ then B leaves **Exch** and executes **Res** with T. On the other hand, if A has not received any message from B or T at time $t + \Delta$, then she exits the protocol.

---

[7] However, we are not giving any security proof in the multi-user setting.
[8] We assume both can potentially act as signers or verifiers, although A never uses τ and h.

– **Res.** B refers to T for resolving the partial signature $\rho_A = (r, d, c)$ on M. After identifying himself, he must send t, ID_A, M together with ρ_A and his partial signature ρ_B on m to T. T non-interactively checks the validity ρ_A and ρ_B for $m = H(M||ID_A||ID_B||ID_T||t)$. If the protocol is not timed out (with respect to the deadline t) and **Res** has not been invoked before for the same m, then T runs **Conv** for both partial signatures and sends the resulting b to B (i.e., $\sigma_A = (r, b, c)$) and σ_B to A. T temporarily stores the tuple (m, ID_A, ID_B, t) until time t, to prevent further executions of **Res** on the same contract.

5.1   Security Analysis

Correctness and *ambiguity* are straightforward from the description of the protocol. Moreover, *setup-freeness* is implied by the noninteractive nature of **PKeyGen**.

Security Against A. (Proof sketch.) If B accepts a partial signature $\rho = (r, d, c)$ on a message m, then $e(d, Xg_2^r) = e(g_1, Z_2)$ and by the soundness of the zero-knowledge argument, $e(d, U) = e(c, Z_2)^{y+m+rs}$ so $e(d, U) = e(c^z, Yg_2^m S^r)$. Thus T will always accept ρ as valid and he can always compute $b = d^{1/z}$, which allows B to get the valid ordinary signature $\sigma = (r, b, c)$. Notice that the only way to break the soundness of the zero-knowledge argument is by using the trapdoor information of the trapdoor commitment scheme. Indeed, an adversary doing so can be used to get two different openings of the same commitment (via rewinding), and then compute the discrete logarithm of Z_2 on base g_2.

Security Against B. (Proof sketch.) As defined before, we assume that B asks only for executions of **PSign**, **PVer** and **Res**. Indeed, whenever B wishes to know an ordinary signature on a message m, he simply needs to ask **PSign** to obtain a partial signature, and then to ask **Res** on that signature. We consider two different adversaries F_1 and F_2 which use B as a subroutine: F_1 breaks the strong unforgeability of BB signature scheme, while F_2 directly breaks the SDH assumption. Basically F_1 extracts a BB forgery from any partial signature computed by B using a 'fresh' randomness r, while F_2 breaks SDH by tying the SDH instance description to one of the values of r used by the signing oracle simulator, provided B uses exactly that value in the forgery. In either case, a q-SDH instance is solved, since it is shown in [6] that any BB existential forger can be used to break a q-SDH instance, with the same success probability.

Security against T. (Proof sketch.) We show that for any honest but curious T we can build a DBB forger F which perfectly simulates T's (eavesdropping) view of A and B in some contract signing protocol instances. Indeed, F starts receiving the public key (X, Y, S, U) of a DBB instance, and completes it to obtain A and B's keys $pk_A = (X, Y, S, U, h = g^\tau)$, $sk_B = (x', y', s', u', \tau')$ and $pk_B = (X', Y', S', U', h')$. Then, F extracts z and (Z_1, Z_2) from T(by means of the knowledge extractor for the proof of knowledge of the secret key, perhaps involving rewinding of T) and sends him pk_A and pk_B. Now F can trivially simulate everything for T except the partial signatures normally issued by A and the transcripts of **PVer**. However, a partial signature on any message m selected by F is computed by querying the DBB signing oracle to obtain σ_A, and then converting it to ρ_A by means of z. The transcripts of **PVer** are simulated by means of the trapdoor τ'. Eventually, the malicious T outputs a forged signature σ'_A on a new message m', which is forwarded by F thus winning the unforgeability game with the same probability as T(which in turn would imply that q-SDH Assumption is false).[9]

Abuse-freeness. If the transcript of **PSig+PVer** is simulatable by B (without interacting to A) then abuse-freeness is guaranteed. Observe that assuming that nobody can issue valid partial signatures on behalf of A, simulatability of **PSig** requires that valid and invalid partial signatures for a given message m cannot be distinguished in probabilistic polynomial time. Moreover simulatability of **PSig+PVer** also implies that a simulated validity proof for an invalid partial signature must be indistinguishable from a real proof of validity of a valid partial signature.

In our scheme the transcript of a successful execution **PVer** on a given (valid or invalid) PDBB signature can be easily simulated due to the zero-knowledge property of the concurrent Chaum-Pedersen proof (provided B knows his secret key, which is guaranteed by the key registration process). Indeed, to compute the simulated transcript $((C, f, \alpha, v_1, v_2, \delta)$ in the notation used in Section 3.2), B first chooses random challenge f and response δ of the Chaum-Pedersen proof, then computes the witness (v_1, v_2) according to the verification equations, and finally computes the commitment $C = g^\alpha h'^{\hat{H}(v_1, v_2)}$ for a randomness α. Observe that no secret key is involved in those computations.

Therefore, simulatability of **PSig+PVer** depends only on the invisibility of PDBB signatures, *i.e.*, no polynomial time adversary can tell apart a valid PDBB signature $\rho = (r, d, c)$ on a message m from a valid signature $\rho' = (r, d, c')$ on a random (unknown) message m', given m. We show that no external party D can distinguish ρ from ρ' given m. Actually, any such distinguisher D can be used to build an adversary F which breaks the Decisional Tripartite Diffie-Hellman Assumption (DTDH). A description of F follows:

After receiving the description $(X_0 = g_2^{x_0}, Y_0 = g_2^{y_0}, Z_0 = g_0^{z_0}, U_0 = g_2^{u_0})$ of an instance of the DTDH problem for $\mathsf{psys}_0 = (p, G_1, G_2, G_T, g_0, g_2, e, \psi, g_{T0})$ such that $\psi(g_2) = g_0$, F picks m and random $\alpha, s, \epsilon \in \mathbb{Z}_p^*$ and $r \in \mathbb{Z}_p$, and computes $\mathsf{psys} = (p, G_1, G_2, G_T, g_1 = g_0^\epsilon, g_2, e, \psi, g_T = g_{T0}^\epsilon)$, $pk_A = (X = X_0 g_2^{-r}, Y = Y_0 g_2^{-m-rs}, S = g_2^s, U = U_0)$ and $pk_T = (Z_1 = \psi(X_0)^{\alpha\epsilon} = g_1^{x_0\alpha}, Z_2 = X_0^\alpha)$ and

---

[9] Actually, we are proving a stronger version of the security against T. Indeed, an honest but curious T cannot launch a chosen message attack, but he can only collect some message/signature pairs. However, we could think on a Trusted Party who influences the content of the contract signed by A. And this behavior must be seen as a mild chosen message attack in which the adversary cannot choose the message to be signed, but he can influence its probability distribution.

sends psys, pk_A, pk_T them to D, along with m and $\rho = (r, d = g_1^\alpha, c = Z_0^\epsilon)$. Clearly d is a well-formed PDBB signature, since $e(d, Xg_2^r) = e(g_1, X_0)^\alpha = e(g_1, Z_2)$. Moreover, ρ is valid for m if and only if $e(d, U) = e(c, Z_2)^{y+m+rs}$. But $e(d, U) = e(g_1, U_0)^\alpha = e(g_1, g_2^\alpha)^{u_0}$ and $e(c, Z_2)^{y+m+rs} = e(Z_0^\epsilon, X_0^\alpha)^{y_0} = e(g_1, g_2^\alpha)^{x_0 y_0 z_0}$. So ρ is valid for m if and only if $u_0 = x_0 y_0 z_0$. Then, F forwards D's output bit and, since the simulation of D's environment is perfect, both D and F have the same advantage.

6   Efficiency Considerations

In this section we compare our protocol's performance compared to other existing abuse-free protocols, based on on-line/off-line computations. Comparing to non abuse-free protocols is nonsense, since achieving abuse-freeness is the most costly task.

We have provided a table for comparison of efficiency between our scheme and the abuse-free contract signing protocols [16,31], which are proven secure in the random oracle model, and the standard-model one in [20]. The comparison is based on the number of exponentiations and pairings computed by both signers during the **Exch** protocol, and also the number of rounds and the amount of data exchanged. The number of exponentiations given in [31] differs from our estimate because they have not considered the two exponentiations included in each commitment computation. On the other hand the construction in [16] is a generic construction based on the so-called OR-proofs and designated verifier signatures. We analyze an instantiation based on El-Gamal cryptosystem and the designated verifier proofs in [21], which use the signature by Chaum in [8]. The number of exponentiations computed by both the prover and verifier in the proof in [21] is 10, and they need almost the same number for the encryption.

An estimation of the overall computational cost of our **Exch** results in 6 exponentiations and 2 pairings to be computed on-line by A plus 6 off-line exponentiations. On the other hand, B has to compute 8 exponentiations and 4 pairings on-line, and 4 off-line exponentiations. The total communicated data in our **Exch** is around 460 bytes (5 scalars, 6 points in G_1, one in G_2 and 1 pairing result) for the usual sizes of pairing groups (160 bit finite field and embedding degree 6), while the RSA-based protocol in [31] uses about 1220 bytes to be exchanged.

Taking into account that our protocol is secure in the standard model and that the number of rounds is only 5, our protocol is comparable with most existing practical protocols. More precisely, our protocol has better round complexity and communication complexity, while it is about 4 times slower. This shows that our scheme is not only of theoretical interest but also it is suitable for practical applications.

As for the scheme in [20], although it achieves a similar security level in only 3 rounds and in the standard model, the use of Groth-Sahai non-interactive zero-knowledge proofs increases the computational complexity beyond 162 pairing computations[10], and the parties have to exchange more than 82 group elements,

---

[10] Only the NIZK proof is counted.

Table 1. Efficiency comparison

	Garay et al [16]	Wang [31]	Huang et al [20]	Our Protocol
Computational cost	20 exp.	15 exp.	> 162 pair.	24 exp. + 6 pair.
Bytes exchanged		1220	> 1600	460
Number of rounds	4	7	3	5
Security	ROM	ROM	Std. Model	Std. Model

or more than 1600 bytes[11]. Hence, from a practical point of view it cannot be compared to our scheme.

References

1. Asokan, N., Shoup, V., Waidner, M.: Optimistic fair exchange of digital signatures. In: Nyberg, K. (ed.) EUROCRYPT 1998. LNCS, vol. 1403, pp. 591–606. Springer, Heidelberg (1998)
2. Asokan, N., Shoup, V., Waidner, M.: Optimistic fair exchange of digital signatures. IEEE Journal on Selected Areas in Communication 18(4), 593–610 (2000)
3. Bao, F., Deng, R.H., Mao, W.: Efficient and practical fair exchange protocols with off-line TTP. In: IEEE Symposium on Security and Privacy, pp. 77–85 (1998)
4. Ben-Or, M., Goldreich, O., Micali, S., Rivest, R.: A fair protocol for signing contracts. IEEE Transaction on Information Theory 36(1), 40–46 (1990)
5. Boneh, D., Boyen, X.: Short Signatures Without Random Oracles. In: Cachin, C., Camenisch, J.L. (eds.) EUROCRYPT 2004. LNCS, vol. 3027, pp. 56–73. Springer, Heidelberg (2004)
6. Boneh, D., Boyen, X.: Short Signatures Without Random Oracles and the SDH Assumption in Bilinear Groups. Journal of Cryptology 21(2), 149–177 (2008)
7. Camenisch, J., Michels, M.: Confirmer Signature Schemes Secure against Adaptive Adversaries. In: Preneel, B. (ed.) EUROCRYPT 2000. LNCS, vol. 1807, pp. 243–258. Springer, Heidelberg (2000)
8. Chaum, D., Antwerpen, H.V.: Undeniable Signatures. In: Brassard, G. (ed.) CRYPTO 1989. LNCS, vol. 435, pp. 212–216. Springer, Heidelberg (1990)
9. Chaum, D., Pedersen, T.P.: Wallet Databases with Observers. In: Brickell, E.F. (ed.) CRYPTO 1992. LNCS, vol. 740, pp. 89–105. Springer, Heidelberg (1993)
10. Damgård, I.: Practical and provably secure release of a secret and exchange of signatures. Journal of Cryptology 8(4), 201–222 (1995)
11. Damgård, I.: Efficient concurrent zero-knowledge in the auxiliary string model. In: Preneel, B. (ed.) EUROCRYPT 2000. LNCS, vol. 1807, pp. 418–430. Springer, Heidelberg (2000)
12. Deng, R., Gong, L., Lazar, A., Wang, W.: Practical protocol for certified electronic mail. Journal of Network and System Management 4(3), 279–297 (1996)
13. Dodis, Y., Lee, P., Yum, D.: Optimistic Fair Exchange in a Multi-user Setting. In: Okamoto, T., Wang, X. (eds.) PKC 2007. LNCS, vol. 4450, pp. 118–133. Springer, Heidelberg (2007)
14. Dodis, Y., Reyzin, L.: Breaking and repairing fair exchange from PODC 2003. In: Proc. of ACM Workshop On Digital Rights and Management (DRM 2003), pp. 47–54 (2003)

---

[11] Not taking into account the one-time signature included in the partial signatures.

15. Galbraith, S., Paterson, K., Smart, N.P.: Pairings for cryptographers. Discrete Applied Mathematics 156, 3113–3121 (2008)
16. Garay, J.A., Jakobsson, M., Mackenzie, P.: Abuse-free optimistic contract signing. In: Wiener, M. (ed.) CRYPTO 1999. LNCS, vol. 1666, pp. 449–466. Springer, Heidelberg (1999)
17. Goldreich, O.: A simple protocols for signing contracts. In: Advances in Cryptology — CRYPTO 1983, pp. 133–136. Plenum Press, New York (1984)
18. Groth, J., Sahai, A.: Efficient non-interactive proof systems for bilinear groups. In: Smart, N.P. (ed.) EUROCRYPT 2008. LNCS, vol. 4965, pp. 415–432. Springer, Heidelberg (2008)
19. Huang, Q., Yang, G., Wong, D.S., Susilo, W.: Efficient optimistic fair exchange secure in the multi-user setting and chosen-key model without random oracles. In: Malkin, T. (ed.) CT-RSA 2008. LNCS, vol. 4964, pp. 106–120. Springer, Heidelberg (2008)
20. Huang, Q., Yang, G., Wong, D.S., Susilo, W.: Ambiguous Optimistic Fair Exchange. In: Pieprzyk, J. (ed.) ASIACRYPT 2008. LNCS, vol. 5350, pp. 74–89. Springer, Heidelberg (2008)
21. Jakobsson, M., Sako, K., Impagliazzo, R.: Designated verifier proofs and their applications. In: Maurer, U.M. (ed.) EUROCRYPT 1996. LNCS, vol. 1070, pp. 143–154. Springer, Heidelberg (1996)
22. Laguillaumie, F., Paillier, P., Vergnaud, D.: Universally convertible directed signatures. In: Roy, B. (ed.) ASIACRYPT 2005. LNCS, vol. 3788, pp. 682–701. Springer, Heidelberg (2005)
23. Liskov, M., Micali, S.: Online-Untransferable Signatures. In: Cramer, R. (ed.) PKC 2008. LNCS, vol. 4939, pp. 248–267. Springer, Heidelberg (2008)
24. Lu, S., Ostrovsky, R., Sahai, A., Shacham, H., Waters, B.: Sequential aggregate signatures and multisignatures without random oracles. In: Vaudenay, S. (ed.) EUROCRYPT 2006. LNCS, vol. 4004, pp. 465–485. Springer, Heidelberg (2006)
25. Markowitch, O., Saeednia, S.: Optimistic Fair Exchange with Transparent Signature Recovery. In: Syverson, P.F. (ed.) FC 2001. LNCS, vol. 2339, pp. 329–350. Springer, Heidelberg (2002)
26. Micali, S.: Simple and fast optimistic protocols for fair electronic exchange. In: Proc. of the 22th Annual ACM Symp. on Principles of Distributed Computing (PODC 2003), pp. 12–19 (2003)
27. Park, J.M., Chong, E., Siegel, H.J., Ray, I.: Constructing Fair Exchange Protocols for E-commerce Via Distributed Computation of RSA Signatures. In: Proc. of the 22th Annual ACM Symp. on Principles of Distributed Computing (PODC 2003), pp. 172–181 (2003)
28. Pedersen, T.P.: Non-interactive and information-theoretic secure verifiable secret sharing. In: Feigenbaum, J. (ed.) CRYPTO 1991. LNCS, vol. 576, pp. 129–140. Springer, Heidelberg (1992)
29. Pfitzmann, B., Schunter, M., Waidner, M.: Optimal efficiency of optimistic contract signing. In: Proc. of the 17th Annual ACM Symp. on Principles of Distributed Computing (PODC 1998), pp. 113–122 (1998)
30. Piva, F.R., Monteiro, J.R.M., Dahab, R.: Regarding timeliness in the context of fair exchange. In: Proc. of Int. Conf. on Network and Service Security (N2S 2009), pp. 1–6 (2009)
31. Wang, G.: An Abuse-Free Fair Contract Signing Protocol Based on the RSA Signature. In: Proc. of WWW 2005. ACM, New York (2005) 1-59593-046-9/05/0005
32. Waters, B.: Efficient identity-based encryption without random oracles. In: Cramer, R. (ed.) EUROCRYPT 2005. LNCS, vol. 3494, pp. 114–127. Springer, Heidelberg (2005)

Attribute Based Signatures
for Bounded Multi-level Threshold Circuits

Swarun Kumar, Shivank Agrawal, Subha Balaraman, and C. Pandu Rangan

Indian Institute of Technology, Madras

Abstract. Attribute based signature (ABS) permits users produce signatures using any predicate of attributes issued from an attribute authority. ABS disallows any group of colluding users to forge a signature based on a predicate of attributes which they do not individually satisfy. Earlier schemes in this direction are either in the generic group model or support only single-level threshold predicates. In this paper, we propose the first attribute based signature schemes that support bounded flexible multi-level threshold predicates. Our first scheme is proved in the random oracle model and the second does not rely on random oracles. We provide security models for unforgeability and attribute-privacy and formally prove the same under the Computational Diffie-Hellman assumption.

Keywords: attribute-based, signature, threshold, multi-level.

1 Introduction

Attribute based signatures (ABS) is a recently proposed cryptographic primitive in which users produce signatures using any predicate of attributes issued from an attribute authority. For example, consider a company where employees are issued attributes based on their department, designation, etc. Suppose Alice required a document to be signed by an employee who is a part of the administration department and at least a junior manager or a board member in the company. In this scenario, it is sufficient if a valid signature proves that the signer possesses an appropriate set of attributes without revealing any further information about the signer. This requirement is very similar to signature variants like group signatures [1] and ring signatures [2]. The common theme of all these signature primitives is that they allow the signer fine-grained controlled over how much of her personal information is revealed by the signature.

Several ABS schemes are present in literature. In [3], Maji et al. introduced the first ABS scheme which supports predicates having AND, OR and threshold gates, but the security of their scheme is in generic group model. The scheme in [4] is proven secure under the standard computational Diffie-Hellman assumption but considers only (n, n)-threshold, where n is the number of attributes purported in the signature. In [5] Safavi-Naini extended [4] and presented an ABS scheme supporting (k, n)-threshold. In [4,5] every secret attribute component included in a signature has to be used to sign the message one by one making

J. Camenisch and C. Lambrinoudakis (Eds.): EuroPKI 2010, LNCS 6711, pp. 141–154, 2011.
© Springer-Verlag Berlin Heidelberg 2011

it inefficient. Recently Li et al. [6] explore a new signing technique integrating all the secret attributes components into one, so that only one signing operation is required to generate a complete signature, thus improving the efficiency of the scheme. However given construction in [6] works only for single level threshold predicates of the form k-of-n among a certain set of attributes.

Support for multi-level threshold circuits permits a wide range of applications for ABS. For example, an important national document signed with a security clearance level, lets say "$Z3$" can be signed only by few of the defense personnel satisfying the following multilevel predicate:

("Army" AND "General") OR [2-out-of("Navy","Major","Pilot")]

Our contributions. In this paper, we propose the first attribute based signature schemes that support bounded flexible multi-level threshold predicates [7] with and without random oracles. Our schemes use constructs defined in [6], however the latter supports only a single level threshold predicate. We provide the security model for unforgeability and attribute-privacy and formally prove the same under the Computational Diffie-Hellman assumption.

2   Preliminaries

2.1   Computational Diffie-Hellman Assumption

Let $\mathbb{G}$ be a cyclic group generated by g of order p. Let $\mathcal{F}$ be an algorithm which when given a generator $g \in \mathbb{G}$ and elements $g^a, g^b \in \mathbb{G}$, where $a, b \in \mathbb{Z}_p$, outputs g^{ab}. Let $\mathbf{Succ}_{\mathcal{F}}^{cdh} = |Pr[\mathcal{F}(g, g^a, g^b) = g^{ab})]|$ be called the success of $\mathcal{F}$ in breaking the CDH problem. We say that the (t, ϵ)-CDH assumption holds in $\mathbb{G}$ if no adversary running in time less than t can solve the CDH problem with success probability greater than ϵ.

2.2   Bilinear Pairing

Let $\mathbb{G}_1$, $\mathbb{G}_T$ be cyclic multiplicative groups of prime order p. The element $g \in \mathbb{G}_1$ is a generator of $\mathbb{G}_1$. A bilinear pairing is a map $e : \mathbb{G}_1 \times \mathbb{G}_1 \rightarrow \mathbb{G}_T$ with the following properties:

1. **Bilinear:** $e(g_1{}^a, g_2{}^b) = e(g_1, g_2)^{ab}$ for all $g_1 \in \mathbb{G}_1$, $g_2 \in \mathbb{G}_1$, where $a, b \in \mathbb{Z}_p$.
2. **Non-degenerate:** There exists $g_1 \in \mathbb{G}_1$ and $g_2 \in \mathbb{G}_1$ such that $e(g_1, g_2) \neq 1$; in other words, the map does not send all pairs in $\mathbb{G}_1 \times \mathbb{G}_1$ to the identity in $\mathbb{G}_T$.
3. **Computability:** There is an efficient algorithm to compute $e(g_1, g_2)$ for all $g_1 \in \mathbb{G}_1$ and $g_2 \in \mathbb{G}_1$.

2.3   Lagrange Interpolation

Let $q(x)$ be a $d - 1$ degree polynomial with each coefficient in $\mathbb{Z}_p$. Then, given any set of d points on the polynomial $\{q(i) : i \in S\}$, where S is a set of indices such that $|S| = d$, we can use Lagrange's interpolation to find $q(j)$ for any $j \in \mathbb{Z}_p$ as follows:

$$q(j) = \sum_{i \in S} q(i) \Delta_{i,S}(j) \quad, \text{where} \quad \Delta_{i,S}(j) = \prod_{j' \in S \setminus \{i\}} \frac{j - j'}{i - j'}$$

2.4   Scheme Outline

An attribute based signature scheme consists of four algorithms: setup, key generation, signing and verification algorithms. These are defined as follows:

- **Setup.** On input 1^λ, where λ is the security parameter, this algorithm outputs public parameters *params* and SK as a master secret key for attribute authority.
- **Key Generation.** Suppose that a user requests an attribute set $\theta \subseteq \mathcal{U}$. The attribute authority computes SK_θ as the attribute private key with SK if the user is eligible to be issued with these attributes.
- **Signing.** Assume a user wants to sign a message m with a bounded multi-level threshold circuit $\mathcal{T}$. He outputs a signature σ on m if and only if his secret key SK_θ (corresponding to the set of attributes θ) satisfies $\mathcal{T}$.
- **Verification.** After receiving a signature σ on a message m and associated bounded multi-level threshold circuit $\mathcal{T}$, the signature is considered valid if and only if the signer's attributes satisfy $\mathcal{T}$. We require that σ does not reveal any additional information about the identity of the actual signer. This property is called *attribute-signer privacy*. This algorithm outputs a boolean value *accept* or *reject* to denote if the signature is verified or not.

2.5   Security Models

Attribute based signatures have two security requirements: unforgeability and attribute-signer privacy.

2.6   Unforgeability

Informally, unforgeability requires that no polynomial time adversary be allowed to produce a signature with an associated bounded multi-level threshold circuit $\mathcal{T}$ when his attributes do not satisfy the threshold circuit. In this work, we also consider a weaker security notion called Selective-Threshold Circuit Model. Specifically, the adversary has to select a bounded multi-level threshold circuit in advance before Setup phase. This model has also been used in many other protocols such as [7] [6] [8].

- **Initial Phase.** $\mathcal{F}$ chooses and outputs a threshold circuit $\mathcal{T}^*$ on which it will attempt to forge.
- **Setup Phase.** After receiving the threshold circuit $\mathcal{T}^*$, $\mathcal{C}$ chooses a sufficiently large security parameter 1^λ and runs Setup to generate key pair (SK, PK). $\mathcal{C}$ retains the secret key SK and sends public key PK and public parameters *params* to $\mathcal{F}$.

- **Training Phase.** After receiving the public parameters, $\mathcal{F}$ can perform a polynomially bounded number of queries on attribute set, θ (not satisfying the circuit $\mathcal{T}^*$) and $(m, \mathcal{T})$ to the private key generation oracle and signing oracle, respectively. These queries will be answered by $\mathcal{C}$ with secret key SK.
- **Challenge Phase.** Finally, $\mathcal{F}$ outputs a signature σ^* on message m with respect to $\mathcal{T}^*$, which is the threshold circuit sent to $\mathcal{C}$ in the Initial phase. Note that m must not have been queried to the signing oracle in the training face.

The adversary wins the game if σ^* is a valid signature on message m for $\mathcal{T}^*$, $(m, \mathcal{T}^*)$ has not been queried to the signing oracle and no attribute set θ^*, where $\theta^* \subseteq \theta$ satisfying $\mathcal{T}^* = 1$ has been submitted to the private key extraction oracle. The advantage $\mathbf{Adv}_{\mathcal{F}}(1^{\lambda})$ is the probability that it wins the game.

Selective-Threshold circuit Unforgeability. *A forger $\mathcal{F}(t, q_k, q_s, \varepsilon)$ breaks an attribute based signature scheme if $\mathcal{F}$ runs in at most time t, and makes at most q_k private key extraction queries, q_s signature queries, while $\mathbf{Adv}_{\mathcal{F}}(1^{\lambda})$ is atleast ϵ. An attribute based signature scheme is $(t, q_k, q_s, \varepsilon)$ existentially unforgeable if there exists no forger that can (t, q_k, q_s, ϵ) break it.*

2.7   Privacy

To guarantee a strong privacy for the signer, the signature reveals nothing about the identity or attributes of the signer beyond what is explicitly revealed by the claim being made. Its definition is formalized as follows:

Attribute-Signer Privacy. *An Attribute based signature scheme satisfies attribute-signer privacy if for any two attribute sets θ_1, θ_2, a message m, a signature σ on a threshold circuit $\mathcal{T}$ satisfying $\mathcal{T}_{\theta_1}$ and $\mathcal{T}_{\theta_2}$, any adversary $\mathcal{F}$, even with unbounded computational power, cannot identify which attribute set is used to generate the signature with probability better than random guessing. That is, $\mathcal{F}$ can only output the attribute set used in the signature generation with probability no better than $1/2$.*

This holds even if the adversary gets access to the signer's private keys, that is, the signature is simply independent of everything except the message and the threshold circuit.

3   Bounded Multi-level Threshold Circuit

In our constructions, signer's secret key will be associated with a set "θ" of attributes. Any signature σ is associated with a tree structure $\mathcal{T}$ which we call a *bounded multi-level threshold circuit* [7]. A signer could have produced a signature σ if and only if his attributes θ satisfy the associated tree structure $\mathcal{T}$. We now proceed to explain the threshold circuit used in our constructions.

Multi-level threshold circuit. Let $\mathcal{T}$ be a tree representing a multi-level threshold circuit. Every non-leaf node of the tree represents a threshold gate, described by its children and a threshold value. If num_x is the number of children of a node x and k_x is its threshold value, then $0 < k_x \leq num_x$. The term *cardinality* refers to the number of children of a node. Each leaf node x of the tree is associated with an attribute.

Let $\Phi_{\mathcal{T}}$ denote the set of all the non-leaf nodes in the tree $\mathcal{T}$. Further, let $\Psi_{\mathcal{T}}$ be the set of all the non-leaf nodes at depth $d - 1$, where d is the depth of $\mathcal{T}$. To facilitate working with the threshold circuits, we define a few functions. We denote the parent of the node x in the tree by $par(x)$. The threshold circuit $\mathcal{T}$ also defines an ordering between the children of every node, that is, the children of a node x are numbered from 1 to num_x. The function $index(x)$ returns such a number associated with a node x, where the index values are uniquely assigned to nodes in an arbitrary manner for a given access structure. For simplicity, we provision that $index(x) = att(x)$, when x is a leaf node and $att(x)$ is the attribute associated with it. If a set of attributes θ satisfies the tree $\mathcal{T}_x$, we denote it as $\mathcal{T}_x(\theta) = 1$.

Universal threshold circuit. Given a pair of integer values (d, num), define a complete num-ary tree $\mathcal{T}$ of depth d, where each non-leaf node has a threshold value of num. The leaf nodes in $\mathcal{T}$ are empty, i.e., no attributes are assigned to the leaf nodes. Next, $num - 1$ new leaf nodes $\Delta_{u,x}$ are attached to each non-leaf node x, thus increasing the cardinality of x to $2.num - 1$ while the threshold value num is left intact. These newly added leaf nodes $\Delta_{u,x}$ are associated with a special set of attributes called *dummy attributes*. We define the set of all *dummy child nodes* as: $\Delta_u = \bigcup_{x \in \Phi_{\mathcal{T}_u}} \Delta_{u,x}$. Dummy attributes are used to vary the threshold of nodes with respect to other real attributes. This will be explained in detail in the next section. The resultant tree $\mathcal{T}$ is called a (d, num)-universal threshold circuit, where d, num are initialized during setup.

Normal Form. A $\mathcal{T}'$ is a (d, num)-*bounded threshold circuit* if it has a depth $d' \leq d$, and each non-leaf node in $\mathcal{T}'$ exhibits a cardinality at most num. Consider a (d, num)-bounded threshold circuit $\mathcal{T}'$. We say that $\mathcal{T}'$ exhibits the (d, num)-normal form if: It has a depth $d' = d$ and all the leaf nodes in $\mathcal{T}'$ are at depth d. Any (d, num)-bounded threshold circuit $\mathcal{T}'$ can be converted to the (d, num)-normal form by prefixing a vertical chain of nodes (each with cardinality and threshold 1) to leaf nodes not at depth d.

Map between threshold circuits. Consider a (d, num)-universal threshold circuit $\mathcal{T}_u$ and another tree $\mathcal{T}'$ that exhibits the (d, num)-normal form. A map between the nodes of $\mathcal{T}'$ and $\mathcal{T}_u$ is defined in the following way in a top-down manner:

1. First, the root of $\mathcal{T}'$ is mapped to the root of $\mathcal{T}_u$.
2. Now suppose that a node x' in $\mathcal{T}'$ is mapped to a node x in $\mathcal{T}_u$.

3. Let $z'_1, \cdots, z'_{num'_x}$ be the child nodes of x', ordered according to their index values. Then, for each child node $z'_i, i \in [1, num_{x'}]$ of x' in T', set the corresponding child node z_i (i.e. with index value $index(z'_i)$) of x in T_u as the map of z'.

4. This procedure is performed recursively, until each node in T' is mapped to a corresponding node in T_u.

To capture the above node mapping procedure between T' to T_u, we define a public function $map(.)$ that takes a node (or a set of nodes) in T' as input and returns the corresponding node (or a set of nodes) in T_u.

4   Scheme

Our scheme allows a signer whose attributes satisfy a threshold circuit T to sign a message m using T. During setup, the signer is given secret components with respect to the universal threshold circuit T_u. The leaf nodes of this tree map to attributes (we call these "real" attributes) and we have additional $num - 1$ "dummy" children attached to each node. We know from the previous section that any tree T in (d, num)-normal form can be mapped to T_u. Furthermore, we can support any threshold from 1 to num on each of these nodes by mapping an appropriate number of *dummy attributes* to the dummy children. This technique is similar to the one introduced in [7]. Now, the signer can produce signature on any (d, num)-bounded threshold circuit T by mapping it to T_u.

4.1   Setup

Define the universe of real attributes as $\mathcal{U} = (1, \cdots, n)$. We define a (d, num) universal bounded threshold circuit T_u. We define a universe of $num - 1$ dummy attributes δ. Select a random generator $g \in \mathbb{G}_1$. Choose $\chi \in_R Z_p^*$ and set $g_1 \leftarrow g^\chi$, $g_2 \in_R \mathbb{G}_1$.

Two hash functions H_1 and H_2 are chosen such that $H_1, H_2 : \{0,1\}^* \to \mathbb{G}_1$. Define $Z = e(g_1, g_2)$. The public parameters are $params = (g, g_1, g_2, Z, num, H_1, H_2)$ and the master secret key is χ.

4.2   Key Generation

The key generation algorithm outputs a private key that enables the signer to sign on any message m under a bounded threshold circuit T, as long as $T(\theta) = 1$. Choose a random polynomial q_x for each non-leaf node x in the universal bounded threshold circuit T_u. These polynomials are chosen in the following way in a top-down manner, starting from the root node r. For each x, set the degree c_x of the polynomial q_x to be one less than the threshold value, i.e., $c_x = num - 1$. Now, for the root node r, set $q_r(0) = \chi$ and choose c_r other points of the polynomial q_r randomly to define it completely. For any other non-leaf node x, assign $q_x(0) = q_{par(x)}(index(x))$ and choose c_x other points randomly to completely define q_x.

The secret values are given to the user by generating a new attribute set $\theta^* = \theta \cup \delta$. For all $i \in \theta^*$:

1. If $i \in \theta$, for each $x \in \Psi_{T_u}$
   (a) Choose $r_{x,i} \in Z_p{}^*$
   (b) Compute $d_{x,i0} = \{g_2{}^{q_x(i)} H_1(x||i)^{r_{x,i}}\}$, $d_{x,i1} = g^{r_{x,i}}$
2. If $j \in \delta$, for each $y \in \Phi_{T_u}$
   (a) Choose $r_{y,j} \in Z_p{}^*$
   (b) Compute $d_{y,j0} = \{g_2{}^{q_y(j)} H_1(y||j)^{r_{y,j}}\}$, $d_{y,j1} = g^{r_{y,j}}$

Thus the private key is $\{d_{x,i0}, d_{x,i1} | x \in \Psi_{T_u}, i \in \theta\} \cup \{d_{y,i0}, d_{y,i1} | y \in \Phi_{T_u}, i \in \delta\}$.

4.3   Signing

To generate a signature on message m with a bounded threshold circuit T, the signer first finds a mapping between T and the universal threshold circuit T_u. We require that T has depth $\leq d$, where each non-leaf node x in the tree is a k_x-out-of-num_x threshold gate, where $num_x \leq num$. The signer then chooses an assignment of real attributes to the leaf nodes in T_u.

Before signing message m with the bounded threshold circuit T , the signer first converts it to the normal form (if required). A map between the nodes in T and the universal threshold circuit T_u is defined as explained in section 3. Finally, for each non-leaf node x in T, the signer chooses an arbitrary $(num - k_x)$-sized set $\Delta_x \subseteq \Delta_{u,x}$ of dummy child nodes of $map(x)$ in T_u . Denote $\Delta = \bigcup_{x \in \Phi_{T_u}} \Delta_x$ the set of all dummy attributes under consideration, Θ'' to be the set of all leaf nodes corresponding to real attributes in T and Θ' to be the set of leaf nodes in T corresponding to attributes in Θ. Since the set of attributes θ satisfies the tree T, there exists $\Lambda = \{\lambda_i | i \in \Theta' \cup \Delta\}$, such that the master secret key $\chi = \sum_{y \in \Theta' \cup \Delta} q_{par(y)}(index(y))\lambda_y$. Note that the signer may compute Λ by applying the Lagrange's interpolation formula recursively. The signer, then chooses $s \in Z_p{}^*$ and computes:

$$\sigma_0 = \prod_{y \in \Theta' \cup \Delta} d_{par(y),att(y)0}^{\lambda_y} \prod_{y \in \Theta'' \cup \Delta} H_1(par(y)||att(y))^{r'_y} \ H_2(m)^s$$

$$\sigma_y = \begin{cases} d_{par(y),att(y)1}^{\lambda_y} g^{r'_y} & \text{if } y \in \Theta' \cup \Delta \\ g^{r'_y} & \text{if } y \in \Theta'' \backslash \Theta' \end{cases}$$

$$\sigma'_0 = g^s$$

Finally the signer outputs a signature $\sigma = (T, map(\cdot), \sigma_0, (\sigma_y)_{y \in \Theta'' \cup \Delta}, \sigma'_0)$.

4.4   Verification

The verifier obtains the signature $\sigma = (T, map(\cdot), \sigma_0, (\sigma_y)_{y \in \Theta'' \cup \Delta}, \sigma'_0)$ of a message m with a bounded multi-level threshold circuit T. Once again, Θ'' denotes the nodes corresponding to set of attributes in the leaf node and Δ denotes the set of dummy attributes selected by the signer in T_u. The signature can be verified by the following equation:

$$\frac{e(g, \sigma_0)}{\{\prod_{y \in \Theta'' \cup \Delta} e(H_1(par(y)\|att(y)), \sigma_y)\} e(H_2(m), \sigma_0')} = e(g_1, g_2)$$

This proves the threshold circuit T is satisfied by the signer of σ.

5   Security

We prove the unforgeability and attribute signer privacy of our schem.

5.1   Unforgeability

Theorem 1. Suppose that the (t', ϵ')-CDH assumption holds in $\mathbb{G}_1$ and the adversary makes at most q_{H1}, q_{H2}, q_K and q_S times queries to random oracle H_1, H_2, private key extraction and signature queries, respectively. Then, the Attribute Based Signature scheme is $(t, q_{H1}, q_{H2}, q_K, q_S, \epsilon)$-EUF-STC-CMA, where $t' < t + (q_{H1} + q_{H2} + 2q_K + 3q_S num) t_{exp}$, t_{exp} is the maximum time for an exponentiation in $\mathbb{G}_1$, and $\epsilon' \approx \epsilon/(q_{H2} \prod_{y \in \Phi_{T_u}} \binom{d-1}{d-k_y}))$

Proof. The construction is proven under selective-threshold circuit security model. Suppose the forger $\mathcal{F}$ can sign on the message m, then we build a challenger $\mathcal{C}$ that uses $\mathcal{F}$ to solve the CDH problem. Given $(g, A = g^a, B = g^b)$ and $\mathcal{C}$ has to compute g^{ab}.

Setup Phase. First $\mathcal{F}$ challenges on the bounded multi-level threshold circuit $\mathcal{T}$ with depth $d' \leq d$, where each non-leaf node x in the tree is a k_x-out-of-num_x threshold gate, where $num_x \leq num$.
The challenger obtains the normal form of $\mathcal{T}$, if required, and uses the mapping $map(\cdot)$ between $\mathcal{T}$ and the universal access structure $\mathcal{T}_u$. For each non-leaf node $y \in \Phi_T$ with threshold k_y, $\mathcal{C}$ selects an arbitrary subset of Δ_y^* of the dummy child nodes of $map(y)$ such that $|\Delta_y^*| = d - k_y$. Define $\Delta^* = \bigcup_{y \in \Phi_{T_u}} \Delta_y^*$. Then, $\mathcal{C}$ sets $g_1 = A$ and $g_2 = B$. Also set Θ^* to denote the set of children of Ψ_{T_u} mapped to real attributes, which are associated with the leaf nodes of the normal form of $\mathcal{T}$.

Training Phase. Assume that $\mathcal{F}$ makes at most q_{H_1} times to the H_1 oracle and q_{H_2} times to the H_2 oracle. The challenger maintains lists $\mathcal{L}_1$ and $\mathcal{L}_2$ to store the oracle's queried outputs. Also $\mathcal{C}$ selects a random integer $\gamma \in [1, q_{H_2}]$. This γ is the challenger's guess of the index of the query m^* made to oracle H_2, where m^* is the message on which the signature is forged. If $x\|i$ is sent as a query of H_1, $\mathcal{C}$ checks the list $\mathcal{L}_1$ and works as follows:

1. If an entry is already found in $\mathcal{L}_1$, then the same answer is returned to $\mathcal{F}$.
2. Otherwise:
   (a) If $y \in (\Theta^* \cup \Delta^*)$, let $i = att(y)$, and choose $\omega_{x,i} \in_R \mathbb{Z}_p$ and set $H_1(x||i) \leftarrow g^{\omega_{x,i}}$.
   (b) If $y \notin (\Theta^* \cup \Delta^*)$, $i = att(y)$, and choose $\omega_{x,i}, \gamma_{x,i} \in_R \mathbb{Z}_p$ and set $H_1(x||i) \leftarrow g_1^{-\omega_{x,i}} g^{\gamma_{x,i}}$.

If m_i is sent as a query of H_2, $\mathcal{C}$ checks the list $\mathcal{L}_2$. It functions as below:

1. If an entry for the query is found in $\mathcal{L}_2$, the same answer will be returned to $\mathcal{F}$.
2. Otherwise:
   (a) If $i \neq \gamma$, it chooses random $v_i, \omega_i' \in \mathbb{Z}_p$ and answers $H_2(m_i) = g_1^{v_i} g^{\omega_i'}$.
   (b) If $i = \gamma$, it chooses random $\omega_i' \in \mathbb{Z}_p$ and returns $H_2(m_i) \leftarrow g^{\omega_i'}$.

Key Generation Oracle. A key can be requested for upto q_K private key generation queries on any set of attributes not satisfying the challenge threshold circuit $\mathcal{T}$. Our aim is to provide decryption key components of the form $\{d_{x,i0}, d_{x,i1}|x \in \Psi_{\mathcal{T}_u}, i \in \theta\}$ for real attributes and $\{d_{y,i0}, d_{y,i1}|y \in \Phi_{\mathcal{T}_u}, i \in \delta\}$ for dummy attributes.

The challenger first needs to set up a family of $num - 1$ degree polynomials $q_x(\cdot)$ for all $x \in \Phi_{\mathcal{T}_u}$ such that $q_r(0) = \chi = a$, where r is the root and $q_x(0) = q_{par(x)}(index(x))$, otherwise. Let the set of attributes corresponding to the key requested be "θ". The attributes, may or may not satisfy $\mathcal{T}_x$ (i.e. the challenge threshold circuit rooted at node x), but will definitely not satisfy $\mathcal{T}_r$ (i.e. the challenge threshold circuit $\mathcal{T}$). We now define two algorithms KEYGENSAT and KEYGENUNSAT which award the decryption keys for satisfied and unsatisfied threshold circuits respectively.

- KEYGENSAT($\mathcal{T}_x, \phi_x, \theta$): The algorithm considers two cases based on whether $x \in \Psi_{\mathcal{T}_x}$:
  - If $x \in \Psi_{\mathcal{T}_x}$: Define a random $num - 1$ degree polynomial $q_x(\cdot)$ such that $q_x(0) = \phi_x$. Now set the decryption keys for the each attribute i attached to child y of x as $d_{x,i0} = g_2^{q_x(index(y))} H_1(x||i)^{r_{x,i}}$ and $d_{x,i1} = g^{r_{x,i}}$.
  - If $x \notin \Psi_{\mathcal{T}_x}$: Define a random $num - 1$ degree polynomial $q_x(\cdot)$ such that $q_x(0) = \phi_x$. Now set the decryption keys for every dummy attribute i attached to a dummy child y of x as $d_{x,i0} = g_2^{q_x(index(y))} H_1(x||i)^{r_{x,i}}$ and $d_{x,i1} = g^{r_{x,i}}$. For the every other child y of x, recursively call KEYGENSAT($\mathcal{T}_y, q_x(index(y)), \theta$).

- KEYGENUNSAT($\mathcal{T}_x, g^{\phi_x}, \theta$): The algorithm considers two cases based on whether $x \in \Psi_{\mathcal{T}_x}$:
  - If $x \in \Psi_{\mathcal{T}_x}$: Let θ^* denote the real attributes attached to the leaf nodes of $\mathcal{T}_x$ and k_x denote the threshold on x. As the sub-tree $\mathcal{T}_x$ is unsatisfied, we have $|\theta^* \cap \theta| < k_x$. We first define three sets Γ, Γ', S in the following manner: $\Gamma = (\theta \cup \theta^*) \cup \Delta_x^*$, and Γ' such that $\Gamma \subseteq \Gamma' \subseteq S$ and $|\Gamma'| = num - 1$. Let $S = \Gamma \cup \{0\}$. Next, simulate the decryption key components D_i as follows:

* For $y \in \Gamma'$: Let $i = att(y)$. Output $(g_2^{\tau_{x,i}} H_1(x||i)^{r_{x,i}}, g^{r_{x,i}})$, where $\tau_{x,i}, r_{x,i}$ are randomly chosen from $\mathbb{Z}_p$.

* For $y \notin \Gamma'$: Let $i = att(y)$. We define a polynomial $q_x(\cdot)$ with $q_x(0) = \phi_x$ and $q_x(j) = \tau_{x,j}$ for all $j = att(z) : z \in \Gamma'$. The challenger outputs the following:

$$(g_2^{\frac{\Delta_{0,S}(i)\gamma_{x,i}}{\omega_{x,i}}+\sum_{j \in \Gamma', k=att(j)} \Delta_{k,S}(i)q_x(k)} (g_1^{-\omega_{x,i}} g^{\gamma_{x,i}})^{r'_{x,i}}, g_2^{\frac{\Delta_{0,S}(i)}{\omega_{x,i}}} g^{r'_{x,i}})$$

Here, $q_x(i) = \sum_{w \in \Gamma', j=att(w)} \Delta_{j,S}(i)q_x(j) + \Delta_{0,S}(i)q_x(0)$. This key is valid with $r_{x,i} = \frac{\Delta_{0,S}(i)}{\omega_{x,i}}b + r'_{x,i}$.

- If $x \notin \Psi_{\mathcal{T}_x}$: Let Δ'_x denote the set of dummy child nodes of x which are satisfied in $\mathcal{T}$ and Δ''_x denote the set of nodes which are not satisfied. Let N'_x be the set of other child nodes which are satisfied and N''_x be the set of unsatisfied child nodes. Then we consider four cases:

* For $y \in \Delta'_x$: Let $i = att(y)$. Output $(g_2^{\tau_{x,i}} H_1(x||i)^{r_{x,i}}, g^{r_{x,i}})$, where $\tau_{x,i}, r_{x,i}$ are randomly chosen from $\mathbb{Z}_p$.

* For $y \in N'_x$: Choose $\tau_{x,i} \in_R \mathbb{Z}_p$. Now recursively call KEYGEN-SAT$(\mathcal{T}_y, \tau_{x,i}, \theta)$.

* For $y \in \Delta''_x$: Let $i = att(y)$, $S = \Delta'_x \cup N'_x \cup \{0\}$. We define a polynomial $q_x(\cdot)$ with $q_x(0) = \phi_x$ and $q_x(j) = \tau_{x,j}$ for all $j = att(z) : z \in \Delta'_x \cup N'_x$. The challenger outputs the following:

$$(g_2^{\frac{\Delta_{0,S}(i)\gamma_{x,i}}{\omega_{x,i}}+\sum_{j \in \Gamma', k=att(j)} \Delta_{k,S}(i)q_x(k)} (g_1^{-\omega_{x,i}} g^{\gamma_{x,i}})^{r'_{x,i}}, g_2^{\frac{\Delta_{0,S}(i)}{\omega_{x,i}}} g^{r'_{x,i}})$$

Here, $q_x(i) = \sum_{w \in \Gamma', j=att(w)} \Delta_{j,S}(i)q_x(j) + \Delta_{0,S}(i)q_x(0)$. This key is valid with $r_{x,i} = \frac{\Delta_{0,S}(i)}{\omega_{x,i}}b + r'_{x,i}$.

* For $y \in N''_x$: Let $S = \Delta'_x \cup N'_x \cup \{0\}$, $i = index(y)$. We obtain $g^{\tau'} \leftarrow g_1^{\Delta_{0,S}(i)} g^{\sum_{j \in S} \tau_{x,j} \Delta_{j,S}(i)}$. Now recursively compute KEYGE-NUNSAT$(\mathcal{T}_y, g^{\tau'}, \theta)$

Clearly, the challenger may obtain the required decryption keys by invoking KEYGENUNSAT$(\mathcal{T}_r, A, \theta)$.

Signing Oracle. Suppose a signature is requested on a message m such that $H_2(m) = g_1^{v_{i_k}} g^{w'_{i_k}}$. The challenger provides a signature of the form $(g_2^a \prod_{y \in \Theta \cup \Delta} H_1(par(y)||att(y))^{r_y} H_2(m)^s$, $\{g^{r_y}\}_{y \in \Theta \cup \Delta}, g^s)$ as follows: Choose $s', r_y \in \mathbb{Z}_p$ and let $s = -\frac{1}{v_{i_k}}b + s'$. Then compute:

$$\sigma_0 = g_2^a \prod_{y \in \Theta \cup \Delta} H_1(par(y)||att(y))^{r_y} H_2(m)^s$$

$$= (g_1^{v_{i_k}} g^{w'_{i_k}})^{s'} \prod_{y \in \Theta \cup \Delta} H_1(par(y)||att(y))^{r_y} g_2^{\frac{-w'_{i_k}}{v_{i_k}}}$$

$$\sigma'_0 = g^s = g_2^{\frac{-1}{v_{i_k}}} g^{s'}$$

Challenge Phase. Finally, the adversary outputs a forged signature σ^* on message m^* for attributes Θ^* with dummy attributes mapped on to $\bar{\Delta}^*$. If $H_2(m) \neq g^{\omega'_\gamma}$ or $\bar{\Delta}^* \neq \Delta^*$, the challenger will abort. Otherwise, it satisfies the verification equation, which means that $\sigma^* = (\sigma_0, \{\sigma_y\}_{y \in \Theta^* \cup \Delta^*}, \sigma_0^*) = (g_2^a \prod_{y \in \Theta^* \cup \Delta^*} H_1(par(y)\|att(y))^{r_y} H_2(m)^s, \{g^{r_y}\}_{y \in \Theta^* \cup \Delta^*}, g^s)$.

Hence, the challenger can compute $g^{ab} = \sigma_0^* / \prod_y (\sigma_y^*)^{\omega_{y,i}} (\sigma_0^*)^{\omega'_\gamma}$ as $H_1(par(y)\|att(y)) = g^{\omega_{y,i}}$ and $H_2(m) = g^{\omega'_\gamma}$.

Probability Analysis. For the success of $\mathcal{C}$, we require that forgery signature on message m^* such that $H_2(m^*) = g^{\omega'_\gamma}$ and $\Delta^* = \bar{\Delta}^*$. For the correct guess of the subset Δ^* from the set of dummy attributes, the probability is the constant $1 / \prod_{y \in \Phi_{T_u}} \binom{d-1}{d-k_y}$. Therefore, we can get the probability of solving CDH problem as $\epsilon' \approx \epsilon / (q_{H_2} \prod_{y \in \Phi_{T_u}} \binom{d-1}{d-k_y}))$, if the adversary's success probability is ϵ.

5.2   Privacy

Theorem 2. Our Attribute based signature scheme achieves signer-attribute privacy.

Proof. In our construction, for a bounded multi-level threshold attribute-based signature, it is easy to see that the signature will not reveal which set of attributes are really used to sign the message using a threshold circuit $\mathcal{T}$, because any subset of attributes among the attributes attached to the leaves of $\mathcal{T}$ and satisfying $\mathcal{T}$ can generate the signature. Hence, we only need to prove that the signer's identity among all the users with these attributes is kept anonymous even the circuit is an "and" gate.

First, the attribute center runs *Setup* to get the public parameters *params* and the master key χ. It gives the adversary *params* and χ. After these interactions, the adversary outputs two attributes θ_1 and θ_2, where $\theta_a = \theta_1 \cap \theta_2$. Private key for each user should include keys corresponding to the default attribute set δ. Assume the challenger or adversary has generated the private keys as $sk_1 = (d^1_{x,i0}, d^1_{x,i1} \forall x \in \Psi_{T_u}, i \in \theta_1) \cup (d^1_{y,i0}, d^1_{y,i1} \forall y \in \Phi_{T_u}, i \in \delta)$ and $sk_2 = (d^2_{x,i0}, d^2_{x,i1} \forall x \subset \Psi_{T_u}, i \in \theta_2) \cup (d^2_{y,i0}, d^2_{y,i1} \forall y \in \Phi_{T_u}, i \in \delta)$. Let $d^\rho_{x,i0} = g_2{}^{q_x(i)} H_1(x\|i)^{r_{x_\rho i}}$ and $d^\rho_{x,i1} = g^{r_{x_\rho i}}$ for each $i \in \theta_\rho$ where $\rho \in (1,2)$, $r_{x_\rho i} \in \mathbb{Z}_p$ and each q_x is a $num - 1$ degree polynomial with $q_r(0) = \chi$.

Then the adversary outputs a message m^* and a subset $\theta_a^* = (i_1, \cdots, i_k) \subseteq \theta_a$, where θ_a^* satisfies $\mathcal{T}$. It asks the challenger to generate a signature on message m^* with respect to θ_a^* from either sk_1 or sk_2. The challenger chooses a random bit $b \in (1,2)$, and an appropriate subset Δ' of dummy child nodes. Let θ^* denote the set of nodes mapped to real attributes in $\mathcal{T}$. The challenger outputs the signature by running algorithm *Signing* using the secret key sk_1 on attributes θ_1 as follows:

$$\sigma_0^* = g_2^\chi \prod_{i \in \theta^* \cup \delta'} H_1(i\|att(i))^{r_i} \; H_2(m)^s$$

$$\sigma_y^* = g^{r_y'} \text{ for } y \in \Theta^* \cup \Delta'$$

$$\sigma_0^{*'} = g^s$$

Based on the Lagrange interpolation, it is obvious that this signature could be generated either from sk_1 or sk_2. Therefore, we have proved the signature could also be generated from the private key sk_2 for attributes θ_2. By using similar proof, we infer that if a signature is generated by the private key sk_2 for attributes θ_2, then it can also be generated for private key sk_1 for attributes θ_1. From the proof, we have shown that the attribute based signature scheme satisfies unconditional attribute-signer privacy.

6   Removing Random Oracles

The above scheme may be readily modified to be provably secure without random oracles. We highlight the modifications below:

Setup. In addition to the public parameters, pick a random element $u' \in \mathbb{G}$. Next, instead of the hash functions, choose a set of random vectors $\mathbb{H}_y = (h_{y,i})\ \forall y \in \Phi_{T_u}$ and a random n-length vector $\mathbb{U} = (u_i)$. Clearly, $|\mathbb{H}_y| = l+num-1$, for $y \in \Psi_{T_u}$ and $|\mathbb{H}_y| = num-1$, otherwise. The public parameters are $params = (g, g_1, g_2, Z, num, u', \mathbb{U}, \mathbb{H})$ and the master secret key is χ.

Key Generation. The private key $\{d_{x,i0}, d_{x,i1}|x \in \Psi_{T_u}, i \in \theta\} \cup \{d_{y,i0}\ , d_{y,i1}\ |y \in \Phi_{T_u}, i \in \delta\}$ is calculated as:

$$d_{x,i0} = \{g_2{}^{q_x(i)}(g_1 h_{x,i})^{r_{x,i}}\}, d_{x,i1} = g^{r_{x,i}}$$

$$d_{y,j0} = \{g_2{}^{q_y(j)}(g_1 h_{y,j})^{r_{y,j}}\}, d_{y,j1} = g^{r_{y,j}}$$

Signing. Let the message be $m = (\mu_1, \cdots, \mu_n) \in \{0,1\}^n$. The signer computes:

$$\sigma_0 = \prod_{y \in \Theta' \cup \Delta} d_{par(y),att(y)0}^{\lambda_y} \prod_{y \in \Theta'' \cup \Delta} (g_1 h_{par(y),att(y)})^{r_y'} \ (u' \prod_{j=1}^{n} u_j^{\mu_j})^s$$

$$\sigma_y = \begin{cases} d_{par(y),att(y)1}^{\lambda_y} g^{r_y'} & \text{if } y \in \Theta' \cup \Delta \\ g^{r_y'} & \text{if } y \in \Theta'' \backslash \Theta' \end{cases}$$

$$\sigma_0' = g^s$$

Finally the signer outputs a signature $\sigma = (\mathcal{T}, map(\cdot), \sigma_0, (\sigma_y)_{y \in \Theta'' \cup \Delta}, \sigma_0')$.

Verification. The signature can be verified by the following equation.

$$\frac{e(g, \sigma_0)}{\{\prod_{y \in \Theta'' \cup \Delta} e(g_1 h_{par(y),att(y)}, \sigma_y)\} e(u' \prod_{j=1}^{n} u_j^{\mu_j}, \sigma_0')} = e(g_1, g_2)$$

7 Conclusion and Open Problems

In this paper, we proposed the first attribute based signature scheme that supports flexible multi-level threshold circuits with and without random oracles. We have shown unforgeability and attribute-privacy of the scheme based on the Computational Diffie-Hellman assumption. An interesting open problem is to find an attribute based encryption scheme that supports general unbounded multi-level threshold circuits or a general monotone span program.

References

1. Camenisch, J.: Efficient and generalized group signatures. In: Fumy, W. (ed.) EUROCRYPT 1997. LNCS, vol. 1233, pp. 465–479. Springer, Heidelberg (1997)
2. Rivest, R.L., Shamir, A., Tauman, Y.: How to leak a secret. In: Boyd, C. (ed.) ASIACRYPT 2001. LNCS, vol. 2248, pp. 552–565. Springer, Heidelberg (2001)
3. Maji, H., Prabhakaran, M., Rosulek, M.: Attribute-based signatures: Achieving attribute-privacy and collusion-resistance. Cryptology ePrint Archive, Report 2008/328 (2008) http://eprint.iacr.org/
4. Li, J., Kim, K.: Attribute-based ring signatures (2008), http://eprint.iacr.org/2008/394
5. Shahandashti, S.F., Safavi-Naini, R.: Threshold attribute-based signatures and their application to anonymous credential systems. In: Preneel, B. (ed.) AFRICACRYPT 2009. LNCS, vol. 5580, pp. 198–216. Springer, Heidelberg (2009)
6. Li, J., Au, M.H., Susilo, W., Xie, D., Ren, K.: Attribute-based signature and its application. In: ASIAN ACM Symposium on Information, Computer and Communications Security 2010 (ASIACCS 2010) (2010)
7. Goyal, V., Jain, A., Pandey, O., Sahai, A.: Bounded ciphertext policy attribute based encryption. In: Aceto, L., Damgård, I., Goldberg, L.A., Halldórsson, M.M., Ingólfsdóttir, A., Walukiewicz, I. (eds.) ICALP 2008, Part II. LNCS, vol. 5126, pp. 579–591. Springer, Heidelberg (2008)
8. Sahai, A., Waters, B.: Fuzzy identity-based encryption. In: Cramer, R. (ed.) EUROCRYPT 2005. LNCS, vol. 3494, pp. 457–473. Springer, Heidelberg (2005)
9. Bellare, M., Goldreich, O.: On defining proofs of knowledge. In: Brickell, E.F. (ed.) CRYPTO 1992. LNCS, vol. 740, pp. 390–420. Springer, Heidelberg (1993)
10. Boneh, D., Franklin, M.K.: Identity-based encryption from the weil pairing. In: Kilian, J. (ed.) CRYPTO 2001. LNCS, vol. 2139, pp. 213–229. Springer, Heidelberg (2001)
11. Boyen, X.: Mesh signatures. In: Naor, M. (ed.) EUROCRYPT 2007. LNCS, vol. 4515, pp. 210–227. Springer, Heidelberg (2007)
12. Camenisch, J., Lysyanskaya, A.: An efficient system for non-transferable anonymous credentials with optional anonymity revocation. In: Pfitzmann, B. (ed.) EUROCRYPT 2001. LNCS, vol. 2045, pp. 93–118. Springer, Heidelberg (2001)
13. Camenisch, J., Lysyanskaya, A.: A signature scheme with efficient protocols. In: Cimato, S., Galdi, C., Persiano, G. (eds.) SCN 2002. LNCS, vol. 2576, pp. 268–289. Springer, Heidelberg (2003)
14. Chase, M., Chow, S.S.M.: Improving privacy and security in multi-authority attribute-based encryption. In: ACM Conference on Computer and Communications Security, pp. 121–130 (2009)
15. Cheung, L., Newport, C.C.: Provably secure ciphertext policy abe. In: ACM Conference on Computer and Communications Security, pp. 456–465 (2007)

16. Goyal, V., Pandey, O., Sahai, A., Waters, B.: Attribute-based encryption for fine-grained access control of encrypted data. In: ACM Conference on Computer and Communications Security, pp. 89–98 (2006)
17. Shanqing, G., Yingpei, Z.: Attribute-based signature scheme. In: ISA 2008: Proceedings of the 2008 International Conference on Information Security and Assurance (ISA 2008), pp. 509–511 (2008)
18. Yang, P., Cao, Z., Dong, X.: Fuzzy identity based signature (2008),
    http://eprint.iacr.org/2008/002
19. Shamir, A.: Identity-based cryptosystems and signature schemes. In: Blakely, G.R., Chaum, D. (eds.) CRYPTO 1984. LNCS, vol. 196, pp. 47–53. Springer, Heidelberg (1985)
20. Ostrovsky, R., Sahai, A., Waters, B.: Attribute-based encryption with non-monotonic access structures. In: ACM Conference on Computer and Communications Security, pp. 195–203 (2007)

User-Centric Identity Management Using Trusted Modules

Jan Vossaert[1], Jorn Lapon[1], Bart De Decker[2], and Vincent Naessens[1]

[1] Katholieke Hogeschool Sint-Lieven, Department of Industrial Engineering
Gebroeders Desmetstraat 1, 9000 Ghent, Belgium
`firstname.lastname@kahosl.be`
[2] Katholieke Universiteit Leuven, Department of Computer Science,
Celestijnenlaan 200A, 3001 Heverlee, Belgium
`firstname.lastname@cs.kuleuven.be`

Abstract. Many service providers want to control access to their services and offer personalized services. This implies that the service provider requests and stores personal attributes. However, many service providers are not sure about the correctness of attributes that are disclosed by the user during registration. Federated identity management systems aim at increasing the user-friendliness of authentication procedures, while at the same time ensuring strong authentication to service providers. This paper presents a new flexible approach for user-centric identity management, using trusted modules. Our approach combines several privacy features available in current federated identity management systems and offers extra functionality. For instance, attribute aggregation is supported and the problem of user impersonation by identity providers is tacked.

Keywords: user-centric identity management, privacy, security.

1 Introduction

Many service providers want to control access to their services and critical resources. A trivial solution compels users to go through a registration phase. After a successful registration, the user receives a credential that is required to consume certain services or to access resources. The credential can either be a login and password, or a strong authentication token (such as a private key and corresponding certificate). However, this approach has many drawbacks. First, the number of tokens increases linear to the number of service providers. Either the user has to remember many passwords or store a lot of certificates (and their corresponding key). Passwords and certificates can be stored on the user's workstation. However, this decreases the accessibility of services (i.e. services cannot be accessed from a remote location). Second, an increasing number of service providers want to offer personalized services. This implies that the service provider requests and stores personal attributes. However, many service providers are not sure about the correctness of attributes that are disclosed by the user during registration.

J. Camenisch and C. Lambrinoudakis (Eds.): EuroPKI 2010, LNCS 6711, pp. 155–170, 2011.

Some approaches and initiatives aim at solving these drawbacks. First, *federated identity management systems* [1,2] aim at increasing the user-friendliness of authentication procedures, while at the same time ensuring strong authentication to service providers. In fact, identity providers keep a set of personal attributes of registered individuals. They release a subset of those attributes when the user authenticates to a service provider. However, in many architectures, the user only has limited (or even no) control about the attributes that are exchanged between the identity provider and the service provider. Moreover, the identity provider is informed about which services are consumed by that user. Second, many countries are rolling out *electronic identity technology*. A majority use a smart (or SIM) card that contains a few certificates (and private keys) that can be used to authenticate the user to multiple services. Service providers develop authentication and authorization modules that are eID compliant. Although each user now has the credentials required to authenticate to multiple services, current solutions have many drawbacks. First, eID cards typically store only static attributes (i.e. personal properties that do not change during a user's lifetime such as name, date of birth ...). Moreover, users often have little impact on the attributes that are released during authentication. In some architectures, they are always identifiable and need to release attributes that are not required for the particular service (e.g. all attributes including a unique identifier embedded in an authentication certificate). An overview of the privacy features of European eID initiatives is given in [3].

This papers proposes *a new approach for user-centric identity management* that tackles several privacy and security problems of current federated identity management systems (FIMs) and also adds extra functionality. First, our approach combines several privacy features available in current FIMs. For instance, identity providers can no longer profile users and the disclosure of personal attributes is controlled by multiple parties (including the user). Second, identity providers can no longer impersonate users. Third, attribute aggregation [4], in which attributes can be retrieved from multiple identity providers and released to a service provider, is supported. Further, the system can also be used in offline settings under limited conditions.

The rest of this paper is structured as follows. The general approach is clearly defined in section 2. Section 3 points to related work. The roles and requirements are described in section 4. Section 5 discusses the protocols in more detail. Next, the approach is evaluated in section 6. This paper ends with general conclusions.

2   General Approach

This paper proposes a privacy friendly user-centric federated identity management approach based on a trusted secure element. It is a federated identity management system (FIM), as multiple identity providers can endorse the user's personal information to multiple service providers. The secure element is the mediator between identity providers and service providers. More precisely, an identity provider can store some of the user's personal attributes (or properties thereof) in her secure element. Information that is endorsed by identity providers can then be disclosed to service providers. The latter use the information to provide fine-grained access control and offer personalized services. For instance, when acquiring a ticket for a soccer contest, a student can request certain personal attributes from identity providers and release them to the ticketing service get reductions. A university can vouch that the user is a registered student, while the government can guarantee that the user is not a hooligan.

The secure element controls access to identity information. Before the user is authenticated, the service provider first has to authenticate to the secure element and prove that it is authorized to access certain personal attributes. The secure element verifies the acceptability of the service provider's information request. This verification ensures that only information from identity providers is queried, for which the identity providers (or their representative) gave their consent. The authorization info is included in the certificate (or credential) of the service provider. The certificate can be issued by the identity provider or a trusted third party. Additionally, the user may further restrict access to personal information through a policy or an explicit consent. If the query is acceptable, the secure element forwards this request to the identity provider(s) that can provide the information. In this scheme, the service provider remains hidden to identity providers. However, the latter are ensured, by the trusted element, that only trustworthy service providers can request their information.

Our approach combines several privacy features of current FIMs. First, *an identity provider cannot profile the user's actions*, as there is no direct link between identity providers and service providers (i.e. the secure element mediates personal information requests). Moreover, collusion of identity and service providers is prevented by means of service specific pseudonyms. Second, *the disclosure of personal information is controlled by multiple parties*. Service providers cannot retrieve personal data from identity providers without their prior consent. The identity provider only grants (limited) access to trustworthy service providers by means of authorization via certificates. For instance, an identity provider in the eHealth domain can restrict information retrieval to service providers in the same domain. Each eHealth provider can only access a subset of attributes endorsed by the identity provider (namely the attributes that are strictly required for that particular service). However, no commercial service provider can access information stored by that identity provider. Moreover, it is conceivable that the access rights are not issued by the identity provider itself but by a trusted *audit authority* that grants access to service providers on behalf of a federation of identity providers. Users can further restrict the disclosure of personal information or explicit user consent is required prior to data release. Each user can configure its own privacy policy.

Attributes can be cached temporarily in the secure element. This makes the scheme more efficient and usable in an offline environment. A flexible and scalable revocation procedure is foreseen; even offline services can check whether a trusted module is revoked. The mechanism is based on a validation service that regularly updates status information in the secure element. Our approach is also flexible and scalable in the sense that new service providers and identity providers can easily be added. Moreover, a service provider can also play the role of an identity provider for other service providers. A trusted audit authority can also grant access to the service provider on behalf of an entire group. When a service provider wants to retrieve personal information, it can be supplied by any identity provider in that group. For instance, an individual can prove to be a student, without revealing the university, as it can be any of the universities in the group.

The beneficial privacy properties that this scheme provides, originate in the use of a secure trusted element. Such a secure element can be for instance a smart card, a SIM card or even a trusted module in an embedded device, and is issued by a trusted third party. It acts as a gateway between identity providers and service providers. Figure 1 provides an overview of the proposed architecture.

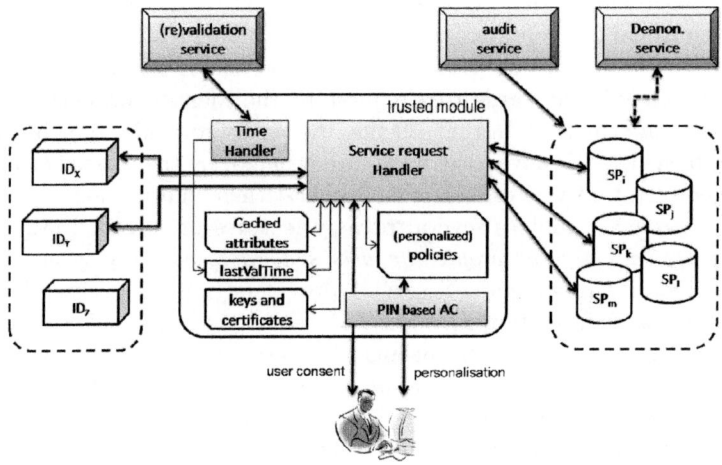

Fig. 1. Overview of the architecture

3   Related Work

A taxonomy of different identity management strategies is given in [5] together with a detailed discussion of their respective usability and privacy features. The systems that are relevant with respect to our contribution are summarized below.

Jøsang and Pope [6] present a user-centric identity management model using a *personal authentication device (PAD)*. Each service provider can store an authentication token on the PAD of the user. Our work generalizes the PAD concept to a personal identification device with extended functionality (e.g. support for multiple identity providers, deanonymization,...) and a concrete implementation is presented.

OpenID [7] is a prototypical example of a decentralized SSO identity model. In OpenID, each user has a global identifier (i.e. an URL) that is released to the service provider. The latter can use the global identifier to locate the corresponding OpenID provider and handle the authentication procedure. However, the system is vulnerable to phishing attacks and TLS is not required during the authentication process. Moreover, the identity provider learns which services are consumed by a user and attributes are not endorsed by the identity provider.

In the federated identity management model [1,2], of which Shibboleth [8] and CardSpace [9] are common examples, a user is known to at least one organization (i.e. the identity provider) in the federation (i.e. a group of organizations with mutual trust agreements). If a user contacts a service provider, authentication is delegated to the identity provider of the user. The identity provider releases the personal data that are requested by the service provider. Shibboleth and CardSpace realize a high level of security, scalability and interoperability (e.g. based on standards, easy integration in Web services, support for a multitude of authentication systems) but also have major drawbacks. For instance, a high level of trust is required in the identity providers. They are trusted to release only the required attributes and they can impersonate the user since typically no authentication between user and service provider is required. They may also know which services a user is accessing. Moreover, combining attributes from different identity providers is not possible in Shibboleth. In CardSpace, this requires the user complete several authentication procedures. Further, the possibilities for offline use are limited and many identity providers still support a weak login procedure (based on passwords) because often no infrastructure for strong authentication is available. Therefore, a significant amount of trust is still required in the workstation (e.g. key loggers can compromise user secrets) impeding the security when used on public computers (e.g. in libraries, . . .).

Several European countries are issuing governmental eID cards to tackle these shortcomings. A trusted module approach is used by the German eID. A common key pair (SK_{Co}, PK_{Co}) is shared by a large set of smart cards and is used to set up a secure channel with service providers. The service provider can only query a limited subset of the personal information that is stored on the card. This subset is approved by the government and stored in the service provider's certificate $Cert_{SP}$. Moreover, service provider specific nyms are generated by the card, based on a personal master secret in the card and data in $Cert_{SP}$. The Austrian eID [10] is a technology neutral concept that can be deployed on different valid physical tokens (i.e. devices that comply with Austrian legislation for serving as eID card). Moreover, multiple organizations can issue identity cards (e.g. banks issue ATM cards and one of the telecom operators issues SIM cards that are considered valid eID cards).

Governmental identity cards mitigate multiple drawbacks of the presented federated identity management systems. However, many designs are not flexible as service providers can only request attributes that are stored in the card itself. Attributes are typically stored in the card during the whole card's lifetime. This implies that only immutable attributes can be stored in the card. Our approach aims at eliminating the drawbacks of existing federated identity management systems and current eID initiatives.

Suriadi et al. [11] propose a user-centric federated single sign-on system based on the private credential system proposed in Bangerter et al [12]. However, the computationally expensive nature of the credential scheme limits the feasibility in mobile solutions. Similar concerns apply to the identity management system [13] proposed in the PRIME project [14]. Moreover, this system is less flexible since attributes are embedded in immutable credentials. Multiple credentials need to be used if not all the requested attributes are contained in a single credential.

4 Assumptions, Roles and Requirements

Each user owns a trusted module that contains logic for processing requests from the different parties in the scheme. The card issuer is trusted to ensure the proper working of the trusted module. Essentially, adversaries should not be able to influence the inner working or deviate from the imposed protocols. Nor can they directly access the memory of the trusted module. Hence, a service provider can trust the data that was returned by the trusted module. A related discussion about trust in trusted computing platforms is given in [15,16]. Note that the German eID requires similar trust assumptions.

Common trusted modules such as SIM and smart cards do not have a user interface. A host is required for user interactions such as entering a PIN. This implies that the user has to rely on the host or a sophisticated card reader (e.g. with PIN-pad and screen).

4.1 Roles

Each *user (U)* has a *trusted module (TM)*, in this text also referenced to as *card* since a prototype implementation was made on a smart card. *Middleware (M)* is installed at the client side (i.e. host or card reader). It allows users and remote parties to interact with the card. The *service provider (SP)* offers personalized services to authorized users. The *identity provider (IP)* returns endorsed personal attributes to trusted modules which can be released to service providers. The *card issuer (CI)* issues trusted modules to users. The *(re)validation authority (RA)* can (re)validate and block trusted modules. The *audit authority (AU)* grants rights to service providers to retrieve personal data from specific identity providers. The *certification authority (CA)* issues certificates to the different actors.

4.2 Functional Requirements

F_1 Service providers can retrieve personal attributes either stored in the card and/or managed by an identity provider.

F_2 Cards can be personalized (e.g. through privacy policies and preferences).

F_3 Adding new services and identity providers is straightforward.

F_4 The card can be used *online* and *offline*.

4.3   Security and Privacy Requirements

S_1 Mutual and strong authentication between the card and other actors.

S_2 Controlled access to personal attributes that are accessible through the card (i.e. based on rights/privileges).

S_3 Secure communication. An adversary should not be able to gain valuable information by monitoring the communication.

P_1 A trusted party, namely the audit authority, restricts the information that can be retrieved by service providers.

P_2 Users can further restrict the personal data that may be released.

P_3 The solution supports one-time anonymity, pseudonymity as well as identifiability of users towards service providers.

P_4 The card issuer only provides the trusted environment. This should not give him advantage in gaining information about the owner.

P_5 Support for conditional anonymity. This allows for identifying suspects in case of abuse.

P_6 The disclosed information should be trustworthy without the need for proof (e.g. signatures), reducing its economic value towards third parties.

4.4   Trust Assumptions

This scheme changes some of the trust assumptions that are inherent to traditional schemes without a trusted module. Besides the trust in the identity provider, to provide correct information about the user, some important assumptions are listed below.

The *card issuer* is trusted by all stakeholders to manufacture and deploy trusted modules that complies with the specifications. Additionally, the *re(validation) authority* is trusted to block stolen and lost cards, and to revalidate valid cards. The *audit authority* is trusted by IP and partially by U to give fair access rights to service providers. The *host* and *middleware* are trusted to securely accommodate a user interface for the trusted module, and an anonymous channel [17] to the remote parties.

4.5   Notation

The following notation will be used when describing the protocols. Note that the integrity of encrypted messages is assumed.

$\rightarrow$ or $\leftarrow$	denote the direction of the data flow.
$\overset{\circ}{\rightarrow}$ or $\overset{\circ}{\leftarrow}$	assume communication over an anonymous channel.
$\boxed{U}$	indicates physical interactions with the card holder.
Variables	are shown in italic.
`card attributes`	are shown in teletype font.
"String"	represents a string constant.
$\{a, b, \ldots\}_K$	denotes the symmetric encryption of variables $(a, b \ldots)$, under the session key K. This key has been established between the two communicating parties.

5   Protocols

The keys and certificates that are maintained in the scheme are listed below:

- Each service provider (SP) generates a key pair, the public key of which is certified by the audit authority (AU) in a certificate $Cert_{SP}$. The certificate also lists the access rights of SP to the user's personal information (which is approved by AU, IP or a set of IPs). The access rights restrict the set of queries (i.e. the set of attributes or properties thereof) that can be requested from the card.
- Each identity provider (IP) generates a key pair, the public key of which is certified by certificate authority CA. If required, the certificate may also include access rights. These access rights allow the identity provider to obtain personal information from the user during enrollment.
- The public keys of root CAs in the system are placed on the card during initialization. This allows the card to verify the certificates.

5.1   Card Issuance

A card issuer CI issues cards to users. The cards contain a keypair (SK_{Co}, PK_{Co}) – certified by CA – that is identical for a large set of cards. Since the private key is kept inside the trusted environment, making a valid signature with it proves that the card is genuine. Hereby, no uniquely identifying information about the card nor the card owner is released.

Before an individual can use the card, it needs to be activated. At this phase, a card specific pseudonym S_C is generated on the card, which is later used to generate service(-provider) specific pseudonyms. Additionally, the user has to confirm a personal PIN.

At the end, the CI can already store a set of immutable attributes (of the card or the card holder) in the card. Alternatively, if the card is used as a *governmental identity card*, CI may cooperate with a governmental identity provider IP_{Gov} to bind the card to a specific user. The card discloses the provider specific nym_{Gov} and chip_number to IP_{Gov}. The former allows IP_{Gov} to bind the citizen to the card. The card can now request attributes from IP_{Gov} (cfr. section 5.5). The latter enables revocation of stolen and lost cards by IP_{Gov}.

5.2   (re)Validation of the Card

The card (re)validation protocol confirms that a card is still valid at a given time. The validity of the card is verified by the (re)validation authority RA, which keeps track of the revoked cards, based on the chip_number. Note that the chip numbers of stolen and lost cards are sent to RA. If a card is revoked, RA will block the card such that further authentications are no longer possible. Otherwise, the lastValTime is updated with the current time. Whenever the card contacts a relying party, it ensures that the lastValTime lies within a certain time frame, that is acceptable for that party (see section 5.4). Table 1 shows in detail how this `lastValTime` is updated when the card is inserted in the card reader.

When the card has not been revalidated recently, user confirmation is requested[1] to start the revalidation protocol (1–6). Next, an authenticated key agreement protocol is executed. Therefore, *TM* uses (SK_{Co}, $Cert_{Co}$) and *RA* uses (SK_{RA}, $Cert_{RA}$). This step results in a shared session key K_s (7). *TM* then sends the `chip_number` (encrypted with K_s) to *RA* (8). Next, the issuer checks the revocation status of the card, encrypts the current time with K_s and sends it to the card (9–11). Finally, upon receiving the encrypted time, the card decrypts it, and updates its `lastValTime` (12). The actual revalidation time is sent to the card since common trusted modules such as SIM and smart cards do not have a real-time clock. The `lastValTime` can be used to verify the validity period of certificates.

Table 1. The card is regularly revalidated by the government

revalidateTrustedModule():

(1)	*TM*	:	inserted in reader
(2)	*TM* ← *M*	:	"Hello", *currentTime*
(3)	*TM* → *M*	:	*reqRevalidation* := (`lastValTime` < *currentTime* - δ)
(4)	*M* → ⬚*U*	:	**if** (*reqRevalidation*) showRevalWindow() **else** abort()
(5)	*M* ← ⬚*U*	:	**response** [*assume* **Yes**; otherwise abort()]
(6)	*M* $\overset{\circ}{\to}$ *RA*	:	"RevalidationRequest"
(7)	*TM* $\leftrightarrows$ *M* $\overset{\circ}{\leftrightarrow}$ *RA*	:	K_s := authKeyAgreement(SK_{Co}, $Cert_{Co}$; SK_{RA}, $Cert_{RA}$)
(8)	*TM* → *M* $\overset{\circ}{\to}$ *RA*	:	{chip_number}$_{K_s}$
(9)		*RA*	:	**if** (**not** isValid(chip_number)) sendBlockCommand(), abort()
(10)		*RA*	:	*time* := getCurrentTime()
(11)	*TM* ← *M* $\overset{\circ}{\leftarrow}$ *RA*	:	{*time*}$_{K_s}$
(12)	*TM*	:	`lastValTime` := *time*

5.3 Authentication

During authentication, the card only proves to be genuine. Authentication between the card and relying party, which can be either a service provider or an identity provider, is accomplished as follows: if the card is not blocked, the card and relying party *P* initiate a standard authenticated key agreement protocol (1–2). The relying party, therefore, uses its certificate $Cert_P$, while the card uses the common certificate $Cert_{Co}$, preserving the privacy of the user. The resulting session key is used to encrypt all messages sent between *TM* and *P*.

After key agreement, a new session is started (3-4), and the session identifier *sesId*, is communicated to *P* (5). Then, *P* will send the earliest acceptable validation time, `accValTime`(6). The card verifies whether it has been revalidated more recently than `accValTime`(7). This ensures that the card was at least valid until `accValTime`, without revealing the precise value of `lastValTime`. If the

---

[1] Note that steps 4–5 are optional. If they are omitted, the card will automatically be revalidated or blocked.

Table 2. Authentication between relying party P and card TM

$sesId :=$ Authenticate():

(1) TM	:	**if** (**not** isActivated() $\vee$ isBlocked()) abort()
(2) $TM \leftrightarrows M \overset{\circ}{\leftrightarrow} P$	:	$K_s :=$ authKeyAgreement(SK_{Co}, $Cert_{Co}$; SK_P, $Cert_P$)
(3) TM	:	$sesId :=$ startNewSession()
(4) TM	:	$\underline{\text{session}}[sesId].K_s := K_s$
(5) $TM \rightarrow M \overset{\circ}{\rightarrow} P$	:	$\{sesId\}_{K_s}$
(6) $TM \leftarrow M \overset{\circ}{\leftarrow} P$	:	$sesId, \left\{ \text{"validatedAfter"}, \text{accValTime} \right\}_{K_s}$
(7) TM	:	**if** (lastValTime $<$ accValTime) abort()
(8) TM	:	$\underline{\text{session}}[sesId].\text{rights} := Cert_P.\text{rights}$
(9) TM	:	$\underline{\text{session}}[sesId].\text{subject} := Cert_P.\text{subject}$

card has been revalidated recently enough, the card stores the name of the relying party, and if available, its access rights, in the temporary session object (8-9). The former can later be used to create a service specific nym.

5.4 Access to (Personalized) Services

Before an individual can use an online service, the service provider may require the user to release certain personal attributes either stored in the card or available at identity providers. If no persistent pseudonym is used throughout several service consumptions, different attributes may be requested each time the individual wants to use that particular service. Moreover, this also allows the service provider to minimize data retention which reduces potential damage done by hackers. This is realized as follows and illustrated in Table 3.

The card and the service provider mutually authenticate (see 5.3) (1). Consequently, the service provider sends its "attributeQuery"-command to the card (2). This query can contain an explicit request to disclose the service specific pseudonym nym_{SP}. Note that not every service provider should be able to link different service requests by the same user. For instance, for some sites it is sufficient to prove that you are older than 18, in order to access the service. Next, the card verifies that the service provider is allowed to query this information, based on the access rights obtained during authentication (3). User-policies may further impose restrictions on the disclosure of these attributes. For instance, the user policy may specify that a valid PIN code is required before the attributes (or properties thereof) are released (4). Optionally, based on the user's policies the card may send the query together with ses_{SP} and SP's name to the host M to be displayed to the user. After the user's consent, the (possibly modified) query (actually, the delta) is returned to the card (5-8). The card removes the delta from the query (9) and if a PIN was required, it is verified (10). The card then checks which attributes are locally available on the card (11) and which attributes have to be fetched from identity providers using attributeMap. This is a table that indicates which attributes can be retrieved from which identity providers. This strategy was proposed as a *Linking Service* in [4]. The service(-provider) specific nym_{SP} is generated locally and certain cached attributes that are still valid are retrieved (12). Generating service(-provider) specific pseudonyms can be kept very simple: $nym_{SP} := \mathsf{hash}(\mathcal{S}_C \| Cert_{SP}.\text{subject})$ where `subject` is the name of the service provider as it is kept in its certificate; $\mathcal{S}_C$ is a card specific secret. Note that in case the service specific nym_{SP} is revealed during registration, disclosing this nym may be sufficient to use the service. The card then authenticates to all identity providers from which data has to be fetched (using the protocol defined in section 5.3), and sends the attribute request together with the identity provider specific pseudonym nym_{IP}. Based on nym_{IP}, the identity provider can fetch the data from its database and return it to the TM(13-21). Finally, the card encrypts all requested attributes with K_s and sends them to the SP(22).

Table 3. The card releases attributes to the authenticated service provider

Identify():

(1) $TM \leftrightarrows M \overset{\circ}{\leftrightarrow} SP :$		$ses_{SP} := \mathsf{Authenticate}()$
(2) $TM \leftarrow M \overset{\circ}{\leftarrow} SP :$		$ses_{SP}, \big\{$ "attributeQuery", $query \big\}_{\underline{\text{session}}[ses_{SP}].K_s}$
(3) TM	:	**if** (**not** $\mathsf{verifyQuery}(query, \underline{\text{session}}[ses_{SP}].\text{rights}))$ abort()
(4) TM	:	$query_P^* := \mathsf{applyPolicy}(query)$
(5) $TM \rightarrow M$	:	$query_P^*, ses_{SP}, SP = \underline{\text{session}}[ses_{SP}].\text{subject}$
(6) $M \rightarrow \boxed{\text{U}} :$		$\mathsf{showQueryWin}(SP, query_P^*)$
(7) $M \leftarrow \boxed{\text{U}} :$		**response** [Assume **OK** [$delta_U^*$, **PIN**]; otherwise abort()]
(8) $TM \leftarrow M$	:	"deltaQuery", $ses_{SP}, delta_U^*$ [, **PIN**]
(9) TM	:	$query_{P,U}^* := query_P^* - delta_U^*$
(10) TM	:	**if** ($\mathsf{PINincorrect}(\textbf{PIN})$) $\mathsf{handleWrongPIN}()$
(11) TM	:	$attsPerIP := \mathsf{resolveQuery}(query_{P,U}^*, \mathsf{attributeMap})$
(12) TM	:	$atts := \mathsf{getLocalData}(attsPerIP\,[\text{"local"}])$
(13) TM	:	**forall** (IP **in** $attsPerIP$):
(14) $TM \leftrightarrows M \overset{\circ}{\leftrightarrow} IP :$		$ses_{IP} := \mathsf{Authenticate}()$
(15) TM	:	$nym_{IP} := \mathsf{getNym}(\mathcal{S}_C, \underline{\text{session}}[ses_{IP}].\text{subject})$
(16) TM	:	$qry := \mathsf{makeQuery}(attsPerIP\,[IP])$
(17) $TM \rightarrow M \overset{\circ}{\rightarrow} IP :$		$\big\{ nym_{IP}, qry \big\}_{\underline{\text{session}}[ses_{IP}].K_s}$
(18) $IP :$		$atts_{IP} := \mathsf{getData}(qry)$
(19) $TM \leftarrow M \overset{\circ}{\leftarrow} IP .$		$\big\{ atts_{IP} \big\}_{\underline{\text{session}}[ses_{IP}].K_s}$
(20) TM	:	$atts.\mathsf{add}(atts_{IP})$
(21) TM	:	**endfor**
(22) $TM \rightarrow M \overset{\circ}{\rightarrow} SP :$		$\big\{ atts \big\}_{\underline{\text{session}}[ses_{SP}].K_s}$

Offline Use With some minor changes, the card can be used for proving attributes offline. If the service provider only requests immutable attributes stored in the card, the protocol remains unmodified. However, the service provider can request attributes that are not stored by default on the card. A simple solution consists of caching these attributes on the card before they need to be used. The identity provider can define which attributes may be cached together with a retention time. Additionally, the service may impose restrictions on the freshness of the (cached) data; such restrictions can easily be passed to the card by including them in *SP*'s certificate.

5.5   Enrollment

Similar to accessing personalized services, a user may enroll with an identity provider. If so, the card discloses the identity provider specific nym_{IP} and possibly attributes from other identity providers. The identity provider links nym_{IP} to the user's personal attributes. The same pseudonym is used during future requests for personal information by *TM*. The identity providers can update `attributeMap` when a connection with the card is established.

5.6   Deanonymization

It must be possible to revoke the user's anonymity for certain services. One strategy consists of encrypting the `chip_number` together with the service specific nym or a random number (in case no nym is revealed) using the public key of a trusted party entitled to deanonymization. An `"attributeQuery"`-command can include a request to disclose the encrypted `chip_number` (used for deanonymization purposes). In case of abuse (and when the deanonymization option was used), the service provider forwards the encrypted data to the trusted party, which can decrypt the data and use the `chip_number` to obtain the users real identity from the card issuer.

6   Evaluation

This section first matches the solution with the requirements defined before, followed by a discussion on the overall functionality and possible extensions. For an in-depth evaluation of a prototype implementation on a smart card, we refer to [18]. [18] demonstrates the practical feasibility of the proposed architecture, presents concrete protocols that realize the security and privacy requirements and provides insight in the most important design decisions made during the instantiation of the architecture.

6.1   Requirements Review

Functional. Functional requirements F_1 and F_4 are realized by a caching table on the card. The table keeps a set of personal attributes and their retention time. The identity provider defines the validity interval. The retention time of the owner's `name` may be unlimited whereas the retention time of `student related information` may be limited (i.e. one year). Caching attributes allows offline use of the card. Note that mutual authentication and generating service(-provider) specific pseudonyms does not require communication with external entities. The user has substantially more control than in traditional identity management systems (cfr. F_2). This is accomplished through personalization and user-consent.

Users can define the set of attributes that can be disclosed without explicit consent and the set of attributes for which a PIN code is required. Moreover, service and identity providers can be blacklisted or whitelisted, or a combination thereof (cfr. F_3). If whitelisting is used, new service and identity providers have to be added explicitly on a whitelist in the card.

Security and Privacy. The security requirements S_1 and S_3 are trivially fulfilled using standard authentication and encryption mechanisms. However, many PKI systems use X.509 certificates. Verifying the validity of these certificates requires verification of certification chains, and revocation lists or OCSP requests. This verification may hamper the performance of the card. An alternative approach uses simpler card verifiable certificates (CVC) with a short life-time. As such, revocation lists or OCSP requests are no longer required. Moreover, to decrease the length of the certificate chain, the certificate authority could issue short-lived CVCs directly to service providers after authentication with a standard X.509 certificate and a proof of acquired access rights. Personalization, auditing and certification enable effective access control (cfr. S_2).

Multiple measures have been taken to realize the privacy requirements. In contrast to many commercial identity management systems, this solution does not require direct communication between identity providers and service providers. On the contrary, identity providers are unaware about the services that are consumed by the card holders.

Access rights for service providers enable an external control mechanism as specified in P_1. These access rights can be coarse-grained, such as *access to all eHealth data of an individual*, or fine-grained, such as *only allow the verification of certain age properties (e.g. age > 18)*. Moreover, if several trusted identity providers can supply the requested information, the service provider does not know which identity provider was used. For instance, when a service provider queries whether the card owner is a student, proving that property does not reveal the university providing this information. Nevertheless, service providers can restrict the set of trusted identity providers. They can request a permission to retrieve attributes from a single identity provider or a group (or federation) of identity providers to an audit authority. Also, a level of assurance (LOA) can be assigned to each identity provider (coarse-grained) or to each attribute that is kept by the identity provider (fine-grained) as proposed in [1]. A service provider can impose a minimal LOA for the requested attributes. The LOA is then included in $Cert_{SP}$. Additionally, card personalization and user-consent gives the user control on the disclosure of personal attributes as specified in P_2. The card supports one-time anonymity, pseudonymity and identifiability (cfr. P_3). Users are identifiable if uniquely identifying attributes are disclosed; pseudonymity is realized by service specific pseudonyms. Users remain anonymous if they do not reveal the service-specific pseudonym nor any uniquely identifying information. During card issuance and activation, the card issuer obtains only a minimal set of information (cfr. P_4). It cannot calculate the card's pseudonyms, which prevents impersonation of a specific person by the card issuer. Simple extensions to the scheme (such as deanonymization) allow to enforce accountability measures as required by P_5. Finally, as specified in P_6, it is not possible to prove invalid statements with a genuine card. The service provider can be sure about the disclosed information, without the need for verifiable proofs (e.g. signatures). Hence, the information has less economic value for third parties.

6.2   Discussion

The proposed scheme has several advantages but also constraints. In the following, we discuss the most important ones and show how to tackle them.

Trust. The major constraint of the scheme, is the trust that all parties require in the Card Issuer. As he has the common keypair, it could impersonate users. However, the card-specific pseudonyms are not known by the card issuer. As such, he cannot perform directed attacks to a specific user, alleviating the required trust from the user-perspective. Furthermore, more advanced cryptosystems, such as anonymous credentials [19], could be used to prove that a genuine card is used. Anonymous credentials allow to prove the value of attributes included in a credential, or properties thereof. However, these proofs decrease the overall performance significantly. However, the credential could be used only for proving the validity of the card, since all processing happens in the trusted module. Hence, each card can keep a unique credential generated on the card itself. To mitigate the trust required by the user in his workstation, a card reader with pinpad can be used. Alternatively, the trusted module can be a SIM card. The middleware can be (partially) implemented on the mobile which serves as a proxy between the trusted module and the outside world. The mobile can inform the user about authenticating service providers and allow for card personalization.

Scalability. One of the prerequisites of the scheme is that service providers have an agreement with identity providers, eventually intermediated by an audit authority. This authority is trusted by the identity providers to grant reasonable access rights to legitimate service providers. However, the scheme can be very flexible. Multiple audit authorities can authorize service providers to request specific attributes of a subset of identity providers. The authority can bind the privileges to the certificate (e.g. by signing the privileges and a hash of the server certificate), instead of including them in the certificate. Alternatively, an identity provider can also grant privileges to service providers directly. Hence, the scheme is very flexible: new parties can be added dynamically.

In the proposed system, card (re)validation and blocking are handled by a dedicated party. This is a significant advantage for service (and identity) providers since they no longer need to maintain certificate revocation lists or support OCSP responders from different CA's, especially since mobile tokens are easily lost or stolen. The latter results in large revocation lists. Moreover, security threats resulting from outdated certificate revocation lists are avoided. However, sensitive services should require a recent `accValTime` resulting in a short vulnerability window when credentials are compromised. Less sensitive or offline services could accept a more permissive window of vulnerability.

Flexibility. Service(-provider) specific pseudonyms are generated based on a secret. If the secret can be transferred securely to other modules (of the same individual), he can access the same service using multiple alternatives. For instance, the secret can be kept both on a SIM and on a smart card. Moreover, the personalized policy can be tuned for a specific module. For instance, the smart card can be used for financial transactions whereas the SIM cannot. Alternatively, the secret can be module-specific. The secret can be generated on the card and never leaves the module. This approach is more secure as users cannot delegate the secret to other devices (possibly owned by other users). However, users must be able to backup their pseudonyms. If the module is replaced (e.g. when the module was stolen or lost), a dedicated protocol must be foreseen to replace old pseudonyms by the new ones.

Personalization. The proposed solution gives the user control over the disclosure of data. Audit authorities and user-policies assist the user in what data may (not) be disclosed in a specific context. Audit authorities define system-wide access rules, while user-policies may further restrict those rules. Certain service providers may require the user's consent/PIN for retrieving confidential data, while other service providers cannot access this information.

7   Conclusion

This paper presented an approach for a user-centric identity management system using trusted modules. We demonstrated the high flexibility and the superior privacy and security properties of the proposed architecture with respect to existing systems. The release of personal information is controlled at two levels. An audit authority defines system-wide access rules. Users can further restrict those access rules or explicitly ask for user consent. Future research will focus on how the system can be deployed in a real-world setting and evaluate the impact on performance, security and privacy.

References

1. Chadwick, D.W.: Federated identity management. In: Aldini, A., Barthe, G., Gorrieri, R. (eds.) FOSAD. LNCS, vol. 5705, pp. 96–120. Springer, Heidelberg (2008)
2. Ahn, G.J., Ko, M.: User-centric privacy management for federated identity management. In: COLCOM 2007: Proceedings of the 2007 International Conference on Collaborative Computing: Networking, Applications and Worksharing, pp. 187–195. IEEE Computer Society, Washington, DC, USA (2007)
3. Ingo Naumann, G.H.: Privacy Features of European eID Card Specifications. Technical report, ENISA (2009)
4. Chadwick, D.W., Inman, G., Klingenstein, N.: A conceptual model for attribute aggregation. Future Generation Computer Systems 26(7), 1043–1052 (2010)
5. Jøsang, A., Zomai, M.A., Suriadi, S.: Usability and privacy in identity management architectures. In: Brankovic, L., Coddington, P.D., Roddick, J.F., Steketee, C., Warren, J.R., Wendelborn, A.L. (eds.) ACSW Frontiers. CRPIT, vol. 68, pp. 143–152. Australian Computer Society (2007)

6. Jøsang, A., Pope, S.: User centric identity management. In: Asia Pacific Information Technology Security Conference, AusCERT 2005, Australia, pp. 77–89 (2005)
7. Recordon, D., Reed, D.: OpenID 2.0: a platform for user-centric identity management. In: DIM 2006: Proceedings of the Second ACM Workshop on Digital Identity Management, pp. 11–16. ACM, New York (2006)
8. Morgan, R.L., Cantor, S., Carmody, S., Hoehn, W., Klingenstein, K.: Federated security: The shibboleth approach. EDUCAUSE Quarterly 27(4) (2004)
9. Bertocci, V., Serack, G., Baker, C.: Understanding windows cardspace: an introduction to the concepts and challenges of digital identities. Addison-Wesley Professional, Reading (2007)
10. Leitold, H., Hollosi, A., Posch, R.: Security architecture of the austrian citizen card concept. In: ACSAC 2002: Proceedings of the 18th Annual Computer Security Applications Conference. IEEE Computer Society, Washington, DC, USA (2002)
11. Suriadi, S., Foo, E., Jøsang, A.: A user-centric federated single sign-on system. Journal of Network and Computer Applications 32(2), 388–401 (2009)
12. Bangerter, E., Camenisch, J., Lysyanskaya, A.: A cryptographic framework for the controlled release of certified data. In: Christianson, B., Crispo, B., Malcolm, J.A., Roe, M. (eds.) Security Protocols 2004. LNCS, vol. 3957, pp. 20–42. Springer, Heidelberg (2006)
13. Camenisch, J., Shelat, A., Sommer, D., Fischer-Hübner, S., Hansen, M., Krasemann, H., Lacoste, G., Leenes, R., Tseng, J.: Privacy and identity management for everyone. In: DIM 2005: Proceedings of the 2005 Workshop on Digital Identity Management, pp. 20–27. ACM, New York (2005)
14. Leenes, R., Schallaböck, J., Hansen, M.: Privacy and identity management for europe (May 2008),
https://www.prime-project.eu/prime_products/whitepaper/
PRIME-Whitepaper-V3.pdf
15. Pearson, S., Mont, M.C., Crane, S.: Persistent and dynamic trust: Analysis and the related impact of trusted platforms. In: Herrmann, P., Issarny, V., Shiu, S.C.K. (eds.) iTrust 2005. LNCS, vol. 3477, pp. 355–363. Springer, Heidelberg (2005)
16. Pearson, S.: Trusted computing: Strengths, weaknesses and further opportunities for enhancing privacy. In: Herrmann, P., Issarny, V., Shiu, S.C.K. (eds.) iTrust 2005. LNCS, vol. 3477, pp. 305–320. Springer, Heidelberg (2005)
17. Syverson, P.F., Goldschlag, D.M., Reed, M.G.: Anonymous connections and onion routing. In: IEEE Symposium on Security and Privacy, pp. 44–54. IEEE Computer Society, Los Alamitos (1997)
18. Vossaert, J., Verhaeghe, P., De Decker, B., Naessens, V.: A smart card based solution for user-centric identity management. In: Pre-Proceedings of the Sixth International PrimeLife/IFIP Summer School on Privacy and Identity Management for Life (August 2010)
19. Camenisch, J., Herreweghen, E.V.: Design and implementation of the *idemix* anonymous credential system. In: Atluri, V. (ed.) ACM Conference on Computer and Communications Security, pp. 21–30. ACM, New York (2002)

Attaching Multiple Personal Identifiers in X.509 Digital Certificates

Prokopios Drogkaris and Stefanos Gritzalis

Laboratory of Information and Communication Systems Security,
Department of Information and Communication Systems Engineering,
University of the Aegean Samos, GR-83200, Greece
{pdrogk,sgritz}@aegean.gr

Abstract. The appeals for interoperable and decentralized Electronic Identity Management are rapidly increasing, especially since their contribution towards interoperability across the entire "electronic" public sector, effective information sharing and simplified access to electronic services, is unquestioned. This paper presents an efficient and user-centric method for storing multiple users' identifiers in X.509 digital certificates while preserving their confidentiality, allowing for interoperable user identification in environments where users cannot be identified by an all embracing unique identifier.

Keywords: Privacy, Identity Management, Digital Certificate, e-Government.

1 Introduction

The requirements raised by e-Government environments for interoperability, acceptance and coherence have strengthen the demands for underlying Identity Management Systems. As European Union states in [4] "Electronic Identity Management is a cornerstone of the implementation of the full range of e-Government services, for both citizens and businesses, across the Union". As more government, personal and commercial transactions are conducted electronically – especially where documents exist only in digital form – parties need to be sure of a person's or an organization's identity". Several protocols and standards have been proposed towards this direction; however either most of them involve a centralized entity for administrating user identities or attributes or they require the establishment of trust relationships among different Identity Providers (IdP).

In this paper we propose an efficient and user-centric method for storing multiple users' identifiers in X.509 digital certificates while preserving their confidentiality. To the best of our knowledge, similar research work has not been published yet. The rest of the paper is structured as follows: Section 2 presents the Subject Identification Method on which our proposal is based; Section 3 discusses the necessity of being able to store multiple identifiers; Section 4 presents our proposal while Section 5 provides an evaluation on the proposed methodology. Finally, Section 6 concludes the paper providing directions for future work.

J. Camenisch and C. Lambrinoudakis (Eds.): EuroPKI 2010, LNCS 6711, pp. 171–177, 2011.
© Springer-Verlag Berlin Heidelberg 2011

2 Subject Identification Method

RFC 4683: Internet X.509 Public Key Infrastructure Subject Identification Method (SIM) [1] is a request for Comments (RFC) published by the Internet Engineering Task Force (IETF); its current status is 'Proposed Standard". What SIM proposes is to include user's privacy-sensitive identifier in the *otherName* field in the *subjectAltName* extension of user's X.509 certificate. User is being assigned an identifier or Sensitive Identification Information (*SII*) which relates to a certain Sensitive Identification Information type (*SIItype*), an object identifier that specifies the type of SII. User selects a password *P* and along with *SIItype* and *SII* forwards them to the Registration Authority (RA) through a secure channel. After RA validates the association between user, SII and SIItype, generates a random value *R* and calculates the *SIM* value as described in formulas (1) & (2), where *H ( )* is a cryptographically secure hash algorithm. *SIM* value is then passed on from the RA to the user and the Certification Authority (CA) through a secure channel. When user sends a certificate request to the CA, she issues user's X.509 digital certificate including *SIM* value in *otherName* field which is part of *subjectAltName* extension.

$$\text{PEPSI} = H (H (P \parallel R \parallel \text{SIItype} \parallel \text{SII})) . \tag{1}$$

$$\text{SIM} = R \parallel \text{PEPSI} . \tag{2}$$

$$\text{PEPSI}' = H (H (P \parallel R \parallel \text{SIItype} \parallel \text{SII})) . \tag{3}$$

$$\text{SIM}' = R \parallel \text{PEPSI}' . \tag{4}$$

$$H (P \parallel R \parallel \text{SIItype} \parallel \text{SII}) . \tag{5}$$

Every time that the user wishes to request an electronic service from a service provider (SP), she must transmit SP, through a secure channel, her *SII, SIItype, P* and her certificate. SP can then compute *PEPSI'* and *SIM'*, through formulas (3) and (4), using user's submitted values, compare *SIM'* to *SIM* value from user's digital certificate and verify user's *SII*. In cases where the SP already knows user's SII and the user wants to prove that she is the owner of the specific identifier, she must send to the SP only P and her digital certificate. Again, SP can compute *PEPSI'* and *SIM'*, through formulas (3) and (4) compare *SIM'* to *SIM* value and verify user's *SII*. Finally, when the user wants to present proof to SP that she is the subject of a SII, without disclosing the identifier itself to SP, she submits the value of formula (5) to SP, which is an intermediate value of formula (1), along with her digital certificate. The SP can then acquire *R* from *SIM* value in user's certificate, compute the hash of formula (5), compare it to the SIM value and verify user's knowledge of *P* and *SII*.

3 Multiple Identifiers

The aforementioned identification method could be deployed by several European countries which have adopted the utilization of a national unique identifier for each citizen [7]. In fact this identification scheme seems much more suitable for electronic services, since every user can be easily identified, irrespective of the requested service, and can also ease the exchange of information (interoperability) among different public departments. However, not all environments can uniquely identify their users through an all embracing identifier; instead they utilize multiple identifiers, one for each sub-environment where each participant – user can be uniquely identified through a sectorial identifier. Even if the transition towards the introduction of an all embracing identifier is obvious, it is not that straightforward from a technical and also from a legal point of view. Each public service should have to update their records with the new user identifier, a process not only costly but also of high risk. Moreover, in several occasions, an all embracing identifier is not viable due to constitutional or legal constrains. In Greece for example, as described in [9], the dignity and the right to protect personal data [10], according to the Constitution, sets a normative obstacle to the intentions of the Greek Government to deploy such a solution.

4   Proposed Method

In this paper we propose an efficient user-centric method that utilizes a Public Key Infrastructure, for storing multiple users' identifiers in X.509 digital certificates while, at the same time, preserving their confidentiality. This method sets the basis for interoperable Electronic Identity Management (eIDM) by enabling seamless, portable and user-centric digital identity exchange and a decentralized validation. Through the support of multiple identifiers, our proposal is not only applicable to environments which identify users through multiple identifiers but also in cross environment identification. The basis of our proposal is Subject Identification Method (SIM) as described in Section 2, which is applicable to environments where users can be identified through an all embracing unique identifier. The differentiation of our proposal, compared with SIM methodology, lies in the introduction of distinct passwords, PEPSI and SIM values for each identifier along with a master password P_{master}.

4.1   SIM Computation

Let's assume that user A has been assigned n identifiers (ID_1, ID_2 ... ID_n) and each one corresponds to an explicit SIItype. Each one of these identifiers must be related to a unique password P_{IDx}, where $x=\{1,2,3,...,n-1,n\}$. However, the selection of n different passwords (one for each identifier) would be highly impractical from password management point of view. Consequently, the user selects a master password P_{master}, which will be utilized for the generation of the required n unique P_{IDx} passwords, based on formula (6), where $H(\ )$ is a cryptographically secure hash algorithm and SIItype is the identifier type. The concatenation of P_{master} and SIItype ensures that each password will be unique, since two user identifiers cannot correspond to the same type and the utilization of a secure cryptographic hash function $H(\ )$ ensures that master password will not be disclosed to unauthorized parties, enabling them to compute identifier passwords P_{IDx}.

$$P_{IDx} = H (P_{master} \| SIItype).$$

$$x=\{1,2,3,\ldots,n\text{-}1,n\}$$ (6)

$$PEPSI_{IDx} = H (H (P_{IDx} \| R_{IDx} \| SIItype \| IDx)).$$

$$x=\{1,2,3,\ldots,n\text{-}1,n\}$$ (7)

$$SIM_{IDx} : (R_{IDx} \| PEPSI_{IDx}).$$

$$x=\{1,2,3,\ldots,n\text{-}1,n\}$$ (8)

$$SIM_{total} : (SIM_{IDx} \| SIM_{IDx+1} \| SIM_{IDx+2} \| \ldots \| SIM_{IDn\text{-}1} \| SIM_{IDn}).$$

$$x=\{1,2,3,\ldots,n\text{-}1,n\}$$ (9)

After the user has computed her P_{IDx} passwords, she informs the Registration Authority (RA), through a secure communication channel, about her identifiers, their SIItype and their passwords. The user may choose to submit less identifiers than the ones that she has been assigned; for simplicity we assume that she submits all her identifiers. The RA verifies that the submitted identifiers are correctly associated with user and SII type and generates a random value R_{IDx}, one for each submitted identifier. This random value must be created by a Random Number Generator (RNG) that meet the requirements defined in FIPS 140-2 [12] and it's length must mandatory be the same as the output of the secure hash algorithm utilized by RA. Having generated n random values ($R_{ID1}, R_{ID2}, \ldots P_{IDn}$), RA must then compute n PEPSI values, one for each identifier, based on formula (7), where $H( )$ is again a cryptographically secure hash algorithm. RA must then compute SIM_{IDx} value for each identifier, based on formula (8), similarly to SIM method described in Section 2, SIM_{ID} value consists of $PEPSI_{ID}$ value concatenated with Random value. After RA computes n SIM_{ID} values, one for each identifier, concatenates them to each other and creates SIM_{total} value, as shown in formula (9). Since the number of identifiers that could be utilized to identify a user in some environment is predetermined, so is the number of SIM_{ID} that could exist. Consequently, a prearranged sequence of blocks allows easy retrieval of each SIM_{ID} and consequently of each $PEPSI_{ID}$ and R_{ID}. In cases where the user does not wish to submit an identifier, the corresponding SIM_{ID} cannot be replaced by another and must be left blank, preserving the aforementioned sequence. Finally, the RA informs the user of her SIM_{total} value and passes it on to the Certification Authority (CA). When the user sends a certificate request to the CA, she issues user's X.509 digital certificate including SIM_{total} value in *otherName* field.

4.2 Identification from Service Providers

Each time a user wishes to request an electronic service from a Service Provider (SP), she should inform the SP of her identifier and also present proof that she has been assigned the specific identifier. However, there are also cases where the SP has some prior knowledge about user's identifier, either from the user herself or from another electronic service, or more infrequently, cases where only proof that the user has been assigned a specific identifier type is required. The proposed methodology is able of supporting all these cases, based on the amount of information the user submits to the SP during an electronic service request.

The first case, which is the most common, is when the SP does not have any information on user who requests the provision of an electronic service. Thus, during the request, the user must also submit to the SP her identifier, the corresponding SIItype, the identifier password (P_{ID}) and her digital certificate. SP can then compute $PEPSI'_{ID}$ value based on formula (10) and knowing the predefined sequence in which SIM_{ID} are stored in SIM_{total}, compare it with SIM'_{ID}. If there is a match then the user has submitted the correct identifier and if she is eligible, can start using the requested electronic service.

$$PEPSI'_{ID} = H \left(H \left(P_{ID} \parallel R_{ID} \parallel SIItype \parallel ID \right) \right). \tag{10}$$

$$SIM'_{ID} : \left(R_{ID} \parallel PEPSI'_{ID} \right). \tag{11}$$

$$H \left(P_{ID} \parallel R_{ID} \parallel SIItype \parallel ID \right). \tag{12}$$

The second case is when SP already knows user's identifier (ID) and only needs proof that the specific user has been assigned the specific identifier. In that case, the user submits her identifier password (P_{ID}) and her digital certificate. Similarly to the first case, the SP can compute $PEPSI'$ value based on formula (10) and knowing the predefined sequence in which SIM_{ID} are stored in SIM_{total}, compare it with SIM'. The third case is when the user wants to prove to the SP that she is the subject of an identifier, without disclosing the identifier itself to the SP. The user computes the value of formula (12) and submits it to the SP along with her certificate. In order to perform this computation, the user must acquire R_{ID} value from SIM_{ID}, which is stored on her digital certificate. Similarly to her, the SP also acquires R_{ID} from user's certificate, computes the hash function of the value that the user submitted earlier and concatenates it with R_{ID}. If the outcome of this computation matches the value of SIM_{ID} stored in user's certificate, then the user's knowledge of identifier (ID) and SIItype is verified.

5   Evaluation

Since users' digital certificates can be publicly available, the preservation of identifiers confidentiality is compulsory and is achieved through the repetitive usage of secure cryptographic hash functions on identifier (ID), identifier password (P_{ID}) and Random Value (R_{ID}). Since several security flaws have been identified in SHA-1 [16], we propose the utilization of SHA-2 or a more secure hash algorithm. Moreover, another vital aspect of SIM_{total} confidentiality is identifiers' passwords (P_{ID}) strength as users tend to chose easy memorable passwords that relate to personal information. Consequently, users must be encouraged to select strong passwords that will at least comply with FIPS 112 and FIPS 180-1 [2][3]. Finally, Random Value (R_{ID}) should be created through a Random Number Generator (RNG) that meets the requirements defined in FIPS 140-2 [12].

Another vital aspect regarding the viability of the proposed method is the measurement of the computation overhead introduced in the overall environment due to the increased size of the user's certificate. Certificate's size depends on the number of indentifies (n), the size of hash function digest and the length of Random Value (R_{ID}). Currently we are conducting performance simulations using various different values in the aforementioned parameters, in order to estimate the relation between performance and identifier's confidentiality.

6   Conclusions

In this paper we have proposed a user-centric method for storing multiple users' identifiers in X.509 digital certificates. Through our proposal, users' identification can be performed based solely on digital certificates, thus diminishing the necessity for a centralized Identity Provider that will be responsible for managing user identifiers, attributes and roles. Even if the proposed methodology has been designed having in mind the specific needs and requirements of e-Government environments, it can also be applied in cross environment identification, through the deployment of a catholic Public Key Infrastructure. User identifiers' regarding bank institutions or medical environments could also be embodied in digital certificates, allowing for higher levels of interoperability amongst different environments, while preserving their confidentiality. Our next steps, relate to the design of a framework that will support the adaptation of the proposed methodology from organizations outside the initial environment.

References

1. Park, J., Lee, J., Lee, H., Park, S., Polk, T.: Internet X.509 Public Key Infrastructure Subject Identification Method (SIM), National Institute of Standards and Technology (2006)
2. Federal Information Processing Standards, Publication (FIPS PUB) 112, Password Usage (1985)
3. Federal Information Processing Standards Publication (FIPS PUB) 180-1, Secure Hash Standard (1995)
4. Europe's Information Society Thematic Portal. A question of identity, http://www.ec.europa.eu
5. Mont, C., Bramhall, P., Pato, J.: On Adaptive Identity Management: The next generation of Identity Management Technologies, HP Labs Technical Report, HPL-2003-149 (2003)
6. Lips M.: Identity Management in Information age Government exploring Concepts, Definitions, Aproaches and Solutions (2008)
7. Hayat, A., Leitold, H., Rechberger, C., Rossler, T.: Survey on EU's Electronic-ID Solutions, Vienna (2004)
8. Drogkaris, P., Lambrinoudakis, C., Gritzalis, S.: Introducing Federated Identities to One-Stop-Shop e-Government Environments: The Greek Case. In: Cunningham, P., Cunningham, D. (eds.) 19th Conference on eChallenges 2009, Istanbul, Turkey. eChallenges e-2009 Conference Proceedings, pp. 115–121 (October 2009)
9. Drogkaris, P., Geneiatakis, D., Gritzalis, S., Lambrinoudakis, C., Mitrou, L.: Towards an Enhanced Authentication Framework for eGovernment Services: The Greek case. In: Ferro, E., Scholl, J., Wimmer, M. (eds.) EGOV 2008, 7th International Conference on Electronic Government, Torino, Italy, pp. 189–196. Trauner Verlag Schriftenreihe Informatik (September 2008)

10. Greek Constitution Articles 2 § 1 (human dignity) and 9 A (right to protection of personal data)
11. Hayat A., Leitold H., Rechberger C., Rössler T.: Survey on EU's Electronic-ID Solutions', Vienna (2004)
12. Federal Information Processing Standards Publication (FIPS PUB) 140-2, Security Requirements for Cryptographic Modules (2001)
13. Menezes, A., Oorschot, P., Vanstone, S.: Handbook of Applied Cryptography. CRC Press, Boca Raton (1996)
14. Lenstra, A., Verheul, E.: Selecting cryptographic key sizes. Journal of Cryptology 14(4), 255–293 (2001)
15. Federal Information Processing Standards Publication 180-2, Secure hash standard (2002)
16. Schneier on Security, Cryptanalysis of SHA-1, http://www.schneier.com
17. McKenzie, R., Crompton, M., Wallis, C.: Use Cases for Identity Management in E-Government. IEEE Security and Privacy 6(2), 51–57 (2008)
18. Greenwood, D., Dempster, A., Laird, M., Rubin, D.: The context for Identity Management Architectures and Trust Models. In: OECD Workshop on Digital Identity Management (2007)
19. Directive 97/66/EC of the European Parliament and of the Council concerning the processing of personal data and the protection of privacy in the telecommunications sector. Official Journal L L 024, 1–8 (1997)
20. Directive 1999/93/EC of the European Parliament and of the Council of 13 December 1999 on a Community framework for electronic signatures. Official Journal L 013, 00120020 (2000)
21. Directive 01/45/EC of the European Parliament and the Council of Ministers on the protection of individuals with regard to the processing of personal data by the Community institutions and bodies and on the free movement of such data. Official Journal L 008, 122 (2001)
22. Hansen, M., Pfitzmann, A., Steinbrecher, S.: Identity management throughout one's whole life. Information Security Technical Report 13(2), 83–94 (2008)

Observations on Certification Authority Key Compromise

Moez Ben MBarka[1,2] and Julien P. Stern[1]

[1] Cryptolog International
6 rue basfroi, 75011 Paris - France
{moez.benmbarka,julien.stern}@cryptolog.com
http://www.cryptolog.com
[2] LaBRI, University of Bordeaux 1
351, cours de la Libération - 33405 Talence - France

Abstract. The most critical requirement for a Certification Authority (CA) is to protect its signing key from compromise. CA keys are typically stored in tamper resistant Hardware Security Modules (HSM). While, in a realistic deployment, the HSM may prevent the full copy of the key to be copied or stolen, it can not totally prevent illegal access to the key (due to compromise or even operator mistakes). This paper defines multiple compromise levels for the CA key and investigates the damages in each level. First, we show that with the most common revocation setting even the lowest compromise level (a single illegal access) may lead to the end of the CA. Then, we show that other revocation settings permit efficient countermeasures to prevent the revocation of the CA in some compromise levels. Finally, we describe some hints about the implementation of these settings in practice.

Keywords: Public Key Infrastructure, certificate validation and revocation, key compromise, countermeasures.

1   Introduction

A Public Key Infrastructure (PKI) [1] is responsible for all organizational and technical aspects of public key identities management. The relationship between the public key and the owner of the corresponding private key is established through a public key certificate. A certificate is a piece of digital data signed by a publicly trusted entity (called the Certification Authority) which includes the public key, the certificate owner identity, the expiration date and additional data (such as serial number, extensions, etc). Various circumstances (e.g. change of name, compromise or loss of the private key...) may cause a certificate to become invalid prior to the expiration of its validity period. Certificate revocation is a mechanism to inform involved parties about invalid, stolen or compromised keys. The most usual mechanism to publish revocation information is using a certificate revocation list (CRL) [1, 2, 3, 4]. A CRL is most commonly signed by the CA and published to public directories for interested parties to download when verifying the revocation status of a certificate.

J. Camenisch and C. Lambrinoudakis (Eds.): EuroPKI 2010, LNCS 6711, pp. 178–192, 2011.
© Springer-Verlag Berlin Heidelberg 2011

The most critical and obvious security requirement for a CA is to protect its key from compromise to ensure that objects signed by the CA can be trusted by relying parties. This key represents a single point of failure. Once compromised, the CA can be exposed to bogus certificates or CRLs, compromising the validity of all issued digital identities. The replacement of a CA key pair (and all issued certificates) is a severe (and expensive) blow to any PKI. The current best practice for certification authorities is to store the signing key in a secure and tamper resistant device. While, in realistic deployment (e.g. if a FIPS 140 level 4 module [5] is used) this hardware protection may prevent the full copy of the key to be copied or stolen, it can not totally prevent illegal access to the key (due to compromise or even operator mistakes). Therefore, one should wonder if in some compromise scenarios, the compromise of the key does not necessary result in the full replacement of the CA key pair and issued certificates.

This paper defines multiple compromise levels of the CA key and investigates the damages in each level. First, we show that with the most common revocation setting (the same key is used for both certificate and CRL signing), even the lowest compromise level (a single illegal access) may lead to the end of the CA. Then, we show that other revocation settings permit efficient countermeasures to prevent the revocation of the CA in some compromise levels. The analysis focuses on the use of CRL as revocation scheme, as it is widely used in practice. We also give some hints on the implementation of the identified countermeasures for Online Certificate Status Protocol (OCSP).

The investigation done in this paper focus on PKIs deployed to offer authentication services (e.g. web site authentication or access control). Similar results may be obtained for PKIs offering non-repudiation and digital signature services. However, the latter case is more complex since additional parameters must be taken into account such as validation in the past and time-stamping which are out of the scope of this paper.

Organization of the paper. Section 2 surveys many protection modes for the CA's key and presents the considered X.509 settings with the definitions of "attack" and "effective countermeasure". Section 3 defines Total and Partial Compromise levels. Section 4 presents effective countermeasures in case of partial compromise and shows that a particular revocation setting can allow to prevent the revocation of the CA in some compromise levels. Section 5 shows the implementation of this setting in practice. Section 6 concludes the paper.

2   PKI and CA Keys Security

A certification authority performs two basic functions: issuing certificates and issuing CRLs using one or more signing keys. The most critical and obvious security requirement for a CA is to protect these keys from compromise to ensure that objects signed by the CA can be trusted by relying parties. It is important that the CA follows state of the art security and organizational requirements [7]. What that trust means is a matter left to the Certificate Policy (CP) document, and the relying parties themselves.

2.1 Protection Modes of the CA Keys

CA keys are commonly stored and managed in a highly secure and tamper resistant hardware security module (HSM). The security provided by the HSM depends on the physical protection provided by the device (e.g. FIPS 140-2 [5] or EAL 4+ [6]) and also on the policies which manage the access to the stored keys. There are many kinds of CAs requiring different configurations and security policies. Most common configurations fall into one of the following:

offline CA: the signing key is never exposed to a network. Typically this is the case for a root CA where the key is only used to sign subordinate CAs certificates. The access to the key requires to be physically in the same room as the HSM and involves an activation procedure. Usually two offline activation patterns are available:
- the activation procedure is required for each access to the key (for each signature request). For instance, an operator must insert (and then remove) a smart card for each certificate signature.
- the activation procedure is required only once during an access session. It means that we can submit multiple signature requests during this session after key activation.

    Although this setting ensures that the key is offline, it exposes a little more the key to potential attackers. The system may need to be in an office environment where physical access control is difficult (more difficult than in a secure room as in the previous case).

online CA: the key is exposed to a network or does not necessitate an activation procedure to be accessed (and used). This may be the case of a subordinate CA which supports online signature requests of end entity certificates. The security issues are obviously greater for this configuration.

While the key compromise is usually considered in binary (0 means the key is compromised, 1 means the key is still trusted), in this paper, we investigate intermediate compromise levels. In particular, we are interested in the session-based activation and the online patterns. In these patterns, the compromise of the key does not necessary mean that the attacker obtained a full copy of it. For instance, the attacker may only hijack the CA software to submit illegal signature requests without obtaining the signing key itself.

2.2 X.509 Settings

Many PKIs architectures are defined and discussed in the literature [8,9]. In this paper we refer to X.509 standard [2] and its PKIX [1] profiles.

We consider a PKI domain composed of a set of X.509 objects including CA certificates, end entity certificates and CRLs. For the purposes of this paper, a PKI domain is an "autonomous" infrastructure that has been deployed within an enterprise or an organization to offer authentication services. We focus on the security of a "leaf" CA which issues end entities certificates and corresponding CRLs (Fig. 1).

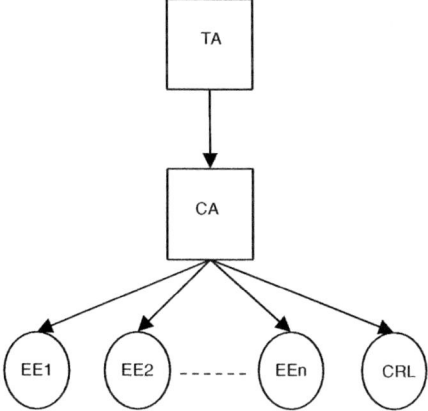

Fig. 1. A PKI domain composed of a *trust anchor (TA)*, a *certification authority (CA)*, a set of *end entities certificates EE1...EEn* and a *certificate revocation list CRL*

Certificate Validation. X.509 specifies a validation algorithm to validate a public key certificate by validating a certification path and the revocation status of each certificate in the path. A certification path is an ordered sequence of certificates such as the subject of each certificate in the path is the issuer of the next certificate. The first certificate is a trust anchor and the last one is the end entity certificate to validate. The path is valid if each certificate in the path is valid (at least not expired and not revoked) at the validation date.

Soundness. The validation algorithm is assumed to be sound. In particular, we assume that, given a PKI domain composed of signed objects honestly issued by honest CAs, any execution of the validation algorithm on each certificate will always output the same validation status. When bogus signed objects are inserted in the domain, the soundness property may be lost. This means that multiple executions of the validation algorithm may output different validation status for the same certificate. In this case, the new domain is said to be unsound to the validation algorithm.

Attacks. Attacking a CA may have many objectives ranging from impersonation and repudiation to simply causing damages to a CA without evident immediate benefits from the attack itself (e.g. by making its PKI domain unsound).

An attack based on key compromise will insert new certificate(s) or CRL(s) in the PKI domain. In the scope of this paper, we will consider a compromise a successful attack if it leads to at least one of the following situations ("old" domain refers to the domain before the attack, "new" domain refers to the domain after the attack - including any signed object issued by the attacker):

1. the new domain is unsound to the validation algorithm.
2. the new domain is sound to the validation algorithm and the validation status of one or more certificates in the old domain changed in the new domain.

3. the new domain is sound to the validation algorithm and the attack inserted one or more certificates with a *valid* status in the new domain.

Countermeasures. A countermeasure is an action enacted by the compromised CA (or a set of CAs from the PKI domain) once the compromise is detected. It consists in inserting additional signed objects into the PKI domain. Intuitively, a countermeasure is effective if it neutralizes any compromise situation described above.

A countermeasure is said effective if, after the execution of the countermeasure, all of the following statements are verified within a reasonable time controlled by the attacked CA ("original" domain refers to the domain before the attack, "new" domain refers to the domain after the countermeasure - including any signed object issued by the countermeasure):

1. the new domain is sound to the validation algorithm.
2. the validation status of every certificate in the original domain is the same as its validation status in the new domain.
3. the validation status of every certificate inserted by the attack is *invalid* in the new domain.

Specifying which time duration can be considered "reasonable" is obviously ambiguous. It depends on the application and trust context in which the credentials issued by the CA are used. While some applications will only accept immediate effective countermeasures, others may tolerate a countermeasure that start to be effective few hours or days after its execution. However, it is important that this duration is controlled by the CA itself and not by the attacker.

3   CA Key Compromise Levels

Key compromise caused by operation mistakes or misconfiguration appears to be unavoidable. This section defines multiple compromise levels. Each level offers to the attacker different capabilities which depend on the way he can access and use the key.

3.1   Total Compromise (TC)

In this model, we assume that a full copy of the CA signing key is out of the control of the CA. Offline CAs are less vulnerable for this kind of attacks than online CAs. However, for the two types of CA, this scenario can still happen through insider attacks. This is the most catastrophic scenario for any CA. The illegal owner of the key is then able to issue bogus certificates and CRLs which allows any of the compromise situations described before. Once detected, the CA must stop issuing certificates or CRLs with the compromised key. The only effective countermeasure in this situation is to revoke the CA itself and reissue all end entities certificates. Thus, this kind of compromise may lead to tricky and expensive recovery procedures (another CA setup, key generation ceremony and associated audit cost...).

3.2   Partial Compromise (PC)

In this model, we assume that the attacker does not know the private key but can make at least one illegal access to submit certificate or CRL signature request. We consider two types of partial compromise: uncontrolled partial compromise and controlled partial compromise.

Uncontrolled Partial Compromise (UPC). In this case, the CA system allows certificate or CRL issuance without secure logging. It means that the illegal access to the key has not been logged (or not in a secure way). We will also consider the compromise as uncontrolled, when the CA logs only signature requests but not what has actually been signed with the key.

Controlled Partial Compromise (CPC). In this case, any access to the key is logged. The logs allow to know that the key has been used and to determine what have been signed with it. Any serious CA should keep secure logs of the secret key access and use. These logs may be used for intrusion and misuse detection or for system audit purposes [10].

Depending on what the attacker has illegally submitted to be signed by the CA's key, the question is if the trust on the credentials issued by the CA may be recovered by taking some countermeasures once the compromise is detected.

The first step in recovering is naturally to detect the compromise. Once a partial compromise is detected, recovering requires from the CA to have secure logs to allow to determine (in a secure way) what the attacker has submitted for signature (which certificates and/or CRLs). This may not be always possible in the case of an uncontrolled partial compromise. Unless issued bogus certificates and CRL are identified shortly after compromise detection, the worst scenario should be considered. Therefore, the uncontrolled partial compromise level may be considered equivalent to the total compromise level.

Next we survey typical attacks in case of partial compromise. The list of attacks below is obviously not exhaustive but includes most typical impersonation and repudiation attacks. Most more complex attacks fall into a combination of these attacks.

Attack 1 (A_1): issue a bogus certificate. The capability to issue bogus certificates may lead to impersonation attacks.

Attack 2 (A_2): issue a bogus certificate + a bogus CRL. This attack requires two illegal signature requests. The attacker may issue a bogus certificate together with a bogus CRL (eventually with a large validity time period) indicating that the certificate is not revoked.

Attack 3 (A_3): issue a bogus CRL. Issuing a bogus CRL allows repudiation attacks. The bogus CRL may either revoke a *valid* certificate or remove a revoked certificate from the revocation list.

Note: The attacks A_2 and A_3 are practical for applications (such as S/MIME) allowing pushing CRLs together with the certificate to be validated by the relying party. However, if the security policy of the application requires to fetch a CRL from the CA at the time of the transaction, then issuing a bogus CRL may have no effect.

4   Countermeasures against Partial Compromise

An obvious countermeasure is the same as in the case of total compromise: we revoke the CA key, issue a new key, use the new key to issue new certificates for all end entities. The objective of this section is to investigate if other (less expensive) countermeasures are possible in case of partial compromise where the attacker has significantly less capabilities than in the case of total compromise.

In all the attacks above, the damages can be neutralized if the CA issues a new CRL with valid revocation information. This CRL must also revoke any certificate issued by the attacker. The CA may issue the new CRL before the previously expected date for the next revocation information update (the *nextUpdate* field). However, an application (such as many browsers [11]) may not attempt to retrieve the latest CRL provided it posses a CRL such as the validation date is in the range [*thisUpdate, nextUpdate*] (we will call the validity interval of the CRL) extracted from the CRL. Therefore, the new CRL may not begin to be effective before the end of the validity interval of the last issued CRL.

The X.509 standard allows many revocation settings related to the processing of CRLs. The traditional setting consists in using the same key for certificates and CRLs signing. First, we investigate if the countermeasure above is effective when the traditional revocation setting is used. Next, we investigate other revocation settings also allowed by the standard but less used in real world PKIs.

4.1   Countermeasure with Traditional Revocation Setting

In this setting the same key is used to issue CRLs and certificates. This allows the attacker to do all the attacks described above.

As a countermeasure, the CA will use the same key to issue a CRL updating the last revocation information. After the countermeasure, the PKI domain may include multiple CRLs with distinct validity intervals that can be used to validate a certificate (Fig. 2):

1. CRL_1: the original CRL (the last honestly issued CRL). We will denote $[T_1, T_1']$ its validity interval.
2. $BogusCRL$: a bogus CRL which may revoke valid certificates or exclude revoked certificates from its revocation list. We will denote $[T_b, T_b']$ its validity interval.
3. CRL_2: the CRL issued to enforce the countermeasure. This CRL contains the last valid revocation information including the revocation of any identified bogus certificate. We will denote $[T_2, T_2']$ its validity interval where T_2 is the date on which the compromise has been detected and the countermeasure enforced $(T_2 \in [T_1, T_1'])$.

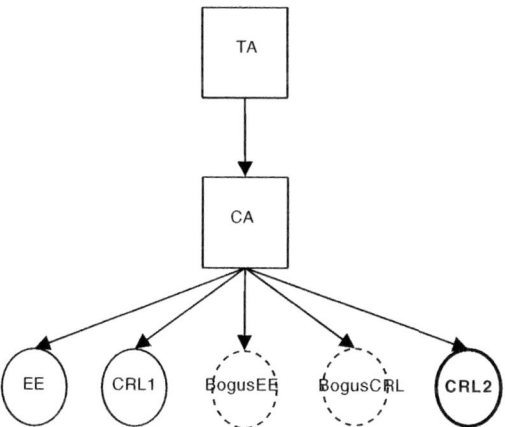

Fig. 2. Compromise countermeasure with the traditional revocation setting. *Dashed objects* are issued by the attacker. The *CRL in bold* is issued by the countermeasure.

In the case of the attack A_1, both CRL_1 and CRL_2 are present in the PKI domain. In the time interval $[T_2, T_1']$, the certificate validation algorithm is unsound as it may output *valid* or *invalid* depending on which CRL is selected to validate the bogus certificate. However, after T_1', the PKI domain is again sound and any bogus certificate is invalid. Therefore, the countermeasure is effective for the attack A_1.

For all other attacks, the PKI domain contains CRL_1, *BogusCRL* and CRL_2. For any date in the interval $[T_b, T_b']$, the certificate validation algorithm is unsound as it may use either the bogus CRL or the valid one. Naturally, the attacker may issue the bogus CRL with an arbitrary large validity interval which is not controlled by the CA. Thus, this countermeasure is not effective for the attacks A_2 and A_3.

Therefore, with this revocation setting, few illegal requests allow to introduce a bogus CRL (1 request) and a bogus certificate (2 requests) leading to demise the trust on the credentials issued by the CA. The only effective countermeasure is the most expensive and tricky one: revoke the compromised CA and reissue all its certificates.

We conclude that with the traditional revocation setting, the partial compromise (even with a single illegal request) can be seen as equivalent to the total compromise despite the big contrast between the attacker capabilities in the two levels.

4.2   Using Other Revocation Settings

X.509 allows two additional revocation settings for CRL signing:

1. The CRL issuer is not the same entity as the certificate issuer (two distinct keys and names are used).

2. The CRL issuer and the certificate issuer are the same entity (the same name) but two distinct keys are used.

In both settings (denoted two-keys setting) the certificate issuer and the CRL issuer do not use the same key. Therefore, the compromise of the certificate issuer's key allows only the attack A_1 and the compromise of the CRL issuer's key allows only the attack A_3. The attack A_2 requires to compromise both keys.

In these settings, the certification and revocation functions are not under the control of the same key. Therefore, we can revoke the revocation issuer without invalidating credentials issued by the certificate issuer. This allows the following countermeasure to any of the attacks A_2 and A_3. Once the compromise is detected:

1. we revoke the CRL issuer.
2. we set up a new CRL issuer (new key pair but same name).
3. and with the new key we issue a new CRL with valid revocation information to neutralize the attack.

This countermeasure starts to be effective at the expiration date of the current CRL indicating the revocation information of the CRL issuer. Before this date, the PKI domain may remain unsound as two CRLs with distinct revocation status are available to validate the CRL issuer certificate. After this date, the only CRL that can be used in any certificate validation is the new CRL. The previous CRL and any bogus CRL inserted into the PKI domain become invalid as its issuer is revoked.

Example: We consider the simple PKI domain depicted in the figure 3. TA is a trust anchor, CA is the certificate issuer and RA is the revocation issuer. An attacker compromised the revocation issuer to issue the bogus CRL $BogusCRL$ which does not include the revoked and not expired certificate EE into its revocation list (the attack A_3). The countermeasure consists in the following:

1. TA revokes RA ($CRL3$).
2. TA sets a new revocation authority RA' with the same name and a new key ($DN2, Key3$).
3. RA' issues a new CRL ($CRL4$) with last valid revocation information (EE is revoked).

The final PKI domain is composed of the following:
$\{TA, CA, RA, RA', CRL1, RA', CRL3, EE, CRL2, BogusCRL, CRL4\}$.

After the expiration date of $CRL1$, the countermeasure is effective due to the following:

— $BogusCRL$ becomes invalid as its issuer is revoked. Therefore, the PKI domain is again sound.
— the revocation status of EE is again "revoked" as it is in the revocation list of $CRL4$.

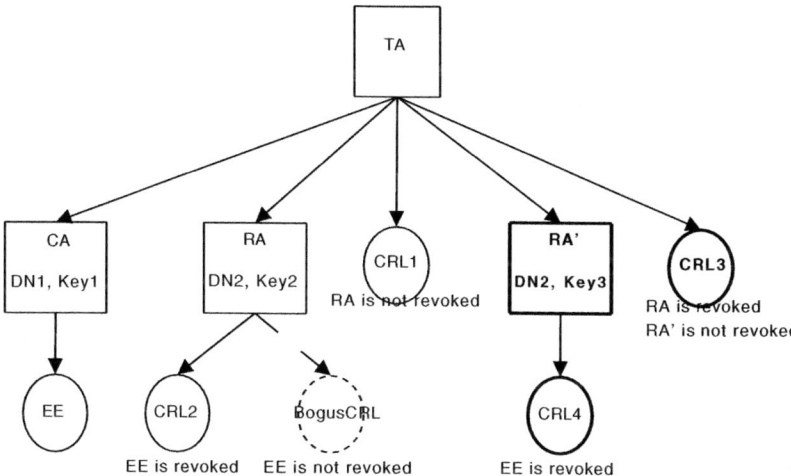

Fig. 3. Compromise countermeasure with the two-keys revocation setting. The *dashed CRL* is issued by the attacker. *Objects in bold* are issued by the countermeasure.

Comparison: The countermeasure involves the issuance of a new revocation key and the publication of two new CRLs. This countermeasure is obviously more efficient (and less expensive) than the previous one which consists on reissuing the CA key and all end entities certificates.

The countermeasure assumes that the compromised CA has secure logs of at least the serial numbers of all bogus certificates. This may not be possible in case of an uncontrolled partial compromise of the certificate issuer. However, the countermeasure does not depend on the content of issued bogus CRLs and therefore can still be applied in the case of total or uncontrolled partial compromise of the revocation issuer.

We conclude that the two-keys revocation setting allows to prevent the fall down of the compromised CA and avoid the fatal countermeasure consisting in reissuing new certificates for all end entities in the following cases:

- controlled partial compromise of the certificate issuer.
- uncontrolled partial compromise of the certificate issuer provided the CA can retrieve (shortly after the compromise detection) the serial numbers of any issued bogus certificate.
- partial or total compromise of the revocation issuer.

Figure 4 summarizes the benefits of the two-keys setting in comparison with the traditional revocation setting.

5   Implementation Considerations

At the CA side, the implementation of the proposed two-setting needs additional organization procedures for the setup phase. Since two keys must be generated

Revocation setting / Compromise	Traditional setting	Two-keys setting
TC of the certificate issuer	Fatal	Fatal
UPC of the certificate issuer	Fatal	Fatal unless serial numbers of bogus certificates can be identified shorter after compromise detection.
TC/UPC of the revocation issuer	Fatal	Effective countermeasure
PC: A_1	Effective countermeasure	Effective countermeasure
PC: A_2	Fatal	Effective countermeasure
PC: A_3	Fatal	Effective countermeasure

Fig. 4. Comparison between the traditional revocation setting and the tow-keys setting

during the CA setup, key generation ceremony and associated audit may be more expensive than in a traditional setup (especially, if the two-key setting involves two entities). However, as we showed above, this setting may prevent the end of the CA (which obviously costs more than the initial setup) in the cases of many partial compromise levels that can happen in the real world.

At the client side (the software that validates a certificate), the implementation of the two-keys setting does not necessary require to update actual versions as the proposed two-keys setting may be implemented using features already present in PKIX standards [1]. This will be showed below.

5.1   Separation between the Revocation and Certification functions

The benefits of the two-keys setting rely on the fact that compromising the certificate issuer does not allow revocation signing and compromising the revocation issuer does not allow certificate signing.

Using CRL. For CRLs, this behavior can be implemented using the $KeyUsage$ certificate extension: the $cRlSign$ bit must not be asserted in the certificate issuer certificate and the $keyCertSign$ bit must not be asserted in the CRL issuer certificate. This extension should be marked as "critical". Therefore, certificate validation software should process it.

Using OCSP. Online Certificate Status Protocol (OCSP) [13] is another mean to provide revocation information for certificate verifiers. OCSP addresses some of the shortcomings of CRLs providing a real-time mechanism for certificate status checking. With OCSP, a validation software will accept an OCSP response if the issuer of the OCSP (also called OCSP responder) is one of the following:

1. the issuer of the certificate to be validated.
2. a locally trusted responder.

3. a designated responder which holds a specially marked certificate (with the bit *id-ad-ocspSigning* asserted in its *ExtendedKeyUsage* extension), issued directly by the issuer of the certificate to be validated, indicating that the responder may issue OCSP responses for that CA.

While OCSP allows the two-keys setting (the cases 2 and 3 above), no mechanism is defined to prevent the use of the CA key to sign an OCSP response. Indeed, the current version of the standard does not mandate the checking of the bit *id-ad-ocspSigning* in the case both the certificate and the OCSP response are signed by the same CA. This means that the verifier may always accept an OCSP response provided it is signed with the same key as the certificate (case 1). Thus, in the general case, even if the two-keys setting is used, the countermeasure proposed above may not be applicable for OCSP. Note however, since OCSP allows local configuration of the accepted OCSP issuer, the two-keys setting may be implemented with OCSP provided the same local configuration is shared by all relying parties.

5.2   Delegation of the Revocation Function

In the two-keys setting, it is necessary that the certificate verifier checks that the CRL issuer is authorized by the certificate issuer to issue CRLs for the certificate.

When the two issuers are not the same entity (this setting is called indirect CRL), PKIX [1] defines certificate and CRL extensions which allow the verifier to verify the authorization. Synthetically, this verification is done by verifying the following:

- One of the *CrlIssuer* fields in the certificate has a value that matches the name of CRL issuer, and
- The certificate issuer entry in the CRL matches the name of the certificate issuer name, and
- The *indirectCrl* flag in the CRL is set to *true*.

The execution of the countermeasure in this setting requires cooperation from both issuers. In general, this is not an issue if they are both in the same PKI domain. Note however that the situation may be more complex in case the bogus certificate redirects to a CRL issuer external to the PKI domain but has a cross certification relationship with a CA from the domain. In this case, cooperation from the external domain may be necessary to execute the countermeasure.

In the case the same entity issues certificates and CRLs but using two distinct keys, the authorization mechanism is implicit (the same name). However, this may raise a known issue in the certificate validation algorithm: if the certificate and CRL are signed using different certificates with different keys but the same name, how the verifier can determine if two different CAs (with the same name) are involved or the same CA is using different keys? A real world assumption is that a CA will not certify two distinct CAs with the same name. Given, this assumption a verifier is certain that if the CRL is signed with a key certified with the same name as the certificate issuer and that the certificate issuer and the CRL issuer certification chains start with the same trust anchor (as mandated by the CRL processing algorithm [1]), then the CRL is signed with a key which belongs to the certificate issuer.

The latter two-keys setting seems to be easier for implementation as it does not require the verifier to validate a certificate chain for the CRL issuer and easier for the execution of the countermeasure as it involves a single entity. However, the fact that the certification and the revocation keys are under the control of the same entity may mitigate the security advantages of separating the revocation and certification functions. In this case, it is important that the two keys are physically separated and can not be accessed by the same employees neither through the same network.

5.3   CRL Validity Interval

The validity interval of a CRL (indicated by the dates *thisUpdate* and *nextUpdate*) is the period of time during which the CRL is considered authoritative by a verifier of a certificate. A CA can issue a new CRL before the *nextUpdate* date announced in the previous CA to quickly publish an updated revocation information. However, as long as the verifier of a certificate has a valid CRL in its local cache, he may not attempt to retrieve another CRL from the directory [11]. This means that a countermeasure based on publishing a new CRL starts to be effective only once the previous CRL expires. When determining the schedule for CRL publishing, there is a trade-off between performance and security. The more often CRLs are published, the more current clients can be with the list of revoked CRLs and the less likely they are to accept recently-revoked certificates which allows the countermeasure to be effective as soon as it is enforced. However, frequent publishing may cause negative impacts on network and client performance [12]. For the countermeasure proposed with the two-keys setting, the CRL issued by the new revocation issuer becomes immediately effective as soon as the last CRL issued by the intermediate CA (the CA that issued the revocation issuer's certificate) expires. Intermediate CAs usually use large CRL validity intervals (larger than the intervals used by leaf CAs). To help mitigate this trade off, delta CRLs [1, 4] can be used if the environment supports them.

A delta CRL is a signed list of incremental changes that have occurred since the last posting of a base CRL. Delta CRLs are generally significantly smaller than the full CRLs and therefore they can be posted much more frequently. The newest revocation information is obtained from the newest base CRL posting and the newest delta CRL. With this mechanism, the CA that will enforce the countermeasure (the issuer of the new revocation issuer) needs only to issue a new delta CRL that revokes the previous revocation issuer. The old cached base CRL can continue to be used by the verifiers.

6   Conclusion

The current best practice for certification authorities is to use hardware security modules to protect signing keys from compromise. While this hardware protection may protect a private key from total compromise (getting a full copy of the key), partial compromise (few illegal access) seems unavoidable, at least when the HSM allows session-based or online access to the key. The paper defined and investigated multiple compromise levels: total compromise and controlled/uncontrolled partial compromise. The first observation is that with the traditional revocation setting (the same key is used for certificate and revocation signing) used by most CAs, the lowest compromise level (1 illegal access) is equivalent to total compromise which leads to the revocation of the compromised CA and may require the issuance of new certificates for all end entities.

Fortunately, this is not the case for other revocation settings. When two distinct keys are used respectively by the certificate issuer and the revocation issuer, the damages caused by some compromise levels can be significantly mitigated in comparison with the damages caused by total compromise. We showed that careful implementation of these settings may allow an efficient and effective countermeasure in case of controlled partial compromise of the certificate issuer or any compromise (partial or total) of the revocation issuer. The countermeasure consists in reissuing a new revocation key and two CRLs, which is more efficient and less intrusive than the countermeasure required for the same compromise levels when the traditional revocation setting is used. Naturally, it is important that the CA enforces additional security and organizational measures simultaneously to the countermeasure in order to avoid that the same compromise affects the new key issued for the revocation issuer. We also described the implementation of the countermeasure using PKIX features. Essentially, the countermeasure requires the separation between the certification and revocation functions. PKIX already defines a mechanism to enforce this separation for CRLs. In the general case, the use of the countermeasure with OCSP requires to define an equivalent mechanism.

While our observations and analysis may appear rather natural, one can be surprised by the fact that most real life certification authorities do not use the two-keys setting (e.g. this is the case for most CAs included in major browsers trust-stores), and therefore do not have a way to recover from a single illegitimate private key access.

We recall that the investigation done in this paper considered only PKIs offering authentication services. It would be interesting to conduct similar investigations for PKIs used in the scope of non-repudiation and digital signature services. In this scope, additional settings and attacks must be taken into account.

Acknowledgment

The authors would like to thank the anonymous reviewers for their valuable comments.

References

1. Cooper, D., Santesson, S., Farrell, S., Boeyen, S., Housley, R., Polk, W.: Internet X.509 Public Key Infrastructure: Certificate and CRL Profile. Technical Report RFC 5280, IETF (2008)
2. ITU/ISO. X.509 Information Technology Open Systems Interconnection-The Directory: Authentication Frameworks. Rapport technique (2000)
3. Aarnes, A., Just, M., Knapskog, S.J., Lloyd, S., Meijer, H.: Selecting Revocation Solutions for PKI. In: Fifth Nordic Workshop on Secure IT Systems (2000)
4. Arnes, A.: Public Key Certificate Revocation Schemes. PhD thesis, Norwegian University of Science on Technology (2000)
5. National Institute of Standards and Technology: Security Requirements for Cryptographic Modules. FIPS 140-2 (2001)
6. CEN European Committee for Standardization, CEN Workshop Agreement: Secure Signature Creation Devices, version EAL 4+. 2004. (CWA 14169 EAL 4+) (2004)
7. ETSI: Electronic Signatures and Infrastructures (ESI); Policy Requirements for Certification Authorities Issuing Public Key Certificates. Technical Report ETSI TS 102 042 v2.12 (2010)
8. Branchaud, M.: A Survey of Public-Key Infrastructures. Rapport technique, Department of Computer Science. McGill University (1997)
9. Agarwal, G., Singh, S.: A Comparison Between Public Key Authority and Certification Authority for Distribution of Public Key. International Journal of Computer Science and Information Technologies 1(5), 332–336 (2010)
10. De Souza, T.C.S., Martina, J.E., Custódio, R.F.: Audit and Backup Procedures for Hardware Security Modules. In: Proceedings of the 7th Symposium on Identity and Trust on the Internet, pp. 89–97. ACM, New York (2008)
11. Wazan, A.S., Laborde, R., Chadwick, D.W., Barrere, F., Benzekri, A.: Which Web Browsers Process SSL Certificates in a Standardized Way? p. 432-+ (2009)
12. Ma, C., Hu, N., Li, Y.: On the release of CRLs in public key infrastructure. In: Proceedings of the 15th conference on USENIX Security Symposium, vol. 15. USENIX Association, Berkeley (2006)
13. Myers, M., Ankney, R., Malpani, A., Galperin, S., Adams, C.: X.509 Internet Public Key Infrastructure - Online Certificate Status Protocol - OCSP. Technical Report RFC 2560, IETF (1999)

An Infrastructure for Long-Term Archiving of Authenticated and Sensitive Electronic Documents

Thiago Acórdi Ramos, Nelson da Silva, Lau Cheuk Lung,
Jonathan Gehard Kohler, and Ricardo Felipe Custódio

Computer Security Laboratory
Computer Science Graduate Program
Federal University of Santa Catarina
P.O. Box 476, 88040-900 – Florianópolis, SC, Brazil
{thg,nelson,lau.lung,jonathan,custodio}@inf.ufsc.br
http://www.labsec.ufsc.br

Abstract. Secure archiving of authenticated and sensitive documents is becoming a necessity due to the dematerialization of paper based documents and processes. Huhnlein et al. combined the Open Archival Information System (OAIS) Reference Model, Evidence Record Syntax (ERS) with Secret Sharing and proposed the Comprehensive Reference Architecture for Trustworthy Long-Term Archiving of Sensitive Data. However, their proposal requires the secret reconstruction and redistribution whenever there are changes in the structure of the servers. In addition, there are some unhandled problems (e.g. compromise of the servers) and open issues (e.g. specification of a protocol) in their proposal. In this article we propose the use of a modified version of Gupta's and Gopinath's protocol G_{its}^2 Verifiable Secret Redistribution (VSR), among other mechanisms, in order to improve the reference architecture, making it suitable for long-term archiving.

Keywords: long-term archiving; secrecy; confidentiality; authenticity; secret sharing.

1 Introduction

The long-term storage of paper based documents requires constant maintenance of the components involved: substratum (paper) and ink. Things are not different when it comes to electronic documents. It is necessary for the document to be constantly preserved, considering its digital nature and its unique characteristics.

With the advancement of Internet, mobility and the equipments we are increasingly more connected, performing tasks from anywhere in the digital environment. Public-key Infrastructure (PKI), digital certificates and signatures contributed to the dematerialization of processes, which were previously only possible in paper, in the electronic environment.

Thus, a treatment similar to the paper based documents one is necessary for electronic documents, considering its digital nature and preservation challenges.

J. Camenisch and C. Lambrinoudakis (Eds.): EuroPKI 2010, LNCS 6711, pp. 193–207, 2011.

However, there is still no appropriate solution to the long-term digital preservation problem, due to the several challenges that must be faced. The letter from United Nations Education, Scientific and Cultural Organization (UNESCO)[1] reinforces the importance of preserving the digital heritage and the migration to this environment, motivating us to work in this research field, aiming the trustworthiness of electronic documents.

The work of Huhnlein et al. [17] propose a comprehensive reference architecture for trustworthy long-term archiving of sensitive data employing the OAIS Reference Model, Evidence Record Syntax (ERS) and Secret Sharing, being an important work due to its attempt of dealing with authenticity and confidentiality of documents, based on this technology, in the same infrastructure. We found some problems and gaps in their proposal and, in this sense, we propose improvements to this reference architecture which we present in this article, incorporating a modified version of Gupta's and Gopinath's [12] protocol and other mechanisms.

We assume there is a private point-to-point connection between clients and servers, and among pairs of servers, a reliable broadcast channel which connects all the servers, and that connections between clients and servers have an unconditional secrecy because traditional methods (e.g. security socket layer) can be eavesdropped and the information will be revealed when the algorithms employed are broken. We require that servers can reliably erase the shares from a previous period in order to prevent an adversary to obtain some information about the secret.

The rest of this work is organized as follows: in section 2, we list the related works. In the next section 3, we provide an overview of the comprehensive reference architecture. In Section 3.1, we address the problems and gaps found in this architecture. An improved reference architecture is proposed in section 4. In section 5, we discuss the management and maintenance of the infrastructure, emphasizing archived objects properties handling, and briefly evaluate our proposal. Finally, we bring the concluding remarks and point some future work in section 6.

2 Related Works

In general, when it comes to the aspects of long-term archiving, there are several publications exploring and discussing strategies for obsolescence and preservation of the basic properties of storage (e.g. conservation of bits), especially projects from archives and libraries [2,4]. Moreover, there is the request for comments (RFC) 4810 [29] which lists a set of long-term archive service requirements, bringing rationales and considerations that must be weighted in such systems. Finally, the Open Archival Information System (OAIS) Reference Model, an International Organization for Standardization (ISO) standard (ISO 14721:2003 [18]),

---

[1] http://portal.unesco.org/ci/en/files/13367/10700115911Charter_en.pdf/
Charter_en.pdf

makes recommendations on what an archive should provide for the long-term preservation of digital information, establishing a common framework of terms and concepts that comprise an OAIS. Some archiving system's projects already implemented are based on the OAIS[2] model.

It is know that digital signatures and certificates have a limited lifetime and need constant maintenance, which can be accomplished by time-stamps [14]. RFC 3126 [26] established the electronic signature formats for long-term electronic signatures which, aftermost, were later extended by technical specifications CMS Advanced Electronic Signatures (CAdES)[9] – also published by the Internet Engineering Task Force (IETF) in RFC 5126 [25] and XML Advanced Electronic Signatures (XAdES)[10] from the European Telecommunications Standards Institute (ETSI). Though, these formats are not effective for large volumes of data since the maintenance of these objects is individual – an archive time-stamp for each signature. In order to cover this gap there was created the Evidence Record Syntax (ERS) [6], which is based on Merkle Trees [21], and consists of a tree of hashes of the objects to be preserved. Thus, preserving the integrity and authenticity provides greater scalability and facilitates the operation by the archives.

Initial works on confidentiality were using encryption to provide secrecy for archived objects [20,8,1,15,19]. However, encryption algorithms are conditionally secure and become weaker in the course of time (increase of computing power and advances in cryptanalysis techniques) and, hence, they are not suitable for long-term. An alternative technique that provides unconditional security is the proposal of Shamir [27]. A hybrid approach was proposed by Wang et al. [30], using secret sharing for the recovery of symmetric keys, but the same obsolescence problem can be found. Some proposed works [22,17,28], for example, use the secret sharing technique, which provides some degree of availability – depending on the threshold adopted. Though, they adopted share renewal mechanisms, except for POTSHARDS[28], in which the secrets are reconstructed for a later redistribution, which leaves them exposed in the reconstruction site (e.g. a central recovery server). POTSHARDS [28] does not have a share renewal mechanism, which is a future work of their proposal.

Herzberg et al. proposed a scheme called proactive secret share [16] in which the lifetime of the secret is divided in shorter periods to avoid mobile adversaries. Their proposal basically employs a sum of polynomial, in one of them the free term is equal to zero, which avoids the reconstruction of the secret. Their proposal has the limitation that the access structure must be maintained, i.e., it needs the same number of available servers before and after a renewal. Another drawback is that Nikov and Nikova [23] investigated the security of proactive secret sharing schemes and found specific weaknesses when a mobile adversary is considered. These weaknesses, which can compromise the secret, can be applied to Herzberg et al. model.

Another approach to the renewal problem is the Verifiable Secret Redistribution (VSR)[31] protocol which combines the secret renovation protocol

---

[2] http://www.oclc.org/research/activities/past/rlg/oaisactivities.htm

without reconstruction from Desmedt and Jajodia [7] with Verifiable Secret Sharing (VSS). This protocol prevents the share renewal to execute a secret sharing technique for each shares held by the servers and allows a different access structure after redistribution. An extension to the VSR (xVSR) was proposed by Gupta and Gopinath [13], because all recipients (in this case, the servers) must be honest, relaxing this requirement only to the needs of the majority. In these protocols the approach of Feldman [11] was used as the VSS technique. Another proposal (G_{its}^2 VSR) from Gupta and Gopinath [12] has revised their protocol and has incorporated Pedersen's VSS approach [24], thus providing information theoretic secrecy.

3   Overview of Comprehensive Reference Architecture

In this section we reproduce an overview of Huhnlein et al.'s [17] work, in which we found problems and gaps that are discussed in section 3.1, in order to solve them and incorporate them into our proposal.

Based on the results of projects ArchiSig [5] and ArchiSafe [32], in joint with the Evidence Record Syntax (ERS) [6], The German Federal Office for Information Security (BSI) has developed a technical directive that regulates the trustworthy long-term archiving for federal agencies in Germany, providing integrity and authenticity of archived data. Huhnlein et al. [17] extended this architecture, combining the different requirements involved, to provide confidentiality and availability as well. Their architecture supports operations for submission, retrieval, evidence request, complementary data request (such as metadata) and deletion of archived objects. The identifier of the archived objects is called Archive Token. Figure 1 illustrates the modules and operations of the proposed infrastructure.

The Archive Gateway Module receives requests from applications and encapsulates the objects to be archived in XML Archival Information Package (XAIP) – if the object is not in that package, it controls the processes and formats using standardized XML Schemas and performs access control. in the case the archival package is already signed in the application layer, the Crypto Module is invoked in order to verify the signatures found. Finally, this module requests evidence services from Evidence Module, and stores the archival package in Storage Module.

The Evidence Module generates hashes of all documents and the resulted hashes are concatenated into hash trees [21]. A time-stamp is generated for the hash resulted from the root of the tree, consolidating the validity of all documents involved. Before algorithms and cryptographic parameters become weak or be compromised, the time-stamp is renewed. When required, this module uses these trees to generate Evidence Records (ER) in concordance with the ERS [6] standard.

The Crypto Module supports cryptographic operations required by the infrastructure, such as hash functions, time-stamping and, optionally, signature generation and verification. The Crypto Interface must be compatible with standard interfaces, ensuring interoperability among others Crypto Modules.

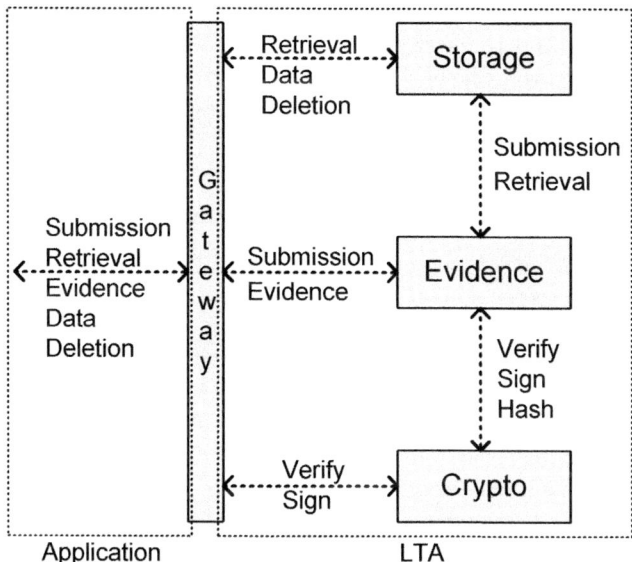

Fig. 1. Overview of modules and operations of the Comprehensive Reference Architecture

The Storage Module (eSafe), in addition to search, deletion and bit-exact reproduction services, should provide a distributed architecture that ensures a (k, n) threshold confidentiality. The Shamir's [27] secret sharing scheme was adopted.

Following the ERS [6] standard, the infrastructure continuously executes the process of Archive Time-Stamp Management, divided into Time-Stamp Renewal and Hash Tree Renewal. The former consists in renewing the time-stamp of the root's tree before events that would invalidate this time-stamp happen – such as the expiration and revocation of certificates and obsolescence of cryptographic algorithms or parameters, happen. The latter occurs when the hash algorithm is considered insecure, requiring the replacement of this algorithm for a secure one.

The Share Renewal mechanism which is described consists in a renewal of the shares whenever a server is added or removed from the system. When a server is added, there is no need to modify the existing shares. However, when a server is removed, the shares must be recalculated to invalidate the share to the removed server. This renovation has impact in Archive Time-stamp Management, depending on the configuration of shared mode that was adopted. There are two modes: inside and outside shared mode.

In Inside Shared Mode the hash is calculated on the data archive and only in eSafe Module the secret share is applied. The size of the tree depends on the number of stored objects. Considering a (k, n) threshold, where n is the total of shares and k is the minimum needed for the reconstruction of the secret, k shares are accessed to a Hash Tree Renewal.

In Outside Shared Mode, the mechanism of secret share is applied at the application layer and the system reads the shares as several documents being the hash tree built from the hash value of each share. The size of the tree depends on the number of shares. For the Hash Tree Renewal it is necessary to access all the n shares.

3.1   Discussion about Reference Architecture

In our analysis of the comprehensive reference architecture from Huhnlein et al. [17] there were detected some problems and gaps that must be solved and filled so that the architecture meets its goals.

Our first concern is related to the suitability of encryption algorithms in the course of time. Although it is true that encryption techniques are designed to be secure for a long time, its suitability degrade over time. Long-term means more comprehensive periods of time than the lifetime designed for encryption techniques, such as indefinitely. As an example of this king of documents, there are the military and government secret files, which needs secrecy against nation-state enemies. Even historical documents leakage can be harmful because the adversaries can learn secrets about the nation. Other examples could be medical records, lawsuits, industrial secrets and so on.

The secret sharing mechanisms are unconditionally secure [27] compared to the security of encryption techniques that provide only conditional security. However, the Share Renewal approach requires that archived object are reconstructed when there is a removal of the servers – to invalidate its shares and for the Hash Tree Renewal – whether the Inside Shared Mode was used, leading to the same problem of the encryption mechanisms. There is a central server for recovery that can be compromised by an adversary who, thus, obtains confidential information [31].

Huhnlein et al. mentioned a variant of the sharing mode, generating shares in the application layer and using the object hash to build the tree. Nevertheless, this approach only postpones the problem, because at some moment it will be necessary to obtain the hash of the objects for the hash tree renewal.

In the proposal, some mechanisms of monitoring and maintenance of the integrity of the shares in the eSafe Module were not mentioned. An attacker that maliciously alters or deletes $(n - k + 1)$ shares will cause the loss of this information.

Also in relation to shares, there are no mechanisms of defense against active and mobile adversaries. The former may compromise the shares before they reach the servers, during a (re)distribution, and this modification will not be detected. The latter can continuously obtain shares in the archive lifetime until she obtains k shares and reconstruct the archived object, since she make it before any changes in the configuration of servers happen.

The hash tree receives a time-stamp at its root that guarantees the long-term maintenance of the objects. However, this tree is not authenticated and it is possible for an attacker to replace it or tamper it, since she has access to the Time-Stamp Authority (TSA) used by the system, e.g. one of a third party.

Malicious Long-Term Archives (LTAs) are not considered in the Reference Architecture proposed. In real systems there is a valid assumption that an intruder can compromise and maliciously control the behavior of the components, especially in long-term systems in which the attacker has an undetermined period to operate.

Another obstacle for long-term archiving is the management of identifications (IDs) of archived objects by the clients, using the Archive Token. This approach is possible if there is a way to recover the IDs, since the clients do not have infrastructure to store information for a long time, even if it were stored on cryptographic tokens.

Finally, a protocol for distribution and renewal of shares was not chosen in the proposed architecture, leaving a significant gap in the system's definition. The interaction between the components of the system, the clients and the servers must be set and secure in order to fulfill the requirements of archival systems.

4   A New Approach of Reference Architecture

The main problem of Comprehensive Reference Architecture [17] is the Share Renewal mechanism, which exposes the secret in a risky way on a recovery central server, being attractive to attackers. Thus, the advantage of using threshold's cryptography is reduced to the security against intrusions on the central server.

Our proposal is the incorporation of a modified version of the protocol (G_{its}^2 VSR) [12] in the Comprehensive Reference Architecture (CRA) – an essential mechanism which was not considered on CRA, thus, solving the Share Renewal problems and mobile adversaries in addition to tolerate faulty LTAs. Afterwards, we will discuss in details each of these problems along with our proposed solutions.

The secret sharing applied is the proposal of Shamir [27]. To share a secret S between n recipients, being k of them required for reconstruct the secret and no information about the secret can be obtained from $k - 1$ shares, choose a polynomial f of order $k - 1$, let the independent term be $f(0) = a_0 = S$ and choose random values to the other coefficients. The shares will be the values obtained from the evaluation of f into i points, for $i = 1...n$, such that $y_i = f(x_i)$. In order to reconstruct the secret it is only necessary to apply an interpolation formula with at least k shares and its identifying indices (i), and, then, evaluate $f(0) = S$.

The secrets being shared are electronic documents, which are split into blocks and have the secret sharing mechanism applied into all of them as follows: divide the file into blocks of the same size, fix values of x_i while varies the polynomial for each block. Subsume in a package called Share all the values of $y_i = f(x_i)$ for each x_i. At the end, distribute these n shares among the n recipients [17].

In order to avoid the Share Renewal a secret redistribution is applied, without having to reconstruct it. A client C has a secret S and divides it into n pieces, storing them on n servers, so that with k or more pieces it is possible to reconstruct S, with $k \leq n$, building an (k, n) access structure. In the course of time, the n secrets are redistributed in n' pieces being that at least k' parts are needed to reconstruct the same secret S, with $k' \leq n'$, forming an (k', n') access structure. These access structures can be of different sizes, depending on the number of servers available when the redistribution process is performed. In some moment the client can reconstruct the secret [31]. Figure 2 illustrates this protocol.

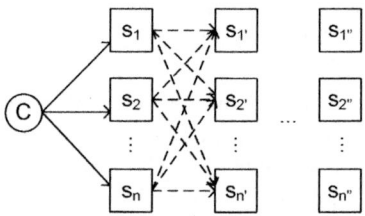

Fig. 2. Overview of VSR protocol

The modification on the protocol G_{its}^2 VSR [12] relates to the use of secret sharing. They calculate the sub-shares $\hat{s}_{ij}$ for then obtain a new share s'_j using Lagrange interpolation. In our approach we simply keep the sub-shares $(\hat{s}_{ij})$ without the computation of a new share (s'_j). When all the servers receive their new shares and all the information is verified, they should erase their shares of the previous period, like PSS scheme [16]. The security against mobile adversaries relies on this erasure and if this procedure is not executed, an adversary can obtain some information or even compromise the secret.

The redistribution process uses the VSS schemes so that members can verify the integrity and validity of the shares without knowing the secret. In the G_{its}^2 VSR protocol, as stated earlier, the approach of Pedersen [24] is applied, thus obtaining information theoretic secrecy. The execution of the chosen protocol is almost identical to xVSR [13], except that twice the information is sent by VSS protocol.

From Wong et al. [31], k non-faulty servers are required, and $k-1$ faulty servers can be tolerated, thus, the constraint is that $k + (k-1) \leq n$, or $k \leq (\frac{n+1}{2})$.

The use of protocol G_{its}^2 VSR [12] solves the Share Renewal problem, since the redistribution can be applied when there is a structural change, either adding or removing a server from infrastructure. Mobile adversaries can be mitigated by applying a secret redistribution before an attacker can obtain k shares and reconstruct the secret S.

Yet, in the proposal of the xVSR protocol, predecessor of G_{its}^2 VSR, malicious LTAs are tolerated in order to cover more realistic situations, requiring only the majority be trustworthy, instead of all recipients (servers) [13]. With this, a protocol for the archive is defined – an existing gap in the Comprehensive Reference Architecture. The verifiable secret share [24] scheme adopted in the protocol makes the verification of shares by the servers possible and also provides information theoretic secrecy.

And how is the Merkle [21] tree, or the maintenance of integrity and authenticity, regarding shares? Suppose you share the secret S with a $(k = 3, n = 4)$ threshold, being the shares (s_1, s_2, s_3, s_4), and that a hash tree was created from the hashes of these shares (h_1, h_2, h_3, h_4), as illustrated in Fig. 3. Any combination of 3 shares or more can prove that they belong to the archived object and, consequently, the integrity and authenticity of this object are established.

Now consider that there was a redistribution of shares with a $(k = 2, n = 3)$ threshold, forming the subset $(s_{11}, s_{12}, s_{13}, s_{21}, s_{22}, s_{23}, s_{31}, s_{32}, s_{33}, s_{41}, s_{42}, s_{43})$. Any combination of 2 sub-shares of 3 shares (e.g. $s_{11}, s_{12}, s_{22}, s_{23}, s_{41}, s_{43}$) or more sub-shares can recover the primary shares (in this case, s_1, s_2, s_4), returning to the previous case. No changes in the tree must be done when there is a redistribution of shares. We reached this result with our modification on protocol G_{its}^2 VSR.

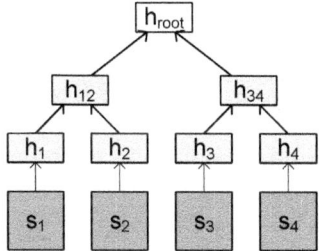

Fig. 3. Merkle tree built from the hash of shares

As previously mentioned in section 3.1, the trees generated in the comprehensive reference architecture are not signed by de system. In our proposal, we added this requirement in order to enhance the security in relation to the authenticity of the trees. In order to do so, we suggested using a distributed signature algorithm, in which a private key S_k is shared between the participating servers by threshold techniques so that, even with possible outages of any server – be them malicious or not, the signature can be performed, provided that it has the necessary quorum.

Concerning the monitoring of the integrity of the shares on the servers, each one of them actively monitors the integrity of its shares through stored hashes [28], in order to reduce the likelihood of tampering in shares, be it intentional or not. In addition, each server must use techniques of mirroring, redundant and/or erasure codes, both local and distributed.

Lastly, a remaining problem of the architecture is the management of the identification of archived objects by the clients instead of by the system. This approach is interesting so that a centralized index of this objects is not required, which is a point to be attacked in the system – such as the recovery central server previously discussed. However, clients do not have infrastructure to store such information for such a long time, e.g. loss of a cryptographic token or formatting of the operational system may occur. One possible way to address this problem is by using the techniques of global name-spaces and approximate pointers of POTSHARDS [28].

5   Discussion and Evaluation of the Proposal

The infrastructure management comprehends the maintenance of the properties that a long-term archiving service must indefinitely preserve. Properties such as integrity, authenticity, confidentiality and availability, need a constant treatment since archiving systems greatest enemy is time.

By using Merkle trees [21] it is possible to manage and maintain the integrity and authenticity of several archived objects at once. However, a maintenance of the tree itself is necessary so that these properties can be maintained.

The time-stamp on the root of the trees must be actively renewed before that the cryptographic algorithms and parameters become weak or the certificate of Time-stamp Authority (TSA) or Certification Authority (CA) belonging to the certification path TSA are revoked or expired [6].

Another necessary maintenance on the trees is related to the hash algorithm adopted. Whenever an algorithm is considered weak it must be replaced by a secure one. However, in order to do so, it is necessary to have access to all the n shares of each archived object and, thus, it becomes possible to reconstruct the trees. These maintenance processes are described in ERS and are adopted by several papers [5,32,17,3].

The integrity and authenticity of the shares are grounded on Merkle trees [21] and ERS [6] which make them attractive to attackers. The replication of these trees must be kept to avoid a single point of failure. Also, in this sense, distinct algorithms must be applied, for example, identical trees applying distinct and secure algorithms, thus avoiding an abrupt crack that compromises the system. The algorithms applied in the infrastructure should be monitored regarding their security and, as soon as they become insecure, they should be replaced by others which are considered secure.

Merkle trees guarantees the authenticity, and partly, the integrity of the shares that compose an archived object. This happens partly because the integrity of the shares requires monitoring and maintenance of the Storage Module, as previously described in section 3.1. Using an active monitoring, redundancy into servers and among them, it is possible to manage the integrity of archived objects.

The shares shall be distributed by distinct LTAs in different geographic locations in order to balance and distribute the load by the infrastructure without a LTA, otherwise a minority may reconstruct the secret, thus achieving the desired confidentiality and availability. Thus, an attacker needs that at least k LTAs maliciously cooperate to reconstruct the secret – an unlikely situation.

The use of threshold cryptography and techniques for redundancy provides the desired confidentiality and a certain degree of availability to the infrastructure. Approaches such as the encryption or the share renewal have points of exposure of confidential information, being a target to attacks. The adopted protocol [12] solves this issue and also provides verification of the integrity of shares by the servers.

Our proposal is just on earlier stages and, thus, more informations and details are not available at this moment. We describe succinctly the amount of disk space required (storage blow-up) and the number of secret sharing operations that are executed at each period, excluding the amount from VSS.

When a client sends a document to the servers this is split into blocks and a (k, n) secret sharing operation for each block of the file is applied. Because secret sharing requires that the shares are at least the same size as the information to reach unconditional security, one secret sharing operation will be executed for each of i blocks (i operations) and the storage blow-up (b) will be $b = i.n.s$, being s the share's size of a block.

At a redistribution, each share is treated as a file and will be split into i' blocks and a (k', n') secret sharing operation will be applied in each of these blocks. Thus, one secret sharing operation will be executed for each i' blocks of n shares ($n.i'$ operations) and the new storage blow-up (b') will be $b' = (n.i'.n'.s')$, being s' the share's size of a block. However, the erasure of the previous shares after the correct execution of the redistribution protocol will free b bytes of disk space. We applied different variables in formulas because the parameters can be changed as wished.

As an example, suppose we have a file with the size of 9.888 bytes, a prime modulus of $s = 48$ bytes and $n = 3$ servers. So, we have $i = 206$ blocks and the resulting blow-up will be $b = 29.664$ bytes after the distribution. Table 1 and the Fig. 4 shows the storage blow-up after redistributions (b'), considering that we keep the same configuration.

Table 1. Blow-up (b') after six rounds of redistributions

rounds	1	2	3	4	5	6
b' (in KB)	57.94	202.78	579.38	1767.09	5272.32	15845.9

Another evaluation is that the size of modulus have a significant impact on the storage blow-up. Table 2 shows the blow-up (b') when we choose different modulus, considering that we keep the same configuration.

Table 2. Blow-up after six rounds of redistribution with different modulus

modsize (bytes)	b'_1	b'_2	b'_3	b'_4	b'_5	b'_6
6	57.9	202.66	579.02	1766.02	5269.11	15836.29
12	57.94	202.78	579.38	1767.09	5272.32	15845.9
24	57.94	202.78	579.38	1767.09	5272.32	15845.9
48	57.94	202.78	579.38	1767.09	5272.32	15845.9
50	58.01	203.03	580.08	1769.24	5278.71	15865.14

We can infer from these informations that the storage blow-up increases quickly, as expected, and the size of modulus has not a great impact on that.

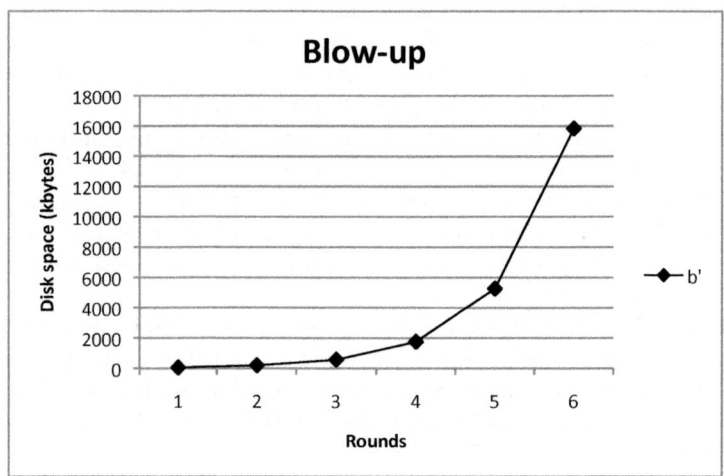

Fig. 4. Blow-up (b') after six rounds of redistributions

Table 3. Secret sharing operations per round (b'_i) with different sizes of modulus (in bytes)

modsize (bytes)	b'_1	b'_2	b'_3	b'_4	b'_5	b'_6
6	4944	14832	44496	133488	400464	1201392
12	2472	7416	22248	66744	200232	600696
24	1236	3708	11124	33372	100116	300348
48	618	1854	5562	16686	50058	150174
50	594	1782	5346	16038	48114	144342

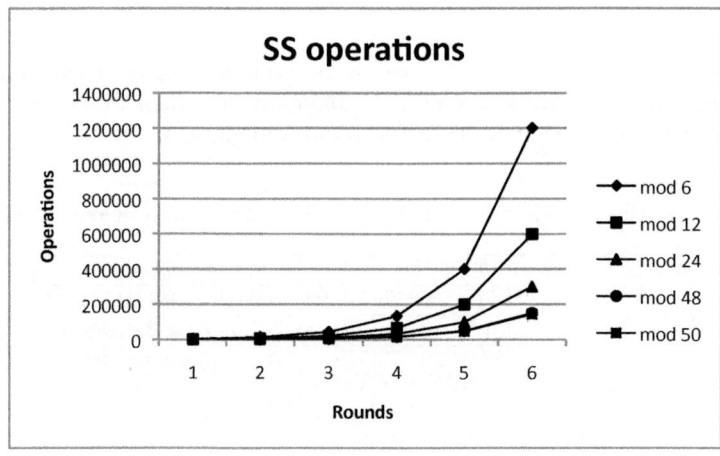

Fig. 5. Secret sharing operations per round with different modulus

However, reducing the modulus' size increases the number os blocks and, consequently, the amount of secret sharing (SS) operations that need to be executed ($n.i'$ operations). Table 3 and Fig. 5 shows this information.

The blow-up shown is considered for the overall system (we can divide it by n to get the blow-up per server) and the costs of storage are decreasing over time, thus, the storage blow-up itself is amortized.

We aim to evolve our proposal and more precisely evaluate it, which will be a subject for future works.

6   Concluding Remarks and Future Works

We presented a new proposal for a reference architecture, based on the Comprehensive Reference Architecture from Huhnlein et al. [17], with the incorporation of a modified version of the verifiable secret redistribution protocol from Gupta and Gopinath [12]. With the adoption of other techniques and mechanisms it is possible to provide a satisfactory approach to the maintaining problem of long-term archiving, especially the integrity, authenticity and confidentially of archived objects.

The appliance of threshold techniques, such as in the approach of Shamir [27], together with the secret redistribution protocol without the need of reconstruction from Desmedt and Jajodia [7], included in protocol G_{its}^2 VSR [12], provides information theoretic secrecy to the architecture for long-term archived objects, without the need of recalculation of the threshold. Thus, a certain degree of availability is obtained, depending on the values of k and n adopted, since the objects are divided into n pieces but can be reconstructed with at least k pieces, in a (k, n) threshold.

Other techniques of redundancy are necessary, such as Internet connections, routers replication, load balancing, among others, which are beyond the scope of this work but must be also equally deployed for the provision of the availability in a comprehensive and appropriate way to a system of this size and importance. Defense mechanisms against denial of service (DoS) and intrusion attacks are also essential to the infrastructure and must be incorporated into the solution.

Problems related to general aspects of long-term archiving were also not ad dressed because the subject is extensive, but must be observed and aggregated to the solution, such as different media technology (e.g. hard drive, solid state drive, optical media, magnetic tape and microfilm), distinct operating systems and software, emulation, notarization and migration strategies, metadata (which are required for most archiving systems, including the OAIS reference model), among others subjects.

As future works we suggest the implementation and evaluation in relation to different subjects of the proposal, tests and refinements regarding the appropriated period for share redistribution, experiments with different techniques and values of k and n at threshold cryptography, incorporating mechanisms against DoS and intrusion, a formalization of the system and its protocols, the extension of the proposal detailing each component and a survey and selection of the most appropriate strategies in issues of general aspects of archiving.

Acknowledgements

We would like to thank the Brazilian Chamber of Electronic Commerce[3] for supporting our research. This work will make part of a master thesis at Computer Science Graduate Program (PPGCC) of the Federal University of Santa Catarina (UFSC).

References

1. Adya, A., Bolosky, W.J., Castro, M., Cermak, G., Chaiken, R., Douceur, J.R., Howell, J., Lorch, J.R., Theimer, M., Wattenhofer, R.P.: Farsite: Federated, Available, and Reliable Storage for an Incompletely Trusted Environment. Operating Systems Design and Implementation (2002)
2. Beagrie, N., Jones, M.: Preservation Management of Digital Materials: The Handbook. Digital Preservation Coalition (2002)
3. Blazic, A.: Long Term Trusted Archive Services. In: First International Conference on the Digital Society (ICDS 2007), pp. 29–29 (2007)
4. Borghoff, U., Rödig, P., Scheffczyk, J., Schmitz, L.: Long-term Preservation of Digital Documents: Principles and Practices (2006)
5. Brandner, R., Pordesch, U.: Long-term conservation of provability of electronically signed documents. Beitrag zu ISSE, pp. 2–5 (2002)
6. Brandner, R., Pordesch, U., Gondrom, T.: Evidence Record Syntax (ERS). Internet Engineering Task Force (IETF) Networking Group, Request for Comments 4998 (2007)
7. Desmedt, Y., Jajodia, S.: Redistributing Secret Shares to New Access Structures and its Applications (1997)
8. Druschel, P., Rowstron, A.: PAST: a Large-scale, Persistent Peer-to-Peer Storage Utility. In: Proceedings of the Eighth Workshop on Hot Topics in Operating Systems, 2001, pp. 75–80 (2001)
9. European Telecommunications Standards Institute: Electronic Signatures and Infrastructures (ESI); CMS Advanced Electronic Signatures (CAdES) (November 2009)
10. European Telecommunications Standards Institute: Electronic Signatures and Infrastructures (ESI); XML Advanced Electronic Signatures (XAdES) (June 2009)
11. Feldman, P.: A Practical Scheme for Non-Interactive Verifiable Secret Sharing. In: 28th Annual Symposium on Foundations of Computer Science (sfcs 1987), pp. 427–438 (October 1987)
12. Gupta, V.H., Gopinath, K.: G_{its}^2 VSR: An Information Theoretical Secure Verifiable Secret Redistribution Protocol for Long-Term Archival Storage. In: Fourth International IEEE Security in Storage Workshop, pp. 22–33 (2007)
13. Gupta, V., Gopinath, K.: An Extended Verifiable Secret Redistribution Protocol for Archival Systems. IEEE, Los Alamitos (2006)
14. Haber, S., Stornetta, W.: How to Time-Stamp a Digital Document. Journal of Cryptology 3(2), 99–111 (1991)
15. Haeberlen, A., Mislove, A., Druschel, P.: Glacier: Highly Durable, Decentralized Storage Despite Massive Correlated Failures. In: Proceedings of the 2nd Conference on Symposium on Networked Systems Design & Implementation, vol. 2 (2005)

---

[3] http://www.camara-e.net

16. Herzberg, A., Krawczyk, H., Yung, M.: Proactive Secret Sharing Or: How to Cope With Perpetual Leakage. IBM TJ. Watson Research Center, 1–22 (1995)
17. Huhnlein, D., Korte, U., Langer, L., Wiesmaier, A.: A Comprehensive Reference Architecture for Trustworthy Long-Term Archiving of Sensitive Data. In: 2009 3rd International Conference on New Technologies, Mobility and Security, pp. 1–5 (December 2009)
18. ISO: ISO/IEC 14721:2003: Space Data and Information Transfer Systems — Open Archival Information System — Reference Model. International Standardization Organization, Geneva, Switzerland (2003)
19. Kotla, R., Alvisi, L., Dahlin, M.: SafeStore: a Durable and Practical Storage System. In: 2007 USENIX Annual Technical Conference on Proceedings of the USENIX Annual Technical Conference (2007)
20. Kubiatowicz, J., Bindel, D., Chen, Y., Czerwinski, S., Eaton, P., Geels, D., Gummadi, R., Rhea, S., Weatherspoon, H., Weimer, W., Wells, C., Zhao, B.: OceanStore: an Architecture for Global-Scale Persistent Storage. ACM SIGPLAN Notices 35(11) (2000)
21. Merkle, R.C.: Protocols for public key cryptosystems. In: IEEE Symposium on Security and Privacy, vol. 0, p. 122 (1980)
22. Miyamoto, T., Doi, S., Nogawa, H., Kumagai, S.: Autonomous Distributed Secret Sharing Storage System. Systems and Computers in Japan 37(6), 55–63 (2006)
23. Nikov, V., Nikova, S.: On proactive secret sharing schemes. In: Handschuh, H., Hasan, M.A. (eds.) SAC 2004. LNCS, vol. 3357, pp. 308–325. Springer, Heidelberg (2004)
24. Pedersen, T.P.: Non-interactive and Information-Theoretic Secure Verifiable Secret Sharing. In: Feigenbaum, J. (ed.) CRYPTO 1991. LNCS, vol. 576, pp. 129–140. Springer, Heidelberg (1992)
25. Pinkas, D., Pope, N., Ross, J.: CMS Advanced Electronic Signatures (CAdES). Internet Engineering Task Force (IETF) Networking Group, Request for Comments 5126 (2008)
26. Pinkas, D., Ross, J., Pope, N.: Electronic Signature Formats for Long Term Electronic Signatures. Internet Engineering Task Force (IETF) Networking Group, Request for Comments 3126 (2001)
27. Shamir, A.: How to Share a Secret. Communications of the ACM 22(11), 612–613 (1979)
28. Storer, M.W., Greenan, K.M., Miller, E.L., Voruganti, K.: POTSHARDS—a secure, recoverable, long-term archival storage system. ACM Transactions on Storage 5(2), 1–35 (2009)
29. Wallace, C., Pordesch, U., Brandner, R.: Long-term Archive Service Requirements. Internet Engineering Task Force (IETF) Networking Group, Request for Comments 4810 (2007)
30. Wang, E., Yau, J., Hui, L., Jiang, Z., Yiu, S.: A Key-Recovery System for Long-term Encrypted Documents. IEEE, Los Alamitos (2006)
31. Wong, T., Wing, J.: Verifiable Secret Redistribution for Archive Systems. In: Proceedings of First International IEEE Security in Storage Workshop, 2002, pp. 94–105 (December 2002)
32. Zimmer, W., Langkabel, T., Hentrich, C.: ArchiSafe: Legally Compliant Electronic Storage. IT Professional 10(4), 2633 (2008)

Author Index